New History in France

New History in France
The Triumph of the *Annales*

François Dosse

TRANSLATED BY PETER V. CONROY, JR.

University of Illinois Press   Urbana and Chicago

L'histoire en miettes: Des "Annales" à la "nouvelle histoire" © 1987 by
Éditions La Découverte, Paris
English-language translation © 1994 by the Board of Trustees
of the University of Illinois
Manufactured in the United States of America
1 2 3 4 5 C P 5 4 3 2 1

This book is printed on acid-free paper.

Library of Congress Cataloging-in-Publication Data
Dosse, François, 1950–
    [Histoire en miettes. English]
    New history in France : the triumph of the Annales / François
Dosse.
       p.   cm.
    Includes index.
    ISBN 0-252-01907-5. — ISBN 0-252-06373-2 (pbk.)
    1. History—Methodology. 2. History—Philosophy. I. Title.
D16.D5813   1994
901—dc20   93-35586
                                                                         CIP

*Originally published in French by Éditions La Découverte, 1 place
Paul-Painlevé, 75005 Paris. ISBN 2-7071-1675-0*

Contents

Translator's Note   vii
Introduction   1

Part 1   Clio Revisited
  1. The Prehistory of the *Annales*   7
  2. The Era of Marc Bloch and Lucien Febvre   42

Part 2   The Braudel Years
  3. The Parry   79
  4. The Paradigm   107

Part 3   The Crumbling of History
  5. Historical Anthropology   139
  6. Serial History   152
  7. A New Interpretive Grid   165
  8. A Metahistory of the Gulag   182
  9. Immobile History   199

Conclusion   215
Index   225

Translator's Note

In translating François Dosse's *L'Histoire en miettes,* my main goal, in addition of course to being faithful and accurate, was to capture as much as possible the verve, the sprightliness, and the near conversational flow of the original. Dosse's style is quite unlike the ponderous academic prose that we might expect for a topic so weighty. His nimble but truculent style complements wonderfully the ideas that he is professing. What I have sought to do is to capture both his style and his words.

The author has read this translation and made a number of suggestions to improve it. Whatever errors remain are due to no one other than myself.

Throughout the book, I have chosen to provide my own translations for all citations, even authors like Lévi-Strauss, Braudel, Bloch, and Febvre, who have already been translated into English. This decision is a bit unusual and requires an explanation. Since so many of the sources cited in the bibliography are available only in French, I did not want to create a possibly invidious distinction between material in English versus that in French. Further complicating the situation, not all the works of Braudel, Bloch, and Febvre quoted here have been translated. To impose some sort of homogeneity on this material, therefore, I decided to translate all the citations myself and to keep Dosse's critical apparatus and references exactly as they were in the French edition. Minor changes were made in accordance with American bibliographical style.

Style—the word keeps reoccurring—is in the end perhaps the prime reason for doing my own translations. When Dosse quotes a source, he often echoes a word or tone from it in his own text. This interplay between citation and commentary is an integral part of his style. Failure to note and attempt to catch this critical dialogue would be a severe shortcoming. While this is not meant in any way as a criticism, available translations did not always render these nuances. Quite understandably, they were conceived for and in an entirely different context and quite rightly they were responding to other needs. As good as they are in themselves, I think I had sufficient reason to attempt my own versions.

Steering a narrow course between the Scylla of accuracy and the Charybdis of style, I have perhaps floundered on one or the other reef. Knowing my intentions and the course I have set, it is for the reader to decide.

Introduction

He who controls the past controls the future.
—GEORGE ORWELL

Clio is inspiring a public that is increasingly eager to know its own history. Crowds are listening to historians talk. Television studios and radio soundstages are welcoming scholars who in the past would have remained anonymous in their archives or been known only within a limited university circle. René Rémond has provided a historian's viewpoint for election returns. Georges Duby was named president of the seventh television channel. While France-Inter has increased the number of historical programs in which professional historians like Pierre Miquel or Henri Amouroux rub elbows, prime time has been left to a woman storyteller who tracks down reveries and daydreams. Every week in her morning program Eve Ruggieri parades Mazarin, la Castiglione, Cleopatra, and Josephine de Beauharnais before a faithful audience that is estimated at 975,000 to 1,200,000 listeners. Alain Decaux's success on television is solid. The communication media has taken over the historian's territory. They are responding to an unmistakable thirst for history. The public's irresistible need has led to prosperity: sales of books and journals that popularize history have increased by 10 percent per year even in the face of an economic slowdown. A first-class journal like *L'Histoire* has runs of eighty thousand copies. This return to history is widespread. After the "year of patrimony"[1] and its attendant activities in 1980, many people traced their genealogical tree or remembered the dictum that every old person who dies represents a library that burns down. They took out their tape recorders to record the older generations and to save the bits of life that were disappearing.

Consumer history has become a remedy that fills in the gaps and breaks the isolation of suburbs without a memory. Here historians assume the task of conservators: they bring security. They are called most often to the bedside of a sick society. If the present is not captivating and the future disquieting, at least the past remains, a place that can be invested with an imaginary identity through times we have lost forever even though they are close to us. This quest has become more individual and local since no collective destiny has captured our interest. We abandon significant periods in favor of the daily life of little people. A new esthetic topography takes over when we speak of villages, of women, of immigrants, of all who are marginalized. In these new fields of investigation, local ethnology feeds on doubts about the notion of progress and flourishes in an "immobile present."[2] We have moved from grand biography of the heroes of history, from Louis XI through Charles V and Napoleon to the biographies of obscure heroes of daily life. Concurrently, the media's presentation of news that changes every day, of rapid and urgent events that take place internationally offers us the image of history that accelerates even as it eludes us. We suffer it more than we live it. Our emotions are engaged, but these events do not confer meaning on our lives; to relieve our anxiety, we search for the calm waters of those mostly medieval, far-away times of our identity. An entire society has refused to become an orphan and has strained to find its origins in history. A recent poll confirms this very pronounced French taste for history. 50.2 percent of those surveyed own books dealing with history; and for 9.6 percent of them, those books are their preferred reading.[3] History means sales, but what kind of history?

Behind the parasite that is pure commercial history or history-as-merchandise, Clio is incarnated in France by one school that has won a dominating position: the *Annales*. Annalists have taken over all the strategic positions in our media-oriented society. The new historians have become merchants as well as scholars: they are deal-makers as well as publicity agents and managers who control the entire network distributing historical works. The editors for historical collections at most publishing houses are Annalists. They occupy the key seats of power; they select the works considered worth publishing and reject the rest. This preeminent school has also taken over the press, where it refers to its own publications and thus ensures them the outreach needed to win over a larger public. From research laboratories to distribution networks, French historical production has become a quasi monopoly of the *Annales*.[4]

This success is the result of a strategy that aimed at capturing the procedures and the language of the neighboring social sciences and of a remarkable capacity to steal another's garb and to dress up an unworthy, dowager cannibal in it. This conquest required constant attention. To better conduct its offensive, this school deployed a strategy it learned from three failures to produce a unified social science at the beginning of this century: e.g., Vidal's geographical school, Durkheim's sociology, and Henri Berr's effort at synthesis. So as not to frighten its eventual partners, this school presented itself at first as a group of martyrs, the victims of ostracism. Militant and marginal, it called upon the social sciences to help it destabilize the then-dominant historical faction. This school refused any dogma, any philosophy or theory of history; hence its plastic mobility and its capacity to infiltrate the largest field of scholarship. This strategy of making alliances combined with its epistemological ecumenism allowed the *Annales* to eliminate its rivals. It has built a vast empire through a war in which the terms of military tactics (frontiers, territories, etc.) are just so many gambits until the final conquest.

In order to understand this triumph, we must relive its stages. Marc Ferro suggests that this school is the embodiment of an experimental science free of ideology or of any world vision. It would like to become an autonomous discipline, above suspicion and beyond influence. Such a self-concept does not allow any questions about its success, its connection with its times, or the function of the historian. However, history depends closely on the place and the time when it is conceived. As Michel de Certeau writes: "The practice of history is completely relative to the structure of society."[5]

More than fifty years old, this school already has a history. As Lucien Febvre said in 1946, "since the world moves, the *Annales* moves also." We have to ask ourselves then how this new historical discourse responded to a social need, and yet we do not want to fall into the kind of mechanical study that would be no more than a game of reflections between society and historians. The latter have their autonomy and a logic proper to their discipline within the field of the social sciences. It is this second parameter that in fact illuminates the critical rifts and the changes in the paradigms of the *Annales* from 1929 until today.

If historical writing is the product of its times (and in Jean Bouvier's words, "there are no innocent historians anywhere") and if historical writing belongs within the social sciences, it should be confronted by a third point of view, that of the historical discipline itself, as an independent discipline having its own professional logic and facing problems of place, innovation, and conservation. Historical writing should study the advance of knowledge as well as its institutionalization, beginning with a sociohistory of the historian's milieu seen from a morphological perspective. It is only when these three viewpoints are situated diachronically that we can uncover the rational forces at work in the *Annales* discourse.

We offer one last remark on the history of the *Annales* for anyone who questions the function of historians and of history. The stakes are important: the very existence of history and its capacity to avoid the double suicide either of fleeing ahead toward dilution within the other social sciences or of retreating back to the old positivistic history of the nineteenth century. Avoiding that fate can only come from transcending empiricism and retooling scientifically. History remains a science under construction in the image of our society from which it cannot be separated. And so the struggle for history continues.

■ NOTES

1. This was an official, year-long event that encouraged the French to become more aware of their French heritage and culture—Trans.

2. J-R. Rioux, *Le Monde du dimanche*, 7 Oct. 1975.

3. Ministry of Culture, *Pratiques culturelles des Français* (Dalloz, 1982). Four thousand persons over fifteen years of age were surveyed between December 1981 and January 1982.

4. F. Dosse, "Les héritiers," in *Lire Braudel* (La Découverte, 1988).

5. Michel de Certeau, "L'Opération historique," in *Faire de l'histoire* (Gallimard, 1974), 1:3–41.

PART I

Clio Revisited

ONE

The Prehistory of the *Annales*

■ BACK TO ORIGINS

Without making any concessions to historians' ritual that Marc Bloch called, using François Simiand's words,[1] the idol of origins, we must understand on what soil the *Annales* grew so as to comprehend how it acquired its hegemonic position.

The creation of the *Annales* journal resulted from two upheavals after 1914–18 that changed the international situation as much as they affected the social sciences. We will find that double influence at each significant change of direction in the evolution of the *Annales* discourse. As Benetto Croce said: "All history is contemporary history."

Jacques Le Goff exaggerates somewhat when he writes: "It is not by chance that the *Annales* was born in 1929, the year of the crash."[2] Marc Bloch and Lucien Febvre's project cannot be reduced to a historian's reaction to the crisis that exploded after the Wall Street crash of October 1929, since the journal appeared in January of that year and had been planned in the years immediately following World War I. Still, Jacques Le Goff is not entirely wrong because the crash was nonetheless the reason for the journal's success, even though it took place after its creation. The dramatic crumbling of the international capitalistic economy affected both America and Europe and forced everyone to rethink the idea of humanity's continual progress toward more material goods. The crash formed the basis for new questions that emphasized economic and social values that had been affected by deflation, recession, and unemployment. In this context where the desire to understand and act is strong, the *Annales*, whose full title is *Annales d'histoire économique et sociale,* answered the questions of an epoch that turned its gaze from politics to economics. Besides, economics did not wait until 1929 to encroach upon politics. The 1920s were punctuated by major debates and decisions in the economic arena. In 1921, as he brought his New Economic Policy to Russia, Lenin claimed that socialism was defined as soviets plus electricity. During these same years, international relations were both dominated and undermined by the question of reparations. Policies were judged more and more by their economic success or failure. The coalition of the Left in France fell on monetary policy (the "mur d'argent"), to Raymond Poincaré's advantage.[3] By reestablishing the franc at its gold equivalent in 1928, he guaranteed his victory in the upcoming elections. Governmental programs were defined by economic policies adopted to fight the depression. Franklin D. Roosevelt owed his election in 1932 to the New Deal, while the victory of the Popular Front was due in part to a reaction against the anti-inflationary policies of Gaston Doumergue and Pierre Laval on the right. The economy became the measure by which the society of the twenties and thirties judged itself. Bloch and Febvre's journal of economic and social history moved like a fish in these waters. Certainly these two great historians followed their intuition, but there was also a specific discourse that fit the social environment in which it was pronounced. The depression was a challenge; it created the need to quantify economic variables and especially changes in prices. During this period three authors published seminal books on this topic: François Simiand, Henri Hauser, and Ernest Labrousse.[4] With these studies a more scientific economic history began to take shape. This was a pivotal point, one from which Pierre Chaunu measures the archeology of this type of history: "Everything begins on the horizon of 1929–30."[5] "Measurement entered into history through prices. The shock hit after the crash of 1929."[6]

This new historical discourse as it was codified by the *Annales* found its origins in the trauma of World War I and its aftermath. The millions who died in that long war rose as in Abel Gance's film *J'Accuse* to remind the living of their responsibilities. For historians, that meant the bankruptcy of a history that focused on battles and that had not prevented the butchery. The resolutely pacifist mentality after the war (the "der des der"), which was at times too pacifist (Munich), incited historians to transcend the purely nationalist and chauvinistic narrative that had been the credo of a generation since the defeat of 1870. In reaction they wanted to reconnect peoples and nations. Historical discourse found a new purpose. After having been the weapon of war, it was now considered a potential instrument of peace. In 1935 Célestin Bouglé summed up the efforts of organizations and international historical meetings working toward this end.[7] The war tolled the knell for the Belle Epoque in a Europe whose decline or decadence was just being noticed.[8] Before the war, everything was decided in Europe. The Eurocentric discourse of historians corresponded to a world unified by capitalism and dominated by Paris or London. At the end of the war, Europe was weakened by bloodshed, several millions dead, immense physical destruction, and the rise of new and more dynamic powers like Japan and especially the United States. The complexity of worldwide problems and the dependency of the old world upon the new made the universal European message more relative and pushed historical discourse toward a repudiation of Eurocentrism and an awareness of destinies (in the plural) and of multiple civilizations. The *Annales* can best be understood in this context of questioning the prewar certitudes and not just as the private evolution of a historical discourse cut off from reality. As Lucien Febvre said: "History's crisis was not a specific malady affecting history alone. It was, it is one of the aspects, the specifically historical aspect of a great crisis in human understanding."[9]

This global crisis did not only affect historians, it upset the certitudes of all the intellectual milieus that were in flux during the thirties as Jean Touchard and Pierre Andreu have shown.[10] We will find many points in common between the *Annales* discourse and this "spirit of the thirties" that inspired a number of disaffected young intellectual groups: "Revolt moved the best part of the youthful intelligentsia."[11] New journals appeared in the thirties: *Plans* edited by Philippe Lamour; *Esprit* by Emmanuel Mounier; *Combat, L'Homme nouveau, Les Cahiers* by Jean-Pierre Maxence; *Réaction* by Jean de Fabrègues; *Critique sociale* and especially *L'Ordre nouveau* by Robert Aron and Arnaud Dandieu. The last two had published together in 1931 *La Décadence de la nation française* and *Le Cancer américain*. Despite the differences separating these diverse intellectual milieus, we can speak of a generation and of common themes: "The solidarity of peril creates among us a unity that neither teachers nor doctrines could have done, a unity of refusal in the face of the disheartening misery of an epoch when all that an individual can love and desire is cut off from its living origins, stained, denatured, inverted, diminished."[12] We find here Marc Bloch and Lucien Febvre's different struggles over history.

First of all, "the major themes of the thirties are anti-themes."[13] The origin of the fundamental *Annales* discourse lies in its systematic opposition to and its total rejection of the dominant historiography called positivistic. The identity of the *Annales* is built in fact upon quarreling with the older generation of Lavisse, Seignobos, and Langlois. The second mark of the thirties intellectuals is their rejection of politics. The political game, parliamentary life, and political parties were all taken to task by these intellectuals. The state was suspect and rejected as external to society. Like a foreign body, it provoked violent reactions: "Whether they be moderates, radicals, socialists, or communists, all the political leaders whose names are displayed on rostrums or atop newspaper editorials carry a mark of shame: a sort of cowardly complicity and a dirty conniving that were too obvious as they called each by first names in the corridors or rubbed elbows at the bar."[14] The journal *L'Ordre nouveau* called for a boycott of the elections in April-May 1936: "It is forbidden to vote just as it is forbidden to spit on the ground."[15] Nonetheless *L'Ordre nouveau*, a fountain of new ideas, expected "to abolish the proletarian condition" and was laying the groundwork for a twentieth-century utopia.[16] The rejection of politics was just as clear in Marc Bloch and Lucien Febvre. They centered their activity on the economic and the social and completely abandoned the political, which became for them superfluous, an appendage, a dead spot. The spirit of the thirties was also a reflection upon decline, decadence, the uselessness of ideology, and the need to give pride of place to man as a unique personality: "It is a question ... in a word of recreating human civilization."[17] This reflection ended with the rejection of both existing realities: both capitalism with its contradictions and crises that led to millions of unemployed and to totalitarian regimes like facism or Nazism, as well as the solution of a collective revolution on the Soviet model: "*L'Ordre nouveau* is preparing the revolution of order against capitalistic disorder and Bolshevik oppression."[18] It was the search for a third way. We find this longing for a future that is new, modern, human, and free of the state in the fundamental themes of the *Annales* discourse. Marc Bloch meditated on a menaced Europe through the bias of medieval history in his *Société féodale*. He extolled comparative history; he belonged to a generation that created institutions capable of advancing international scholarly dialogues.[19] Bloch and Febvre participated fully in this spirit of the thirties alongside "nonconformists," some of whom ended their career in the Académie Française (Thierry Maulnier, Henri Daniel-Rops, Robert Aron, Georges Izard) just as the dissidents of Strasbourg succeeded in imposing their conception of history upon the entire community of historians.

The Prehistory of the *Annales* 11

The other impulsion affecting the historian's milieu was at first a cause of crisis, then of vitality. It came from the social sciences. Questioning evolution and the idea of progress pushed historical consciousness to its furthest limits. This period was marked by new social sciences like linguistics, psychoanalysis, anthropology, and especially that science whose object was society and which situated itself close to the borders of history, i.e., sociology of the Durkheim school: "Bourgeois rationality left history and retreated toward political economics and in part toward sociology."[20]

Emile Durkheim was the instructor of the first sociology class in the college of arts at Bordeaux in 1887. He created a school and, as V. Karady has shown, succeeded in dominating this discipline.[21] But sociology still had far to travel before becoming the equal of the university's traditional disciplines. The strategy of the Durkheim school consisted of winning territory with tactical mobility: it conquered the neighboring territories of the social sciences by proposing interdependent relationships and proffering assistance. Early Durkheimian sociology had the specific ambition of unifying all the humanities under its own aegis around the concept of social causality. In so doing it was attacking the fortress of history, a discipline that was solidly rooted in the university. Starting in 1897 it acquired a voice to broadcast its viewpoints: *L'Année sociologique*. Durkheim did not deny the importance of history, which he considered essential, but he modified its status.

Historians should be happy to gather the materials sociologists would turn into honey: "History cannot be a science except by rising above the individual, at which point it ceases to be history and becomes a branch of sociology."[22] Historians who would attempt to compare and to interpret would become sociologists. History would thus be a subsidiary of the master discipline sociology. Committed to the conquest of a central and dominating position, the Durkheimians demonstrated great cohesion. But they also displayed a certain dogmatic rigidity that eventually scuttled their project. They were fighting on two fronts,[23] as much against the Catholic group of Le Play as against socialism. To Karl Marx's "social division of work" they countered with "the division of social work." They advocated consensus thinking, decorated with modern scholarly discourse and sustained in the closing years of the century by the success of philosophical positivism, which was the birthplace of sociology: "Our society must become aware again of its organic unity. . . . Gentlemen, I believe that sociology is more capable than any other science of restoring these ideas."[24] To the historians, the Durkheimians offered a new field of research, the sociology of religion, which was envisioned as a common language that could break with a tradition of scholastic studies unconnected with the social realm. In addition they had the advantage of a favorable situation at the university.[25] The university was in a period of instability. The sociologists could therefore hope to play key roles since they already enjoyed the prestige of the Ecole Normale Supérieure and held advanced degrees like the *agrégation* in philosophy. They also benefited from the success of Auguste Comte, whom Durkheim claimed as an inspiration. But Clio was too deeply rooted and connected to the destiny of the republic to be marginalized.

The Durkheimians also attacked geography by criticizing its regional monographs. They proposed social morphology as a substitute. François Simiand's ironic comment "It is not enough to say that sheep exist in order to explain that a region has a wool industry"[26] pinpoints the determinism he saw in the great geographers of the time like Demangeon, Blanchard, Vacher, and Sion. To geographical description based on land and climate, the Durkheimians opposed an emphasis that sought causes located within society. Geography was supposed to disappear as a separate discipline. Here too the sociologists floundered on a particularly hard rock, Vidal's school at the apex of its glory. Between the wars the Durkheimians in Paris had to be satisfied with four chairs at the Sorbonne and one position, Marcel Mauss's, at the Collège de France. This situation did not accurately reflect the school's growth. Célestin Bouglé summed up the situation in 1927 by saying that the center was nowhere and the circumference everywhere.[27] Shipwrecked on the shores of the major universities, the sociologists had to retreat to the Ecole Pratique des Hautes Etudes and create in 1924 the Institut Français de Sociologie among whose forty members we find all the founding fathers of the *Année sociologique:* Bouglé, Fauconnet, Davy, Halbwachs, Mauss, and Simiand. This half victory or half defeat prepared the birth of the *Annales* in 1929. Febvre and Bloch picked up the "catch-as-catch-can" strategy of the sociologists. Because careers were blocked at the university between the wars, disciplines like sociology that were not yet firmly rooted were neglected and the focus of innovation moved to the more traditional areas.[28] Paradoxically, success came from the old discipline of history: "I imagine that the *Année sociologique* was, for Marc Bloch, what the *Annales* was for those of my generation."[29] One of the godfathers of *Annales* writing was Emile Durkheim, to whom Block confessed his debt: "He taught us to analyze more in depth, to focus on the problem more tightly, and I would even say, to think less cheaply."[30]

A bomb exploded in 1903 in Henri Berr's new journal, *La Revue de synthèse historique*. It was placed there by a thirty-year-old sociologist, François Simiand. This inflammatory article, "Historical Method and Social Science," constituted the most radical challenge ever to history. It belonged within the larger context of sociology's attack that commanded historians to give up, to submit to their arguments, and to become empirical collectors of materials that sociology, the only social science interested in laws, could interpret. Taking on Charles Seignobos and the methodology of his 1901 book, *La Méthode historique appliquée aux sciences sociales*, Simiand stirred up an enormous controversy. He called on historians to give up their blinders and modernize, and he repeated Bacon's metaphor about "the idols of the tribe of historians." There were three of them, all useless. First was the "political idol," the dominant field or at least the eternal preoccupation with political history. To this was added the "individual idol or the inveterate habit of conceiving history as the history of individuals" and finally the "chronological idol," which was the habit of getting lost in the study of origins.[31]

He thus directly challenged the capacity of history, that old well-established discipline, to become a positive mode of knowledge. In contrast, young sociology presented itself as the "corpus of the social sciences."[32] Sociology invited historians to move from singular to normal phenomena and to those stable relationships that allow the discovery of laws and causes. It asked them to shift their focus from the individual to the social. As the twentieth century began, writing history was in fact limited to the political sphere, which provided the subject for more than half of all history theses and more than three quarters of the Diplôme d'Etudes Supérieures and *agrégation* questions. As for the "individual idol," biographical studies accounted for more than 30 percent of all theses up until 1904, while after the war they diminished significantly and accounted for only 17 percent in the period 1919–38.[33] Simiand's article constitutes one piece in an ongoing debate that touched all the social sciences and especially sociologists and historians who were fighting for the same piece of scholarly turf.

In 1894, Pierre Lacombe began publishing the first edition of *L'Histoire considérée comme science*. To history he assigned a sociological perspective, the search for laws. Even before Simiand, he was inviting historians to turn away from events and from everything that was unique and singular, because science was supposed to establish parallels and fixed laws. The director of the *Revue historique* seemed to be influenced by these criticisms and indicated his hope for a new history open to slow movements and to the social and economic conditions that were more liable to reveal laws. But this was not the direction followed by the historical establishment. It regrouped around a manifesto that tried to parry the sociological offensive. Charles Seignobos's *La Méthode historique appliquée aux sciences* appeared in 1901. Seignobos refused to grant sociology first place among the social sciences and considered historians as the only possible unifying force. With this book, war was declared. It was in this context that Simiand picked up the gauntlet and fought back in what was at first considered a "tactical error." The strategy of the Durkheimian school up to then had been to promote alliances.[34] The effect of this attack was to make the historians close ranks. In addition, Simiand lost potential allies among reform-minded historians like Paul Mantoux and Gabriel Monod, because of the other plank in his polemic, which opposed theoretical economics cut off from facts.[35] Simiand's article took issue with the idiographism of historians as much as with the nomothetism of economists. It had a remarkable fate in that the *Annales* school used it word for word to combat old narrative history and to promote new history. From this diatribe of 1903, the *Annales* drew its main innovations, from history focused on problems to collective research and the use of models. But history and not sociology was to be the unifying force.

Simiand's article "seems to be a sort of theoretical matrix."[36] It must have marked profoundly the generation of Bloch and Febvre. In a rare admission, the latter recognized "the parallel influence" that Simiand exerted on him.[37] Bloch and Febvre reacted against the marginalization of their discipline that Simiand had predicted, not by retreating behind the positions already occupied, but by advancing history into the field of the social sciences. The 1929 response to the Durkheimian challenge consisted then in putting Simiand's program into practice. To show that the lesson was learned and the idols broken, the *Annales* republished Simiand's article in 1960.

There was another particularly vital force at the turn of the century. It came from geography, a discipline that is in France very close to history. Paul Vidal de la Blache was at first a historian who turned to geography after the French defeat in 1872 in order to counter the challenge of a Germany that was keener than France to study the contemporary world. His systemization of geographical subject matter served as a model for the *Annales*.

The geography that was born around 1880 in France had been conceived, like the *Annales* later, as a reaction against the positivism of history. It wanted to eliminate events and politics and take root in contemporary issues. It was interested in the present, in the permanent features that formed the fabric of the countryside at the end of the nineteenth and beginning of the twentieth century. This orientation emphasized certain notions that characterize Vidalian geography: milieu, way of life, daily routine. This geography aspired to be first of all a science of the concrete and of the observable. Here we find the deep wellsprings of the *Annales* inspiration. There is however a contradiction in historians using a science that values "what is fixed and permanent."[38] Of course, Vidal de La Blache did not propose a mechanical connection between the natural milieu and human society that had several ways to adapt to that milieu. Nonetheless, the limits were narrow and "man only triumphs over nature with the strategy that it imposes and with the arms that it provides."[39] Vidal's geography studied man incidentally; before anything else, it was the science of places and of countrysides, of visible effects on the earth's surface that were both natural and human. Man humanizes nature while at the same time man is naturalized.

Vidal's geography was first of all descriptive. The binary code visible/invisible functioned here, reified by the image on a map, a photograph, or a simple walk over the land.[40] The order of Vidalian discourse corresponded to the order of things in the identification process. For Vidal de La Blache, understanding was nothing more than localizing and comparing. Vidalian geography asserted itself then as a discipline of the present in opposition to narrative history.[41]

Vidalian geography was inspired by biological concepts that it used to redefine new ways to delimit and to construct a human geography. In the economy of the Vidalian discourse, the community is compared to the cell, the rural or urban area to body tissue, the region to an organ, and the nation to an organism.[42] There can only be relations of complementarity in an organism, all of whose parts contribute to its life. Just as the parts cooperate in an organism, diverse elements contribute to the harmonious development of the whole in a social body. Reproducing the same belongs within the range of normality, but it escapes historical change. To accentuate what is permanent encourages the development of a geomorphology that emphasizes the countryside's stable structures. To this methodology is added the influence of de Martonne, Vidal's son-in-law who succeeded him at the Sorbonne in 1909. In the same spirit, Vidal's disciples emphasized rural history and sought its permanent traits. More of the country than the city, they preferred the land to the factory, long narrow fields to the tortuous city, bucolic immobility to industrial change.

Another characteristically Vidalian mark, one that we will find later in the *Annales,* was to be wary of any rigid theory and to prefer description and observation. Regional monographs proliferated and made the reputation of this school.[43] They would inspire *Annales* writing and open historians to the land and to what is permanent; they freed historians and allowed them to leave the archives and dusty documents and take to the fields. Febvre recognized this paternity: "You could say that, in a certain manner, it is Vidalian geography that engendered our history."[44] Ever since his first articles in the *Revue de synthèse historique,* Febvre underlined what these regional monographs brought to history.

The close-knit geographers had the advantage over the Durkheimian school in that they were employed by the university. De Martonne was the organizer of this Vidalian takeover, establishing bridgeheads for this new geography both in Paris and in the provinces. The geographers not only had a journal that had been functioning as an official organ since 1891, the *Annales de géographie,* but in the twenties and thirties they increased the number of their regional journals, which extended the impact of their monographs. In addition, de Martonne founded the Association of French Geographers, opened the Institute of Geography in Paris in 1923, presided over the creation of the National Committee of Geography in 1921, and was named by the International Geographical Union to organize the International Congress in Paris in 1931. That was the "culminating point of the French school of geography."[45]

The career of an *Annales* historian like Pierre Vilar demonstrates how extensive an impact the Vidalian school had. He began as a geographer. M. Sorre advised him to go study what would become his specialization, Catalonia. He started a thesis with Albert Demangeon, who introduced him to Marc Bloch.

Geography's last stronghold, which the *Annales* would take over, was its connection with the opinion makers and the depression of 1929.[46] Albert Demangeon was a member of numerous committees concerned with long-term investments. This connection between power and scholars functioned at ground level. Because it filled a societal need, geography benefited greatly even as history was totally disconnected from the present.

The challenge the geographers hurled at historians becomes clearer when we realize that history was not in the best of health. Even if we have to wait to see its efforts crowned by the creation of an *agrégation* of geography in 1941, progress in terms of university chairs is easily noticed. Whereas, in 1914, there was one professor of geography for five in history, the ratio was only one to three in 1938. This increase took place against a background of crisis in history, with careers blocked and no augmentation in the number of positions available. If, as Charles-Olivier Carbonell notes, the number of positions in history increased by 50 percent from 1875 to 1905, the average age was very low (half of the historians were less than forty-two years of age in 1900), and they held those positions for a long time.[47] In contrast to this golden age, the period between the wars was one of severe crisis for history. While between 1919 and 1938 the number of chairs in literature in Paris increased from thirty-nine to fifty-nine, the number in history remained stable at twelve, despite the rising number of students in that discipline. For historians, a university career became a narrow gate that was in danger of closing in their faces. There was a general aging of the teaching body, the average age in 1934 at the Sorbonne being sixty-two. The careers of historians who acquired their credentials young felt the effects. Fernand Braudel obtained the *agrégation* in 1923 but had to wait until 1938 before being hired by section four of the Ecole Pratique des Hautes Etudes, an institution that was marginal despite its intellectual legitimacy. And still he had to make a detour through the lycée in Algiers and the University of Sao Paulo in Brazil. Georges Lefebvre, despite the fame his thesis won for him, had to try his luck three times at the Sorbonne. He was only awarded the chair in the history of the French Revolution in 1937 at the age of sixty-three![48] At the top of the hierarchy sat the Collège de France. The well-known disappointments of the two leaders of the

Annales, Bloch and Febvre, reveal a great deal about blocked careers. Lucien Febvre was elected to the Collège de France on 13 November 1932 after two failures and by emphasizing traditional teaching of modern history, which was paradoxical for an innovator like him. But getting the chair was the main objective. As for Marc Bloch, he was unlucky and never was appointed, despite two attempts.[49] His innovations, in a glutted market, did not win him a higher position within the institution.

Another source that fed the historians of this period should also be mentioned: the evolution of scientific thought. "Our mental atmosphere is no longer the same. The cynetic theory of gases, Einsteinian mechanics, quantum theory have profoundly altered the idea that everyone had about science yesterday."[50] How could this scientific revolution modify the historian's perspective? Febvre and Bloch drew from it an argument against narrative history that had made a fetish out of historical documents to the point of considering them historical explanations. They saw in the theory of probabilities or the relativity of chronological and spatial measurements the possibility of history reaching the status of science, just like the "hard" sciences. But the price was criticizing the witness of the past, of developing schematic reading procedures, of testing hypotheses, and of moving from the given to the created by more aggressive methods: "Historical research, like so many other disciplines of the mind, merges with the royal road of the theory of probabilities."[51] Historical explanation could take the road of research into causes, beginning with the criticism of documents, even if, in the eyes of those promoting the *Annales,* it has to be vaccinated against metaphysics or any theory of single causality.

The other scientific reference point that was a role model for the *Annales* was Claude Bernard's *Introduction à la médecine expérimentale.* In medicine the invisible replaced the visible: "History followed in a sense the same path."[52] Febvre and Bloch tried to substitute for traditional history an experimental history whose object was not immediate knowledge but knowledge mediated by many case studies.

■ THE ERA OF LAVISSE

The definition of history had not known a significant modification from Thucydides until the moment the *Annales* were created. In 1694, the Académie Française's dictionary defined history as "the narration of actions and things worthy of memory," while the eighth edition, in 1935, gave the same meaning: "the story of actions, events, and things worthy of memory." History as story or narrative was still reigning in the 1930s. Historians kept their distance from the other sciences and claimed a very clear but limited territory for their work. Faced with sciences that were looking for the structure of laws and whose object was to find what made for the repetition and the regularity of phenomena, history posed as an idiographic discipline, seeking out the singular, that which cannot be reproduced, and leaving to the nomothetic sciences the task of finding the laws of nature.

This concept of history gave special attention to the critique and classification of sources. Scholarship by the French historical school was solidly supported by the state during the nineteenth century. Before that, historians had been in the service of the king and reflected a flattering image of him. In the nineteenth century, the state facilitated research by financing numerous historical institutions. The number of historians who were remunerated as state employees grew in the nineteenth century: "The state itself became a historian."[53] Guizot created the Committee for Historical Works and the Commission for Historical Monuments; he founded a French school in Athens in 1846. Historical research was becoming organized and rationalized. An unquestionable methodological revolution was taking place inside the state of which it remained a vassal: "How could the historian's discourse not be a state discourse from that point on?"[54] Europe was filled with national sentiment that outweighed analysis. In the first half of the century, French historians had to reconcile the nation and transcend the divisions born of the revolution of 1789 while having to justify that same revolution and make it the foundation of a new era in which contradictions and conflicts would fade behind the satisfied aspirations of a reunified people. This was how the historians Thiers, Mignet, and Guizot defended the revolution of 1830 and Louis-Philippe to the ultraconservatives. While they warned of possible outbreaks, they also declared that class struggle was over. At the heart of this legitimization of power, one reflection upon the revolution, Mignet's *Histoire de la Révolution française* (1824), became the Bible for liberal revolutions. It was translated into twenty languages. Mignet participated in the Three Glorious Days of 1830, a revolution that he considered inevitable. The new party in power rewarded him with the position of perpetual secretary of the Academy of Political and Moral Sciences. The revolution of 1848, however, which shook the throne and transformed France into a republic, filled Mignet with horror: he renounced his deterministic and global vision of history and retreated into a pure description of events and biography that was stripped of any philosophical conception of history. As for Guizot, he placed class struggle at the center of social evolution and called it "the most fertile principle of development in European civilization."[55] According to Guizot, modernity was born out of class antagonisms, which were a source of progress and self-betterment. But, after having established Louis-Philippe's legitimacy and himself at the head of the government, Guizot wanted to consolidate that power. In 1847 he proclaimed that all class struggle had become anachronistic and therefore no longer had the right to exist: "All the major interests have been satisfied.... There is no more class struggle."[56] History writes power, it provides power's limits, its mirror, its meaning. They are the same. The state proclaimed its power in the nineteenth century, which was, as Gabriel Monod said, "the century of history."[57]

Engendered by the defeat at Sedan and the desire to reconquer Alsace and Lorraine, a new kind of history took shape. This methodic school was called, incorrectly, "positivistic." It was grouped around the *Revue historique* started by Gabriel Monod in 1876. It wanted to establish a "positive science" so as to escape from subjectivism.[58] Historians should subject their sources to critical scrutiny in order to establish the truth of what is told, while at the same time they should remain impervious to any philosophical theory. In fact, however, these historians embraced the patriotic Republican party, which they supported against reactionary monarchists. The latter had their own historical journal, the *Revue des questions historiques,* and its members included ultraroyalists and legitimists like the Marquis de Beaucourt, Count H. de l'Epinois, and Count Hyacinthe de Charencey. The partisans of the *Revue historique*, in contrast, favored a moderate and anticlerical republic; they belonged to a republican and secular milieu and shared the same political and scientific interests.[59] Close to power, the methodic school dominated the world of historians and beyond. It contributed to the educational reforms of secondary education carried out by Jules Ferry. Its members occupied university chairs, directed great collective historical works (Ernest Lavisse, *Histoire de France;* A. Rambaut, *Histoire Générale;* Halphen and Sagnac, *Peuples et civilisations*), and fashioned the kind of history that was taught from the first grade onwards. The *Petit Lavisse*, published in 1884, went through its seventy-fifth edition in 1895! All these historians had the same purpose as the state: unite the French around the fatherland. This notion had become the basis of a national consensus whose stability and efficiency could resist the Germans. Such was the mission Gabriel Monod assigned to history when he started the *Revue historique:* "Those events which mutilated the national unity that was slowly created over the centuries inspire us to awake in the nation's soul a consciousness of itself through a deeper consciousness of its history."[60] Underneath the historical archives we find the flag. At the turn of the century history was useful for waging war. Nonetheless, while history appeared to be an instrument of power and concentrated its attention on political and military phenomena, Monod was already looking toward wider fields: "We in history are too used to following the brilliant, earth-shattering, and ephemeral evidence of human activity, great events or great men, instead of insisting upon the great and slow movements of institutions and of economic and social conditions."[61] These words seem to anticipate the epistemological breakthrough initiated later by the *Annales*. Monod's intentions, however, remained a dead letter, sacrificed on the altar of the fatherland. For about fifty years, up until 1926, the journal's orientation remained basically traditional. It continued to be an obligatory rite of passage for "establishment" historians.

This journal anointed the corporation's elite. Despite its proclamations in favor of collective scholarship, despite its innovative desire to open up the spectrum of historical research, the *Revue historique* was impervious to the influence and the soul-searching of the *Année sociologique,* Henri Berr's *Revue de synthèse historique,* and Vidal's geography. The fascination with describing political events was stronger, as Alain Corbin's survey of the *Revue historique* reveals.[62] It seems that the *Revue historique* did not change much until 1926 and kept its traditional approach to history. Two-thirds of its articles from 1901 to 1926 were devoted to biography, politics, or military matters. "The Francocentrism of the *Revue historique* is obvious since on average 54.14 percent of its articles deal with French history."[63] Economics and society played only a minor role. While it favored a time period called modern (the sixteenth to the eighteenth century), the journal was deliberately separated from contemporary society: "I would prefer that our domestic history stop at 1875, with the establishment of the republican constitution and that the scandals of the Panama Canal and of Boulanger be omitted from our schools."[64] Of course, the *Revue historique* did experience a profound renewal in the thirties, especially when Christian Pfister left and Charles-André Julien and Maurice Crouzet took over in 1932.[65] But until then the journal embodied simplemindedly the cult of idols that François Simiand had challenged.

The methodic school defined its methods and ambitions in the *Introduction aux études historiques*, which had been written by Charles Langlois and Charles Seignobos in 1898 with history students in mind. This guide was in a sense the manifesto of the methodic school. History was presented first and foremost as civic instruction: "Events are good tools for civic instruction; they are more effective than studying institutions."[66] Together these two historians wanted to subordinate disciplinary demands to those of civic pedagogy. They defined four stages in historical research. First, historians collect documents and classify them. Second, they treat these documents according to internal criteria. Third, by deduction and analogy, historians connect the facts, fill in the gaps, and fourth, organize those facts into a logical construction. This process restricted historians' ambitions to visible data. It made them slaves of the written document: "History is no more than marshaling documents."[67] Both authors of this manual insisted that priority be given to singular, individual phenomenon: "Literally, every fact is unique."[68] Historians did not have to study the causes of the phenomena they described: "The entire history of events is an obvious and unquestionable chain of accidents."[69] Chance chases away necessity, contingency invalidates any law. Thus the death of Henry II was due to Montgoméry's lance, the Guises' rise to power was made possible by the death of Henry II, and so on. According to this codification, the historian's task was limited to the chain of military and political events without any causal links among them. For Seignobos, the revolutions of the nineteenth century were only accidents. Charles X was imprudent and there were the "flashes in July." Louis-Philippe grew obstinate, by chance a shot rang out on the Boulevard des Capucines, and the monarchy fell. As for the world crisis in 1914, Seignobos reduced it to what was happening at that time. It obliged him to "recognize to what extent the superficial phenomena of political crisis dominate the deep phenomena of economic, intellectual, and social life."[70]

One of the great figures of the methodic school and the author of the Bible for several generations of history students was Ernest Lavisse. He was the linchpin of that holy union of Frenchmen intent on reconquering Alsace and Lorraine. At first he intended to build this union around the imperial idea exemplified by Napoleon III. Victor Duruy, the minister of public instruction, made him chief of staff. Lavisse rose to the top of the state by becoming the tutor of the imperial prince. His connection to the republican regime was in fact late in coming. For a long time he had hoped for Bonaparte's return. He did not defend the republic during the Boulanger crisis and remained uncommitted during the Dreyfus affair. His letters to the imperial prince between 1870 and 1877 bear witness to his hesitations about the newly born republic: "Radicalism is an old mask behind which there are only ignoble passions. The Center-Left is sexless. What to do with all that? . . . You are the only rallying point."[71] His thinking was eventually modified by the force and solidity of republican institutions. Lavisse became the servant of the Third Republic he hated. What most interested him, however, was the revenge that a united France could wreak on the Germans. His history book exalted and exaggerated the steps that led to a national state. Each moment was incarnated in a hero who was a veritable god: "This history book looks like a portrait gallery."[72] History for Lavisse was a call, a foretaste of national mobilization. The veteran of Verdun felt like a worthy heir of Vercingetorix's struggle. History was supposed to fortify the warrior spirit and make clear the simple features that characterized a national superego: "If the schoolboy does not carry within himself the living memory of our national glories; if he does not know that his ancestors have fought on a thousand battlefields for noble causes; if he has not learned how much it has cost in blood and toil to forge our country's unity and to draw out of the chaos of our outmoded institutions the laws that have made us free; if he does not become a citizen who is conscious of his duty and a soldier who loves his rifle, then the teacher will have wasted his time."[73]

The other great builder of this era's national consensus, Fustel de Coulanges, was also marked by the defeat of 1870, which almost ended his career, which had been brilliant under the empire. Victor Duruy had appointed Fustel to teach history at the Ecole Normale and had invited him to give lectures to the Empress Eugénie. The disaster of Sedan led Fustel to break French history off from its Germanic origins and to trace its roots back to Rome. He confirmed the scientific validity of history when it corresponded to the dictates of the methodic school. History "is not an art, it is a pure science."[74] Still it was a science in the service of documents, which supposedly eliminated any form of subjectivity: "The best historian is the one who keeps closest to the texts, who interprets them most accurately, who only thinks and writes according to them."[75] Behind this screen of scientism lies a work that, like Lavisse's, wanted to unify a national community against the hereditary enemy, Germany. The Germans were presented as invaders. To resist them, the French had to transcend their quarrels and take pride in their shared inheritance, either that of the *ancien régime* or of the revolution. Fustel called upon the French to respect their prerevolutionary past and their traditions in order to strengthen their national power and to heal their internal divisions: "True patriotism is not love of the native soil, but love of the past and respect for the generations who have preceded us."[76] Starting with this national reconciliation, history could play a helpful role and guard "the frontiers of our national conscience and the borders of our patriotism."[77] Not only is history difficult to separate from the power of the state but it is also identified with the idea of the nation.

French historicism was nourished in large part by the German historical school, especially by the work of Leopold von Ranke in the middle of the nineteenth century. He greatly influenced French historians who found their theoretic bases in his work. We find in Ranke many of the premises of Langlois, Lavisse, Seignobos, and Fustel: the refusal of theory, the reduction of history to collecting facts, the proclamation of the historian's passivity toward the facts being treated. The French historical school seems to have adopted Ranke's scientific doctrines in order to acquire the Germanic efficiency that was so obvious in the French disaster of 1870.

■ TWO FROM STRASBOURG

As the war receded into the past, Lavisse's methodic school was confronted with questions from several directions. On one side, there were the Durkheimians and their journal, *L'Année sociologique,* on another the Vidalian geographers who wanted to transcend the casual notion of accident and to study the relation of man and his milieu. With the *Histoire socialiste de la révolution française* (1901–8), edited by Jean Jaurès, there was also a socialist approach to history that emphasized social conflicts and economic fluctuations in order to catch the political side effects. Economic history entered the sanctuary of the Sorbonne with Henri Hauser's chair in economic history and Paul Mantoux's thesis of 1906, *La Révolution industrielle au XVIIIe siècle*. All these phenomena hint at the incipient shift in the historian's perspective. They are omens of the break in 1929. Nonetheless, twenty-nine years before the creation of the *Annales*, another journal innovated a radical critique of traditional history.

The *Revue de synthèse historique* was created by Henri Berr in 1900. In the largest sense, the history of the *Annales* begins here at the dawn of the twentieth century.[78] Educated not as a historian but as a philosopher and literary critic, Henri Berr was a professor of literature at the lycée Henri IV in Paris. He defended in 1898 a thesis in philosophy.[79] A free-lance outsider, he was completely at ease when from beyond the institutional and disciplinary pale he demanded that barriers fall and that a real synthesis take place involving all scientific efforts. He considered history the science of sciences whose essential nature was psychological. For him history was the instrument of the synthesis he was promoting, but it had to be new history, the kind that the Durkheimians were calling for. The *Revue de synthèse historique* attacked the sacred cow of facts and the reductionism of the methodic school. Berr extolled history-as-synthesis or a global history that took into account every dimension of reality from economics to *mentalités*, all seen from a scientific viewpoint. He thus picked up the Durkheimian ambition to seek out laws and causes. For this reason historians considered the *Revue de synthèse historique* the "Trojan horse of the sociologists."[80] Nonetheless Berr parted company with the Durkheimians over the excessive importance they gave to social facts. That is what he expressed in his *La Synthèse en histoire, essai critique et théorique*, which appeared in 1911: "When [the Durkheimians] want to introduce all historical phenomena into the same frame and to interpret everything from the same perspective, they are no longer doing science, they are elaborating a new philosophy of history."[81] Berr rejected any form of dogma or rigid theory, and his journal remained the place for ecumenical debate among social scientists until World War I. Moreover, he wanted to reestablish the link between the present and historical studies, which had been undone by the methodic school. Contemporary preoccupations should, for him, guide research. All these new directions adumbrate the *Annales*.

As a young student at the Ecole Normale, Lucien Febvre contributed to this journal. His first article dated from 1905. He quickly became part of the editorial staff and was in charge of the section on "The Regions of France." This experience made him an unmistakable heir of Henri Berr. We find in both these men the same scientific activism, the search for political support, and encyclopedic tastes. In 1914 Berr announced his intention to create a universal and scientific history; in 1925 he founded an international center for synthesis. Febvre, his heir, later directed a French encyclopedia that was proposed by de Monzie. In both men we find the same delight in combat and in polemical debate, in the importance given to book reviews, to the questioning process of history, to psychology. We find in them the same tendency toward synthesis and the search for a total history of subconscious thought that they promoted as an alternative to Marxism. Marc Bloch's first contribution to the *Revue de synthèse historique* was a long article on the Isle-de-France in 1912: "The perspective of the young Bloch, even his terminology, were remarkably similar to Henri Berr's."[82] The parallel with Bloch is noteworthy because of their similar misfortunes as candidates for the Collège de France. Berr made his first attempt in 1905 when Gabriel Monod was elected; he tried again in 1912 with a presentation about teaching based on a historical model. He failed the second time because the guardians of the temple blocked the road against this interdisciplinary agitator.

Why then create the *Annales* in 1929 if a similar journal already existed? Because there were certain lacunae in Berr's effort, from which Febvre and Bloch learned a great deal. First, Berr did not want to found a school around himself, unlike the sociologists around Durkheim. This modesty relegated him to the periphery since it did not incorporate a strategy of taking over university positions and chairs. The revolution in ideas was accomplished, but the essential still had to be done, namely taking over the institutional relays to diffuse those ideas. In addition, World War I made Berr anti-German and vengeful, which caused him to backpedal on some of his original ambitions. He spoke of "a French awakening" and he wanted a "virile science."[83] He proclaimed the superiority of Descartes's country and the victory of 1918 became the victory of the French mind.[84]

This ebb in the desire for change made the *Annales* possible as soon as the war ended. Right from that moment Lucien Febvre conceived the project. Still nothing guaranteed that history would be the rallying point for the social sciences. On the contrary, innovation seemed more likely to come from the sociologists: "The originality of the movement that Bloch and Febvre initiated stemmed more from their manner of presenting their project than from the project itself."[85] In fact, the hope of effecting a multidisciplinary synthesis had already been claimed simultaneously by the Durkheimian school, the geographic school, and the *Revue de synthèse historique*. Febvre and Bloch incorporated the offensive strategy of the Durkheimians, who had been weakened by the death of their leader, while avoiding the dogmatism that had spelled their ruin. To this strategy of conquest they added the ecumenism of Henri Berr so as to win over the various factions in the social sciences and to rally them all behind the flag of a rejuvenated and confederated history. They annexed the geographers by touting their regional monographs. The leaders of the *Annales* understood that to win the game, a tacit alliance with the other social sciences was not enough; it was an outright annexation they needed. This point is critical and can be found at every stage of the *Annales* discourse: their catch-as-catch-can ability to find opportunities, to incorporate what was valuable, and to take over. In order not to frighten their partners and to better absorb them, they dared not tip their hand. In contrast to Durkheim, who led a frontal attack while holding a dominant position within sociology, the *Annales* cultivated its marginality and its antidogmatism, which are part and parcel of its legend and its founding myth. Febvre and Bloch presented themselves as dwarfs confronting a giant and called for help in evicting traditional history. The *Annales* project cannot therefore be separated from its strategy: "No scientific project can be separated from its power project. . . . The will to convince and the will to power are joined like light and shadow."[86] Still the circumstances have to be right for annexation. Such was the case in the thirties when economics was restricted to the law schools and Durkheimian sociology was divided between law and the liberal arts. The geographic school was running out of breath: "The position was up for grabs; the *Annales* took it."[87] The hegemonic desire of the *Annales* sends us back to ideology, to the major themes of this period, to the spirit of the thirties, for "history that wants to dominate cannot go against the dominant ideology."[88]

The two founders of the *Annales* are not, as they and their heirs like to present them, marginal figures. Both were professors at the University of Strasbourg, which had become a showcase since the recovery of

Alsace in 1920. It was supposed to demonstrate that French scholars were capable of doing better than the Germans at the Kaiser Wilhelms Universität (1872–1918). Strasbourg was second only to Paris in the number of its professors. We find there a number of scholars in different disciplines who later collaborated on the *Annales:* the geographer Baulig, the sociologists Maurice Halbwachs and Gabriel Le Bras, the psychologist Charles Blondel, the historians André Piganiol, Charles-Edmond Perrin, and Georges Lefebvre. And of course Febvre and Bloch held strategic positions in this rich pool of university talent.

In addition to the traditional disciplines, new and modern chairs were created. A new spirit, related to that of the *Revue de synthèse historique,* was blowing over Strasbourg, a new desire to break out of the old mold, which Henri Berr had recognized as early as 1921. Saturday get-togethers permitted philosophers, sociologists, historians, geographers, jurists, and mathematicians to get to know each other. Then they inaugurated a regular and institutionalized dialogue around three themes: philosophy and orientalism, the history of religions, and social history. This university was a Parisian enclave, cut off from the local Alsacian reality, whose members only thought of returning to the capital. In 1925 dean Christian Pfister said: "We have to resign ourselves to the fact that we will have the glory of being the waiting room for the Sorbonne."[89] The University of Strasbourg possessed, moreover, a showcase library that was an incomparable tool for research, at least in comparison with other provincial universities. It also enjoyed additional financial support thanks to the Office of Scientific Research, which subsidized the publications of the liberal arts faculty. Another stimulating particularity of Strasbourg was its law school, which attracted the elite of French jurists who wanted to carry on comparative and multidisciplinary research and which bore the unusual title School of Law and Political Science. The sociological jurist Gabriel Le Bras facilitated fruitful contacts between literary scholars and theologians by opening up research on canon law and the sociology of religions. "It is not by chance that the spark of genius of the *Annales* burst forth at Strasbourg, before consuming everything else."[90]

Despite their different personalities, Bloch and Febvre were particularly close at Strasbourg. The Institute for the History of the Middle Ages and the Institute for Modern History were side by side, and the door between them was always open. On one side was a scholar more at ease writing than speaking: "Bloch, with his trip-hammer delivery, seemed cold and distant; what he said was shaded with reservations and hesitations which upset the novices who were looking for certitude."[91] On the other, a born teacher, a caustic and talented public speaker: "Febvre immediately struck his listeners by his fiery temperament and his pedagogical talent and he was not afraid to use physical gimmicks in his teaching."[92] Bloch and Febvre had already acquired by 1929 outstanding reputations since they were collaborating with the *Revue de synthèse historique*. Lucien Febvre had already published two books that had attracted attention: his thesis, *Philippe II et la Franche-Comté* (1911), and another work, *Martin Luther* (1928). He was also a member of the editorial board of the *Revue d'histoire moderne et contemporaine*. As for Marc Bloch, he was eight years younger, the son of one of the best specialists in Roman history, Gustave Bloch. He had defended his thesis in 1920, *Rois et serfs*, and was the author of an innovative and much praised book, *Les Rois thaumaturges* (1924). Their university careers were therefore far from being marginal. Moreover, just after the journal was launched, they took the road to Paris one after the other. It was a full apotheosis for Lucien Febvre with his entry into the Collège de France in 1933; it was only half a triumph for Bloch, who in 1936 became professor of economic history at the Sorbonne, where he replaced Henri Hauser. Lucien Febvre had been introduced into political circles. The minister of national education de Monzie (1932–34) offered him the position of general secretary and director of an *Encyclopédie française*, which put him at the head of six hundred scientific collaborators and two hundred university scholars. Thanks to a schematic diagram drawn by Febvre about his intellectual affinities, we can better understand the connections he has claimed both for himself and the *Annales* in general (see fig. 1). We see in the sketch some circles more or less distant from the center, where he situates himself. Three groups gravitate around him: the *Revue de synthèse*, the *Année sociologique*, and the *Annales*. His fellow students at the Ecole Normale, Jules Sion, Henri Wallon, Jules Bloch, Augustin Renaudet, and Charles Blondel, are right next to him. Then we find other influences, including the geographic school of Vidal de la Blache, the linguistic school of Antoine Meillet, and, of course, Henri Pirenne, whom he asked to be the godfather for the *Annales*.

Febvre had intended to start an innovative journal ever since the end of the war: "The day after the war ended, hardly had I been demobilized when I conceived the idea of an international journal of

Fig. 1. Diagram of Lucien Febvre's Intellectual Affinities

My Authors   *My Mentors and Colleagues*

Renan · Flaubert · Stendhal · Proudhon

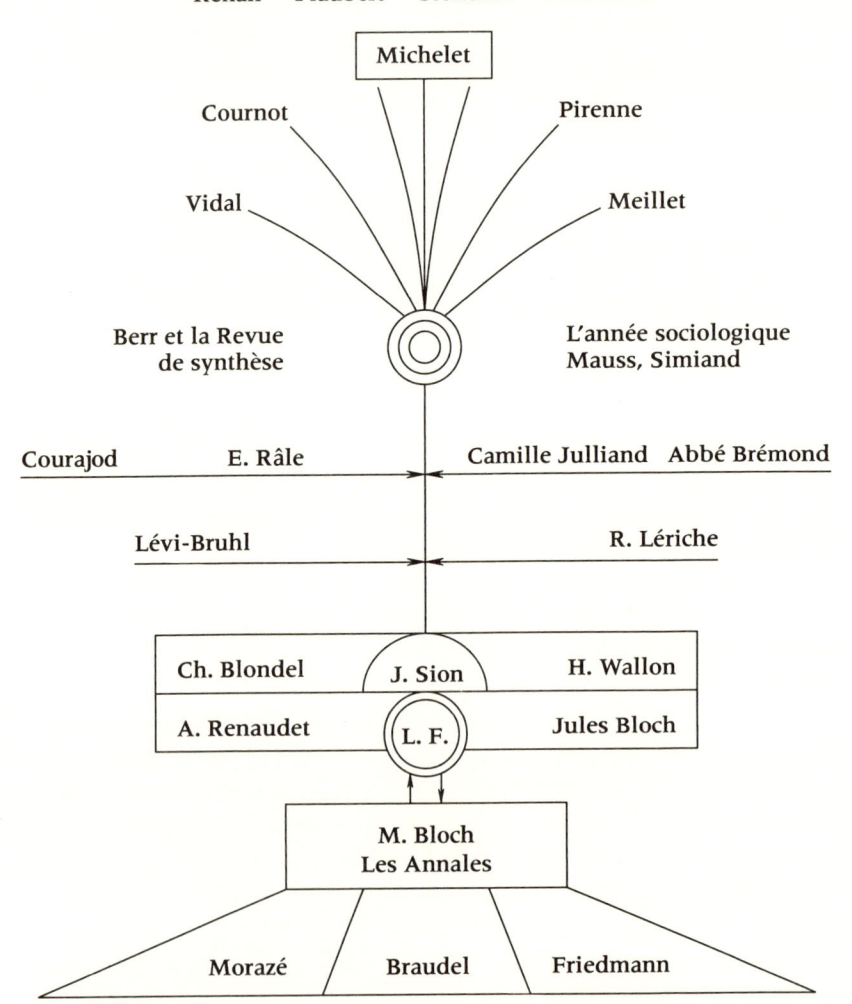

Michelet

Cournot   Pirenne

Vidal   Meillet

Berr et la Revue de synthèse   L'année sociologique Mauss, Simiand

Courajod   E. Râle   Camille Julliand   Abbé Brémond

Lévi-Bruhl   R. Leriche

Ch. Blondel   J. Sion   H. Wallon

A. Renaudet   L. F.   Jules Bloch

M. Bloch Les Annales

Morazé   Braudel   Friedmann

Source: Febvre Archives. Exposition at the Bibliothèque Nationale (1978).

economic history."[93] The primary economic focus of this new history was therefore obvious early on. This is even clearer in the letter Febvre wrote to Armand Colin at the beginning of 1928 and in which he proposed this title for the journal: "Economic Evolution: A Critical Journal of Economic and Social History."[94] In his plan for the journal certain desiderata are evident: break down disciplinary barriers, unify the social sciences around history, and be responsive to the issues of the present. The journal aborning should "establish permanent liaisons among groups of researchers who, most frequently, do not know each other and who remain closed off within the narrow domain of their specialization: historians, economists, geographers, sociologists, and researchers particularly interested in the contemporary world."[95] In a sense this was transposing the Strasbourg model to the entire nation. Marc Bloch was doubtless the force orienting the journal more toward social, sociological studies and not just economics, as in Febvre's project from right after the war. Bloch wrote to André Siegfried: "We insist on the word *social*. I underline the study of the organization of society, of classes in addition to the word *economic*."[96]

The journal finally appeared on 15 January 1929 under the title *Annales d'histoire économique et sociale* (The Annals of Social and Economic History) and with an editorial staff that announced its role as liaison for all the social sciences under the leadership of two historians, Bloch and Febvre. The editors included the geographer Albert Demangeon, who served as a go-between with the publisher, the Durkheimian sociologist Maurice Halbwachs, the economist Charles Rist, the political scientist André Siegfried, and fellow historians André Piganiol for antiquity, Georges Espinas for the medieval period, and Henri Hauser for the modern period (sixteenth to eighteenth centuries). To these must be added the power behind the throne for the whole operation, the Belgian historian Henri Pirenne.[97] The latter's role has been somewhat forgotten. Once the world war was over, at the moment when he wanted to launch his international journal of economic history, Febvre intended to make Pirenne the editor-in-chief because his authority was "incomparable."[98] Early in his career, Pirenne had taken on traditional history and its weaknesses. In 1898 he argued against Langlois and Seignobos that historical science changes depending on its epoch and the spirit of its times. After more than two years of captivity in Germany, which he spent writing his *Histoire de Belgique*, he acquired a good deal of fame. He met Bloch and

Febvre on 1 May 1920: "His refusal to be narrow-minded, the originality of his views in economic and social history, his insistence on affirming the need for comparative history impressed his young colleagues from Strasbourg."[99] The dialogue and the collaboration among these three never varied, whether it was at international meetings, within the *Annales* journal, or at the University of Ghent. Pirenne's death provided an opportunity to express the debt owed to this godfather in the shadows: "He was for us more than an advisor and a protector; he was our own titular genius who gave us the strength and the will to persevere in difficult times and who restored our faith in moments of doubt."[100]

The break between traditional discourse and that of the *Annales* was clean and can be demonstrated by comparing the kind of articles published in the *Annales* with those in the *Revue historique*. The Dutch historian Jean-Louis Oosterhoff has done this.[101] His quantitative analysis of the articles for the period of Bloch and Febvre, 1929–45, shows a spectacular drop in political history, which accounted for only 2.8 percent of the articles in the *Annales* while, for the same period, it comprised 49.9 percent of those in the *Revue historique*. The economic preference of the *Annales* is confirmed: 57.8 percent of its articles dealt with economics compared with 17.5 percent in the *Revue*. The weight of cultural history was still modest because it was less than in the *Revue*: 10.4 percent in the *Annales* versus 16.9 percent for the *Revue*. *Annales* themes began to take over the latter even though they were contrary to its theoretical nature. The traditional sections that had spelled the success of the *Revue historique* began to decline and were replaced by a history more open to economics and society. Biographical history fell off relentlessly. The erosion of political history was real if less spectacular, and it remained the journal's main section.

These figures spell out the success of the *Annales* in opposition to history that focused on battles. Traditional narrative historicism did still hold many positions and honors. Against it the *Annales* took its best shot. Every issue of the journal was another piece of artillery aimed at traditional history. Reviews and the section entitled "Debates and Combats" were so many springboards for polemics in a very militant journal. What kept the sociologists, geographers, and psychologists together, what made their unity, was their rejection of traditional history. Locating the enemy forged the group's cohesiveness. Attacks against narrative history at first were directed at the narrow political focus of its research. The *Annales* declared itself first and foremost hostile to political discourse and to political analysis. The collapse of political history ensued. The *Annales* proposed a wider field for history that, by deserting the political arena, would carry historians' gaze to other horizons: physical nature, the countryside, population, demographics, exchanges, manners. "Thus a material anthropology was formed and the concept of historical materialism was defined."[102] As the concept of materialism became central, it displaced the sources of historians who could no longer limit themselves to the exegesis of written documents belonging to the political sphere. They owed it to themselves to enlarge their sources and their methods by integrating statistics, demographics, linguistics, psychology, numismatics, and archeology: "Of course texts, but not only just texts."[103] This opening-up revealed that the alliance being proposed to the other sciences intended to make them history's servants. In their publications and reviews Bloch and Febvre denounced the shortcomings of the former masters of the French historical school. In his *Société féodale*, Bloch's intention was to show that medieval society could not be reduced to a simple political or judicial definition: "In today's accepted usage, feodality and feudal society cover an intertwined network of customs in which the fief no longer stands in the foreground."[104] The history he yearned for left the battlefields and the preparations for war. In contrast, it chose to reconcile past antagonisms. The previous generation's fear of Germany was left behind: "The theory of predestined frontiers cannot in fact be defended by the study of the past or the observation of the present. France has not always been hungrily poised to conquer the Rhine any more than Germany has. Germany was for a long time unmoved by the mystique of the Rhine, which is a recent creation of mind and heart. France, Belgium, the Low Lands, Germany, Switzerland: all these countries have understood each other, contributed to each other, and enriched each other through the Rhine."[105] Beneath the rejection of politics lay the decision to diminish events to the advantage of long duration, which matched the evolutionary rhythm of historical materialism better. In a 1950 review of the third part of Fernand Braudel's thesis, *La Méditerranée et le monde méditerranéen à l'époque de Philippe II*, whose subject was events, politics, and men, Febvre called this history "froth," as did its author, and spoke of "waves that animated superficially the powerful respiration of an ocean mass."[106] Frequently the tone was very polemical. Seignobos,

Langlois, Lavisse, Fustel, and Halphen became targets on which the Annalists sharpened their arguments and their argumentativeness. Let us judge from this deadly review by Febvre of a book by Seignobos, Louis Eisenmann, and Paul Milioukov published in 1932: "I open *L'Histoire de la Russie*. What a sorry spectacle. Weakling czars straight out of *Ubu Roi;* palace dramas; ministers breaking everything, bureaucrats parroting; all the oukases and prikazes you could want.... History is what I do not find in this history of Russia, which is therefore stillborn."[107] The year before, in 1933, the same Seignobos had been signaled out by Febvre in the same journal for his *Histoire sincère de la nation française*. Febvre said it was more a high school text than a history book: "Through this book I am attacking not a historian but a certain concept of history ... a concept that I reject with all my being."[108] He stigmatized the static approach to history that transformed France into something ready-made, a given, an atemporal invariable removed from the torments of history. This polemic with traditional history remained constant in the *Annales*. In 1946 Febvre took on "diplomatic history per se" apropos of a book by A. Roubaud, *La Paix armée: 1871-1914:* "This book is located at the antipodes of what we in the *Annales* think a good book of contemporary history should be.... Geography, zero.... Economics, zero."[109]

For its second target, the *Annales* took aim at traditional historians' fetish of the fact and at their so-called passivity before the facts that they are supposed to transcribe without any afterthought: "The scholar, the historian in other terms, is asked to disappear before the facts."[110] In contrast, Bloch and Febvre claimed that historians must interact with the documents or the archives. Gaston Bachelard expressed this in a phrase that picked up terms from the *Annales* discourse: "Nothing is self-evident. Nothing is given. Everything is constructed."[111] According to the *Annales*, historians construct their working materials: they classify documents into intelligible groups within a theoretical framework that predates their research and that is adapted to it. Unless they use this questioning procedure, historians are helpless, typists, architects perhaps, but not scientists. Quoting the physiologist Dastre, Febvre claimed: "When you don't know what you are looking for you don't know what you find."[112] Traditional historians' procedures were marked then by weakness, "naiveté," and "laziness," terms that ring of polemics. Febvre insisted on the critical role of historians and on their subjectivity: "Are there any givens? No, all is created by the historian."[113] "It is not the past that engenders the historian. It is the historian who gives birth to history."[114] To the scientific objectivity of Ranke or Seignobos, Bloch and Febvre opposed the subjective relativism in which historians would choose the facts to investigate in the light of their current preoccupations and subject them to a certain number of hypotheses. Failing that, historical knowledge is a meaningless word. Historians do not have to eliminate their individuality to profess doubt; on the contrary, they merely have to confront their hypotheses with the documents they have collected.

To burn down traditional history the *Annales* found any fuel acceptable. Including sociologists, psychologists, and geographers on their team was not a modernist alibi or excuse for seeking a history unique unto itself. The *Annales* was nourished on concepts, methods, and hypotheses taken from the other social sciences. The strategy of Bloch and Febvre included taking over all these new languages and codes that were the indispensable means of winning the battle for power. It began with an appeal to knock down barriers: leave your trenches, we are proposing a treaty to allow fraternizing among the social sciences: "The walls are so high that they often cut off the view. . . . We intend to rise up against these cleavages."[115] Regrouping was primarily a reaction, in this case against the old-fashioned historical school. The journal used the notions most likely to reach far and wide, and it carefully avoided appearing as the incarnation of a new dogma that might frighten its allies: "A code as vague as it was social . . . seemed to have been created to serve as the banner for a journal that did not want to close itself off behind walls."[116] Not content to ally itself with other specialists, the *Annales* wanted to incorporate their methods and their concepts. Febvre was influenced directly by the linguist Antoine Meillet, who collaborated on the *Année sociologique,* when he advanced his notion of a mental tool that, like language, designates the "keyboards of possibilities" that society puts at an individual's disposition.[117]

When Febvre laid the foundations for historical psychology, he used the work of psychologists Henri Wallon or Jean Piaget and gave historians a new perspective: the study of feeling and emotional life in history. This was not picked up immediately, but it did have some success later on. Bloch placed the sociological categories that he was testing historically right in the middle of his *La Société féodale*. Bloch's *Les Caractères originaux de l'histoire rurale* (1931) marked a historiographic breakthrough in which we can see the Durkheimian concept of *social fact* emerge as a tool of history. Febvre defended Vidal de la Blache against the German geopolitical school of Ratzel. He included the geographer's procedures within the historian's scope in *La terre et l'évolution humaine* (1922). In 1953 he even claimed that it was Vidal's geography that begat the kind of history the *Annales* promoted. But such praises masked the attempt to subdue geography as an auxiliary of history. The way to do so consisted in incorporating geography into history and then limiting its subject matter: "The soil and not the state: that is geography's subject. . . . As for the rest, we are free to dip into geographical research . . . for reasons that are not geographic."[118] The geographers felt threatened and reacted so violently that Febvre had to explain himself: "I have been informed from diverse sources recently that I had hatched the particularly nefarious plot to strangle geography. And, adding insult to injury, to strangle it with a garrote borrowed from geography itself."[119] But this round was won even before it began; the geographic school was already in decline.

More than any cartel, the *Annales* succeeded in marshaling the social sciences under its banner. The struggle against historicism resulted in a permanent core of *Annales* discourse: the relativization if not the rejection of narrative and political history. With this rejection the *Annales* defined itself as a recognizable school despite its diverse components. The enemy was always the same: so-called positivistic history. This permitted continuity and cohesion within the movement: "An additional advantage: the enemy is not dangerous, he is dead."[120] The two rejections of this first period, narrative history and political history, are still claimed by the *Annales* today. This condemnation without appeal is seen as a constant in Oosterhoff's analysis of the journal's content in different time periods. Political history accounted for only 2.8 percent of the articles from 1929 to 1945; 5.4 percent from 1946 to 1956; 4.1 percent between 1957 and 1969; and fell to a low of 2.1 percent from 1969 to 1976. In this the *Annales* of today is the heir of the *Annales* of Bloch and Febvre of 1929. This continuity is the reason the school survived the diversity of its component parts.

■ NOTES

1. F. Simiand (1873–1935) was a Durkheimian sociologist and economist and professor at the Collège de France from 1932 to 1935.
2. J. Le Goff in *La Nouvelle Histoire* (Retz, 1978), 214.
3. "Le mur d'argent" means, literally, the wall of money. Popular opinion

thought that rich bankers had conspired through the Banque de France to defeat the Left by not funding its programs in 1924–26—Trans.

4. F. Simiand, *Recherches anciennes et nouvelles sur le mouvement général des prix du XVIe au XIX siècle* (1932). H. Hauser, *Recherches et documents sur l'histoire des prix en France de 1500 à 1800* (1936). A pioneer of the economic history of the sixteenth century, Hauser (1866–1946) studied the origins of modern capitalism in France. E. Labrousse, *Esquisse du mouvement des prix et des revenus en France au XVIIIe siècle* (1933). Born in 1895, he was a professor at the Sorbonne and section six of the Ecole Pratique des Hautes Etudes.

5. P. Chaunu, *Histoire et science sociale* (SEDES, 1974), 56.

6. P. Chaunu, "L'Histoire sérielle: bilan et perspectives," *Revue historique* (1970): 302.

7. C. Bouglé, *Bilan de la sociologie française contemporaine* (1935), 79.

8. A. Demangeon, *Le Déclin de l'Europe* (1920). O. Spengler, *Déclin de l'Occident* (1920).

9. L. Febvre, *Combats pour l'histoire* (A. Colin, 1953), 26.

10. J. Touchard, "L'Esprit des années 1930," in *Tendances politiques dans la vie française depuis 1789* (1960); and P. Andreu, "Les Idées politiques de la jeunesse intellectuelle de 1927 à la guerre," *Revue des travaux de l'Académie des sciences morales et politiques* (1957): 17–35.

11. P. Andreu, "Les Idées politiques."

12. D. de Rougemont, "Cahiers de revendications," *NRF* 20 (1932): 51.

13. J. Touchard, "L'Esprit des années 1930," 101.

14. H. Daniel-Rops, *L'Ordre nouveau* (Oct. 1933), as quoted by J. Touchard, "L'Esprit des années 1930," 102.

15. *L'Ordre nouveau* (Apr. 1936) as quoted by J. Touchard, "L'Esprit des années 1930," 102.

16. P. Andreu, "Les Idées politiques."

17. *Plans*, no. 1, p. 9.

18. The prospectus announcing *L'Ordre nouveau*.

19. For example, the founding of the Institute of Comparative Studies at Oslo in 1930. In 1935, the J. Bodin Foundation in Brussels sponsored a debate between Germans and Poles over the situation in Silesia.

20. A. Guerreau, *Le Féodalisme: Un Horizon théorique* (Le Sycomore, 1980), 142.

21. V. Karady, "Durkheim, les sciences sociales et l'université: bilan d'un semi-échec," *Revue française de sociologie* (Apr. 1976).

22. E. Durkheim, *L'Année sociologique* 6 (1903): 124–25.

23. See D. Linderberg, *Le Marxisme introuvable* (Calmann-Lévy, 1975).

24. E. Durkheim, "Leçon d'ouverture du cours de science sociale," *Revue internationale de l'enseignement* 15 (1888): 48.

25. V. Karady, "Stratégies de réussite et modes de faire-valoir de la sociologie chez les durkheimiens," *Revue française de sociologie* 20 (Jan. 1979): 49–82.

26. F. Simiand, *L'Année sociologique* 11 (1906–9): 729.

27. C. Bouglé, "Comment étudier la sociologie à Paris?" *Annales de l'Université de Paris* (1927): 313–24.

28. J. Heilbron, "Les Métamorphoses du durkheimisme: 1920–1940," *Revue française de sociologie* (Apr.–June 1985): 226.
29. Georges Duby, "Préface," in M. Bloch, *Apologie pour l'histoire* (1941; rpt. A. Colin, 1974), 8.
30. M. Bloch, *Apologie pour l'histoire*, 27.
31. F. Simiand, "Méthode historique et science sociale," *Revue de synthèse historique* (1903); reprinted in *Annales* (1960): 117.
32. R. Chartier and J. Revel, "L. Febvre et les sciences sociales," *Historiens et Géographes* (1979): 430.
33. O. Dumoulin, "Profession historien: 1919–1939," 3d cycle diss. (EHESS, 1984), 233–36.
34. Philippe Besnard, "L'Impérialisme sociologique face à l'histoire," *Journées annuelles de la Société française de sociologie* (Lille, 1984).
35. P. Mantoux (1877–1956), *La Révolution industrielle au XVIII siècle en Angleterre* (1906). G. Monod (1844–1912) was a professor at the Collège de France in 1905 and founded the *Revue historique* in 1876.
36. J. Revel, "Histoire et sciences sociales: les paradigmes des *Annales*," *Annales* (1979): 1362.
37. L. Febvre, *Pour une histoire à part entière* (1940; rpt. SEVPEN, 1963), 311.
38. P. Vidal de La Blache, *Tableau géographique de la France* (1911), 385.
39. P. Vidal de La Blache, "La Géographie politique," *Annales de géographie* (1898), 102.
40. J. M. Besse, "Idéologie pour une géographie," *Espaces-Temps* 12 (1979).
41. C. Grataloup, "Après l'empire, le beau temps," *Espaces-Temps* 30 (1985): 53.
42. Philippe Bachimon, "Physiologie d'un langage," *Espaces-Temps* 13 (1979).
43. 1905: A. Demangeon, *La Picardie;* 1906: R. Blanchard, *La Flandre;* 1907: Felice, *La Basse Normandie;* 1908: Vacher, *Le Berry,* and Passerat, *Le Poitou;* 1909: J. Sion, *Les Paysans de Normandie orientale;* 1913: M. Sorre, *La Notion de paysage dans les Pyrénées méditerranéennes.*
44. L. Febvre, *Annales* (1953): 374n.
45. N. Broc in *Au berceau des Annales* (Presses de l'Université de Toulouse, 1983), 248.
46. A. Demangeon, *Le Déclin de l'Europe* (1920).
47. Charles-Olivier Carbonell in *Au berceau des Annales* (Presses de l'Université de Toulouse, 1983), 89–104.
48. O. Dumoulin, "Profession historien," 89.
49. Bloch was a candidate twice, on 20 January 1929 and 13 January 1935. Unlike Febvre, Bloch played the innovative card, first promoting comparative history, then betting on economic history.
50. Marc Bloch, *Apologie pour l'histoire*, 29.
51. Ibid., 107.
52. M. Ferro, *L'Histoire sous surveillance* (Calmann-Lévy, 1985), 135.
53. Charles O. Carbonell, *L'Historiographie* (Presses Universitaires de France), 94, in Collection "Que sais-je?"

54. Ibid., 95.
55. Guizot, *Histoire de la civilisation en Europe* (1828), seventh lesson.
56. Quoted by G. Mairet, *Le Discours et l'historique* (Repères, 1974), 29.
57. G. Monod, *Revue historique* 1 (1876).
58. Ibid., 36.
59. Members of the editorial board of the *Revue historique* in 1876 included V. Duruy, Renan, Taine, Boutaric, Fustel de Coulanges, G. Monod, Lavisse, Guiraud, Bémond, Rambaut.
60. G. Monod, *Revue historique* 1 (1876): 38.
61. G. Monod, *Revue historique* (July–Aug. 1896): 325.
62. A. Corbin, "Lundis de l'histoire," France Culture, 21 Dec. 1976. This survey was done for the centenary of the *Revue historique*. See also, A. Corbin in *Au berceau des Annales*, 105–7.
63. Ibid., 119.
64. G. Monod, *Revue historique* (1900): 309.
65. Christian Pfister (1857–1933) was a medievalist and a specialist on Lorraine. He was dean and later rector of the University of Strasbourg from 1919 to 1931. Charles-André Julien (born in 1891) was a socialist historian and participated in the Congress at Tours in 1920. He was also dean of the college of liberal arts at Rabat and author of *L'Histoire de l'Afrique du Nord* (1931) and *L'Histoire de l'Algérie* (1964). Maurice Crouzet was an inspector general for the Ministry of National Education.
66. Seignobos to the French Philosophical Society in 1908, as quoted by A. Gérard in *Au berceau des Annales*, 84–85.
67. Charles Langlois and Charles Seignobos, *Introduction aux études historiques* (1898), 275.
68. Ibid., 204.
69. Ibid., 253.
70. Charles Seignobos, *Histoire politique de l'Europe contemporaine* (1924).
71. E. Lavisse in a letter to the imperial prince, 18 Feb. 1877, as quoted by P. Nora, *Revue historique* (June 1962): 79.
72. G. Bourdé and H. Martin, *Les Ecoles historiques* (Le Seuil, 1983), 158–59.
73. Lavisse in the preface to the last edition of his manual (1912).
74. Fustel de Coulanges, *La Monarchie franque* (1888), 32–33.
75. Ibid.
76. Fustel de Coulanges, *Questions historiques* (1893), 3–16.
77. Ibid.
78. Georg G. Iggers, *New Directions in European Historiography* (Wesleyan University Press, 1975), 51.
79. H. Berr, *L'Avenir de la philosophie: esquisse d'une synthèse de la conaissance historique* (1899).
80. M. Siegel in *Au berceau des Annales*, 206.
81. H. Berr, *La Synthèse en histoire, essai critique et théorique* (1911), 43.
82. M. Siegel in *Au berceau des Annales*, 208.
83. H. Berr in the preface to the reappearance of the journal in 1919.

84. H. Berr, *Le Germanisme contre l'esprit français* (1919).
85. A. Burguière, "Histoire d'une histoire: la naissance des *Annales*," *Annales* (Nov. 1979): 1350.
86. Ibid., 1353.
87. Ibid.
88. H. Coutau-Bégarie, *Le Phénomène nouvelle histoire* (Economica, 1983), 126.
89. Quoted by F. G. Dryfus in *Au berceau des Annales*, 11–19.
90. M. Thomann in *Au berceau des Annales*, 33–36.
91. Ph. Dollinger in *Au berceau des Annales*, 65–67.
92. Ibid., 65.
93. L. Febvre, prospectus for the *Annales* (Nov. 1928), as quoted in *Combats pour l'histoire* (A. Colin, 1953), 398.
94. *Catalogue de l'exposition sur L. Febvre*, Bibliothèque National (Nov. 1978), 39.
95. Ibid.
96. Quoted in P. Leuilliot, "Aux origines des *Annales d'histoire économique et sociale*," in *Mélanges en l'honneur de F. Braudel* (Privat, 1972).
97. A. Demangeon (1872–1940) was a Vidalian geographer and professor at Lille, later at the Sorbonne (1911). He wrote *Le Déclin en Europe* (1920) and a 1905 thesis, *La Picardie et les régions voisines: Artois-Cambrésis, Beauvaisis*.

M. Halbwachs (1877–1945) was a Durkheimian sociologist and professor in Paris from 1935. Publications: *Les Causes du suicide* (1930); *Morphologie sociale* (1938); and *Esquisse d'une psychologie des classes sociales* (1939).

Charles Rist (1874–1955) was an economist and an undergovernor of the Bank of France from 1926 to 1929. Publications: *Histoire des doctrines économiques, depuis les physiocrates jusqu'à nos jours* (1909) and *Histoire des doctrines relatives au crédit et à la monnaie depuis John Law jusqu'à nos jours* (1938).

A. Siegfried (1875–1959), professor at the Collège de France, was one of the founders of political sociology. He wrote *Le Tableau politique de la France de l'ouest* (1913) and *Le Tableau des partis en France* (1930).

A. Piganiol (1883–1968) was a historian specializing in classical Rome and professor at the Collège de France from 1942 until 1954. Publications: *Essai sur les origines de Rome* (1917); *La Conquête romaine* (1928); and *L'Histoire de Rome* (1939).

G. Espinas (1869–1948), a medievalist and specialist in urban history, wrote *Les Origines du capitalisme* (1933–49) and *La Vie urbaine à Douai au Moyen Age* (1913).

H. Pirenne (1862–1935) was a Belgian historian and professor at Ghent. He wrote *L'Histoire de la Belgique* (1899–1932).
98. L. Febvre, *Combats pour l'histoire* (A. Colin, 1953), 398.
99. R. Demoulin in *Au berceau des Annales*, 274.
100. L. Febvre, "H. Pirenne: 1862–1935," *Annales* 7 (1935): 529.
101. See H. L. Wesseling, "The *Annales* School and the Writing of Contemporary History," *Review* 1 (Winter-Spring 1978). J. L. Oosterhoff did the quantitative part.

102. B. Barret-Kriegel, "Histoire et politique," *Annales* (Dec. 1973).
103. L. Febvre, "Leçon d'ouverture au Collège de France" in his *Combats pour l'histoire*, 13.
104. M. Bloch, *La Société féodale* (1941; rpt. A. Michel, 1968), 13.
105. L. Febvre, *Le Rhin, problème d'histoire et d'économie* (A. Colin, 1935), 291–92.
106. L. Febvre, *Pour une histoire à part entière* (1950; rpt. SEVPEN, 1963), 167–79.
107. L. Febvre, *Revue de synthèse* 7 (1934); reprinted in *Combats pour l'histoire*, 70–74.
108. L. Febvre, *Revue de synthèse* 5 (1933); reprinted in *Combats pour l'histoire*, 80–98.
109. L. Febvre, *Combats pour l'histoire*, 61–69.
110. M. Bloch, *Apologie pour l'histoire* (1941; rpt. A. Colin, 1974), 117.
111. G. Bachelard, *La Formation de l'esprit scientifique: Contribution à une psychanalyse de la connaissance objective* (Vrin, 1970), 14.
112. L. Febvre, *Combats pour l'histoire*, 59.
113. Ibid, 7.
114. L. Febvre, "Introduction," in Charles Morazé, *Trois Essais sur histoire et culture* (A. Colin, 1948), 8.
115. L. Febvre, *Annales* (1929).
116. M. Bloch and L. Febvre, "A nos lecteurs," *Annales* (1929): 1–2.
117. H. D. Mann, *L. Febvre: la pensée vivante d'un historien* (A. Colin, 1971), 131.
118. L. Febvre, *La Terre et l'évolution humaine* (1922; rpt. A. Michel, 1970), 78.
119. L. Febvre, *Pour une histoire à part entière*, 163.
120. H. Coutau-Bégarie, *Le Phénomène nouvelle histoire*, 296.

TWO

The Era of Marc Bloch and Lucien Febvre

■ HISTORIANS OF THE PRESENT

French historians have a tradition of disliking philosophers. This rejection of any philosophy of history can be found in the *Annales:* "No abstract methodology in the German fashion. . . . Historians draw their ideas from history itself."[1] Despite themselves, however, Marc Bloch and Lucien Febvre did have a conception of history, and therefore a philosophy of history, that can be read in the fundamental concepts of their historical method. Even if the thrust of their writing accented historical method and avoided all historical theory, they still could not avoid the fact that the empiricism they proclaimed was already a choice, a particular concept of history. More than other historical schools, the *Annales* heard the call of contemporary society since its founders had reestablished the link between past and present. This school could not, therefore, ignore the dominant values of the modern and technocratic society that came into being at the beginning of the twentieth century in Europe. We find the coherence of the *Annales* in its connection with modernity.

To better understand this "Popular Front" spirit,[2] it is necessary to follow the career of the first *Annales* historians. At the beginning of his intellectual life, Lucien Febvre was a fervent Socialist; between 1907 and 1909 he wrote for *Le Socialiste comtois*, the weekly journal of the Section Française de l'Internationale Ouvrière in the department of the Doubs. On 21 March 1909, he wrote four articles that filled half of the first page: "Long Live Life! Down with the Authorities," "Until When?" "Propaganda in the Fields," and "The Floquet Demonstration." Both style and content surprise us when we compare them with his subsequent positions. When he frequented the halls of power as a professor at the Collège de France, he kept the vehemence of this polemical tone, but he limited his fight to history and avoided politics. That was not the case in 1909, as can be seen by this citation: "Oh, dear old Proudhon! There are some who say you are dead! Go on, rest easy: that human personality which for so many centuries wallowed in unchanging servility is now standing up. It is speaking, in a voice that is still weak but no longer timid, the liberating cry that you yourself proclaimed: no more authorities!" If, at the moment of the creation of the *Annales* Febvre was no longer politically engaged, that was not true for a certain number of his collaborators at the journal. Georges Friedmann, an admirer of Soviet accomplishments, wrote many articles extolling the benefits of Stalinism; Frantz Borkenau belonged to the Frankfurt school; Georges Bourgin, the historian of the Commune, was a friend of Lucien Herr and of Leon Blum; the sociologist Halbwachs died at Buchenwald in 1945.

As for March Bloch, the encomium that Borislav Geremek, the historian and adviser to Lech Walesa, recently gave him ended with "We can die for Danzig!"[3] The allusion reminds us that neither Geremek nor Bloch avoided history when they found it, whether opposing general Jaruzelski or the Nazi occupation. This total engagement, linking thought and action, cost Bloch his life in 1944. He acknowledged that he belonged to the generation at the end of the Dreyfus affair. He favored the Popular Front in 1936, was hostile to the Munich pact in 1938. When war broke out he was fifty-three. He was a captain during what has come to be known as the "funny war" and what he called the "Strange Defeat." He narrowly avoided capture and rejoined his family at Guéret, in the department of the Creuse.

From this point on the two leaders of the *Annales* followed different paths. Bloch opposed continuing to publish the journal under conditions imposed by the Nazi occupational authorities, that is to say, an editorial staff of Frenchmen without any Jewish blood. "I think we should not allow any appearance of going along."[4] That was not Febvre's opinion, who answered: "The *Annales* has to continue. It must."[5] The journal continued and changed its name. It became *Mélanges d'histoire sociale* and appeared under that title until 1944, with the names of two non-Jewish editors on the cover: Lucien Febvre and Paul Leuilliot. Meanwhile, Bloch contributed to the journal under the pseudonym Marc Fougères. That was not all. He totally committed himself: "I say it frankly: in any case, I hope we have some blood to shed, even if it is the blood of those who are dear to me."[6] Unlike many other intellectuals, he refused to leave for the New School in New York, which had invited him to flee the Nazis. In 1943 he joined the Resistance in the region around Lyons. He became the militant of the *Franc-Tireurs:* "That eminent professor came to put himself at our command simply and modestly."[7] He became a member of the executive committee of the Unified Resistance Movement (MUR) for the Lyons region under the pseudonym Narbonne: "Soon the entire Resistance knew him. Too well, because he saw and wanted to see too many people."[8] In the spring of 1944, the Gestapo arrested many of the leaders of the Lyons MUR. Bloch was arrested, incarcerated at Montluc, and tortured. When the Allies landed, the Nazis executed inmates from the Montluc prison, including Bloch. Next to him "a sixteen-year old kid was trembling, 'It's going to hurt.' Bloch took him by the arm and said kindly: 'No, it doesn't hurt.' He was the first to fall shouting 'Long live France!'"[9] Bloch left a spiritual testament that he wrote in March 1941 and in which he proclaimed first and foremost his French identity: "A stranger to any formal religious belief as well as to any supposed racial solidarity, I have felt myself to be, for my whole life, quite simply French before anything else. . . . I die, as I have lived, like a good Frenchman."[10] Despite this heroic act, the socialist tendencies of the *Annales* in the thirties did not weigh heavy since the group premised its existence on rejecting all that was political: "I always ask myself how a true historian could study politics."[11] The traditional historical school's adhesion to the republic was functional; it served the discourse of power. By refusing political discourse, the *Annales* failed in its mission of producing a historical journal that would help explain contemporary phenomena. Of course, the gulag was not then known, but Stalinism was. Trotsky was its most famous victim as the whole world knew after 1927. The *Annales*, however, continued to praise the totalitarian Stalinist state because the journal limited itself to advances in productivity and the growth of heavy industry, which constituted a partial vision, to say the least, of Soviet reality. Georges Friedmann praised Stakhanovism ("the warm gift of their experience and their knowledge that the Stakhanovists display") and Stalin ("of all the politicians' speeches, the most substantial and solid are those of Molotov and Stalin").[12]

What is even more serious, the *Annales* sidestepped the phenomena of fascism and Nazism. This gap in a journal that wanted to be progressive is particularly significant and hinges also on its denial of politics. In a beautiful book entitled *Etrange défaite*, written in 1940 and published in 1946, Marc Bloch regretted, bitterly but too late, these lacunae that derived from the erroneous postulates of the *Annales*: "We have not dared to be, in the public square, the voice that cries out first in the desert. . . . We have preferred to remain in the fearful calm of our workshops. May the young pardon us the blood that is on our hands."[13] Bloch's comments voiced a self-criticism of the *Annales* positions: "In general, we have the right to say we were good workers. Were we always good citizens?"[14] Here he questioned the fatalism of the *Annales* discourse that gave priority to the interplay of massive forces, denied the role of individuals and their convictions, and shunned both individual and collective actions: "That was incorrectly interpreting history."[15] This page is in itself already a very lucid critique of the insufficiency and the obfuscation of the *Annales* historical discourse. It is all the more valuable in that it was written by one of the uncontested masters of this school at a tragic moment when history knocked at the door and the specialists walked on by and did not see.

If leftist sentiment was dominant between the wars in the *Annales*, we should not therefore make it a cell of Marxist intellectuals as some have tried. Surely, the journal's orientations, i.e., the importance given to the economic and the social, the emphasis on historical materialism, the primacy of underlying structures, could sustain such a belief. Many of these concepts are close to Marxism, but as T. Stoïanowich has shown, Marxist history "is both a rival and a precursor of the *Annales*."[16] Up until the thirties, Marxism was little known. It was of course claimed by the workers' parties, but essentially as praxis. It began to spread in the thirties in university milieus, thanks especially to the *Cercle de la Russie neuve*, a journal founded in 1932 and edited by Daniel Chalonge, Charles Parrain, and Jean Baby; Georges Friedmann, among others from the *Annales*, contributed to it. This group organized a number of conferences that led to the publication in 1937–38 of several volumes entitled *A la lumière du marxisme* that summed up the contribution of historical materialism. The *Annales* adapted many ideas from a diffuse and poorly understood Marxism in order to better resist an efficient historical materialism that itself aspired to be total history. In its efforts to expand, the *Annales* risked joining Marxism purely and simply. The group therefore laid the bases of a specific discourse that would be both offensive and defensive. Reviews of Marxist books written by Febvre denounced their compartmentalized construction and their bias in favor of popular movements and revolutionary leaders. Febvre saw in Marxist discourse simultaneously a form of economic spiritualism and a conception of individual events and wills similar to traditional history's. The review of Daniel Guérin's book on the French Revolution demonstrates what Febvre objected to in Marxism: it was a history of good guys and bad guys and it dared to judge. Under the title "Prancing on the Revolution," he denounced "this collusion between Michelet and Marx, an incest," and he repeated: "The historian is not a judge."[17] When the translation of Engels's *The Peasant War* appeared in 1930, Febvre denied that the book had any historical scope. Under the title "An Out-of-Date Book" he wrote: "For knowing Engels, yes. For knowing the peasant wars, it is a joke."[18] Still the blame did not fall on Marx and Engels, and indeed they were the object of undisguised admiration: "For Karl Marx I have personally the greatest admiration. . . . Is that sufficient, however, to make his lessons the eternal measure for every doctrine?"[19] Besides, the young Marxist historians of those years, like Pierre Vilar and Jean Bruhat, warmly welcomed this new journal that seemed so close to their own preoccupations. In 1934 in the Catholic journal *Foi et Vie*, Febvre vaunted Marx's merits: "The large and powerful question of the rapports between capitalism and the Reformation . . . who first posed it? Let us not hesitate to answer: it's Karl Marx."[20] Nonetheless, he criticized the prophetic character of Marx's thesis, his determination to show only one truth at whatever cost, and to see in historical materials only the proof that supported his argument, namely a reformation engendered by capitalism. For this causal approach Febvre substituted the notion of interdependent phenomena. What Bloch and Febvre had in common with Marx's thought was its desire to be total and entire, to embrace what is real. We are not then astonished to read this from Febvre's pen: "Read Marx, I would say gladly. . . . Read Lenin too, and those who have continued Marx's effort on a few decisive points."[21]

With traditional historical discourse on the right and Marxism on the left, the *Annales* offered a third way and occupied a middle position that was ideal for its power play. It had yet to construct an original paradigm or a specific kind of knowledge that would legitimize its desire for hegemony. In this regard, the *Annales* discourse broke with traditional history and thus constituted a historiographic revolution. An essential innovation of the *Annales* at this time was to break with traditional history's exclusive concern with the past and to correlate past and present by constructing a history that took as its field of study not just the past but also contemporary society. Whereas traditional history thought that, to be scientific, it should be cut off from the present, Febvre invited historians to take their inspiration from the problems of the times in which they were living, working, and writing. To question the past from the present had a heuristic value for the *Annales*. History was a "response to questions that the man of today necessarily asks."[22] The present helped in seeking the past, favored a problem-oriented technique, and enriched the knowledge of the past. Using the heuristic value of the present, the *Annales* defended a relativistic concept of historical discourse. Being immersed in its own time and in the problems of the present, history produces a construction of historical time, perspectives, and periodizations whose limits coincide with those that permitted the research. It is a construction that has to be located each time in the moment and in the place where it was first formulated. Every epoch constructs its own representation of the past according to its own preoccupations. History "seeks out and accentuates the facts, the events, and the tendencies in the past that prepare the present, that permit understanding it, and that help to live it. . . . [History] makes for itself the past that it needs."[23]

The *Annales* did not find that the idea of historians rewriting history in response to the call of the present contradicted the scientific character that the historical enterprise should possess. If the present helped to better understand the past, the present-past link could also work in the other direction. Not to know the past hindered a good knowledge of the present and consequently any effective action. Bloch refused to accept the definition that reduced history to the science of the past: "That is, in my opinion, speaking incorrectly."[24] The heuristic value of the present for knowing the past was pushed further by Bloch, who called for a recurrent procedure from historians, a retrospective approach. Historians leave the present to regress in time back to the societies of the past. He proposed this backwards reading "since the natural method of any investigation is to go from the better or less badly known toward the most obscure."[25] He applied this retrospective procedure to his own research. When he compared the countryside in the north of France to that in England,[26] he began by noticing the contrast between the very long and narrow plowed fields in Picardie and the English meadows that were fragmented and cut up by hedges or fences. Starting with this tangible reality he questioned the past in order to explain this duality in regions that were so close to each other. Taking the agrarian system as his subject, Bloch began with the contemporary countryside before going back to the medieval period. The past was thus consubstantial with the present for the *Annales,* and Bloch contrasted antiquarians sealed within their cult of the past with historians who look around themselves.[27]

The importance conferred on the present was evident in the *Annales,* which was, in this first period, primarily turned toward the study of contemporary society. This orientation distinguished the *Annales* from other journals and especially from the *Revue historique.* A. Corbin's study of *La Revue historique* from 1929 to 1939 reveals the predominance of the sixteenth to eighteenth centuries, which account for 33.8 percent of its articles. The contemporary period, taken in the large sense, i.e., from 1789 on, figures in only a quarter (26.6 percent). Olivier Dumoulin's study of the *Annales* shows that during the same period, the articles on contemporary history account for 42.4 percent of the total.[28] If we use as a measure more contemporary history, i.e., from 1871 on, the comparison for the same period, 1929–39, gives these results: 36 percent of the *Annales* articles, 8 percent for *La Revue d'histoire économique et sociale,* and 7.5 percent for *La Revue historique.* This preoccupation with contemporary problems was omnipresent at the *Annales* as the following titles for the period 1929–39 show: "The Population Problem in USSR" (1929); "The Banking Crisis in Germany" (1932); "The Banking Crisis in Central Europe" (1932); "Causes and Origins for the World Wheat Crisis" (1933); "Agrarian Unrest in the American West" (1936); "The Roosevelt Experience" (1936); "The Banking Crisis and the Great Depression in the United States" (1936); "Collective Agriculture in the USSR" (1938). These titles demonstrate the presence of current problems as much as the absence of politics, in addition to the journal's international preoccupation. The perspective of historians can be used by economists; historians can boast of advising their managers. The use of the future and conditional tenses in the journal illustrates the desire to bring a functional knowledge that is useful to those running society: "If economic history had been better known, the current economic situation would have been more easily understood."[29] The link between past and present was thus ceaselessly reaffirmed by the journal's editors, who made this connection the very meaning of historical procedure: "Why speak of past and present? Reality is one. To allow everyone to touch that unity with a finger will be tomorrow as it was yesterday the aim of the *Annales*."[30] "Between the present and the past, there is no watertight separation: that's the theme of the *Annales*."[31]

The two leaders of the *Annales* increasingly claimed an organic link between past and present as they subscribed to the logic of capitalistic management. They counted on adapting their historical approach to the technological era in which they hoped to play a useful role. In this spirit they surrounded themselves with leaders from both business and government. The journal attracted specialists whose main task was to act on economic and social issues. It asked them to reflect on what they were doing while they learned from contact with historians about the viability of the tools they used daily. "Two classes of workers made to understand each other and who, ordinarily, work side by side without knowing each other."[32] Bankers and financiers wrote in the *Annales* and thus reinforced the technocratic tendency of the journal. Their participation in the *Annales* discourse invalidates the theory that the journal was a forum for Marxism. The *Annales* answered the need of a government in power that was no longer content with a parliamentary mandate after the war. It needed technicians and specialists to solidify its policies more scientifically in the reality of things: "The laws of statistics replaced the spirit of the laws."[33] The young social sciences were evidently better placed than history to meet this social demand. The *Annales* answered this challenge by attempting to connect the interests of historians and managers. It called on the president of the International Swiss Bank in Zurich, G. Backman; the director of the International Bank for Commerce and Industry, A. Pose; the director of the Bank of Central Europe, J. Chappey. The American model inspired the *Annales*: "Will we see one day . . . sitting in the office of special studies of our principal businesses, next to the head of statistics, a specialist in history?"[34] Contributors were also recruited from the League of Nations, especially the Bureau International de Travail, which was then headed by Albert Thomas. Thomas graduated from the Ecole Normale in the same class (1899) as Lucien Febvre. Febvre tapped his old friend Thomas when he launched the *Annales*: "He would drop everything and write to me, Come to Geneva. . . . I will help you all I can."[35] In the proposal for the creation of the journal, Bloch revealed his many connections with the business world, including Raymond Bloch, one of the chief executives for the Paris-Orleans railway line. He also intended to have colonial administrators contribute. Thus the *Annales* adopted quite an original attitude toward the establishment. This juncture with the rising technocracy inspired it to favor mechanisms without regard for the nature of the government involved. The articles of Georges Friedmann on Stakhanovism or the admiring chronicles of Gérard Méquet on the Soviet Union were just some of the signs of this economic reading of society. However, this connection weakened at the end of the thirties. In 1938 Febvre ceaselessly repeated to Bloch, almost as if it were a reproach: "Too much medieval stuff, too many university people."[36]

■ INNOVATORS

The *Annales* transformed historical discourse radically. First, as its title suggests, the journal accented economic and social phenomena that had been neglected before. Jean-Louis Oosterhoff's study clearly shows the fundamental opposition between the *Annales*, which devoted 84 percent of its articles to economic and social history in the period 1929–45, and *La Revue historique* with 21.9 percent or *La Revue d'histoire moderne et contemporaine* with 26.5 percent. Abandoning political history worked then to the advantage of economic and social history. This evolution fit into a favorable context, as we have already seen, and the *Annales* benefited from the contribution of two pioneers in this area, Henri Hauser and François Simiand.

Henri Hauser had succeeded in establishing at the Sorbonne in 1927 the first chair of economic history for a liberal arts institution. Therefore, he played the role of pioneer in institutionalizing economic history within the liberal arts. Bloch replaced him in 1936. Economics was a relatively new subject and was taught in the law schools, where jurists had introduced economic and social sciences in 1878. As a result economics was somewhat isolated, cut off from sociology, social history, and human geography. A member of the *Revue d'histoire économique et sociale* as well as the *Annales*, Hauser was skeptical of the statistical curves that François Simiand was promoting. He remained in this "the last practitioner of preserial economic history."[37]

The real inspiration for economic history was not a historian, but rather François Simiand, the Durkheimian sociologist who had directed that sharp diatribe against history. He was the real precursor of economic history founded on statistical analysis that described regular cycles at work in the large-scale movements that affected the whole of society. He facilitated the connection between monetary studies, social studies on the cost of living, and what he himself called collective psychology for different social groups. As early as 1930 Febvre encouraged historians to forget their injured pride of 1903 and to read Simiand: "For historians, there is one bedside book: Simiand's course on political economy."[38] That did not mean that Febvre thought Simiand's method should be directly transposed to history, but that it could serve as an inspiration, an experiment.

The real revolution in historiography, which absorbed Simiand's inspiration by adapting it to history, came from Ernest Labrousse.[39] Labrousse's career is another sign of the difficulty of integrating economic history into the liberal arts university. A history student of Aulard's at the Sorbonne, Labrousse wrote a thesis on the Paris Commune for his 1913 DES degree in the history of the French Revolution. Interested in political economics, he registered for the law school in 1919. He studied law and received his degree. Then he began research for his doctoral degree on social legislation from 1789 to Year III [i.e., 1795]. In 1926, he changed focus, returned to true economic history, and published his thesis, *Esquisse du mouvement des prix et des revenus en France au XVIIIe siècle* (1932). This turning point was heavily influenced by the work of Simiand and Albert Aftalion, whose assistant he became in law school. We have to wait until 1943, and his *Crise de l'économie française*, to see Labrousse recognized as "docteur ès lettres" and become, in 1945, lecturer and then professor at the Sorbonne. This difficult career path highlights the twists and turns needed at this time to make economic history scientific. Although he was an enthusiastic reader of the *Annales* right from the start, Labrousse kept his distance from the journal. He did not contribute to it until 1945. Nonetheless, he owed his appointment in 1938 as director of studies in section four at the Ecole Pratique des Hautes Etudes to Bloch, who supported his candidacy. Ever since, he has been recognized as one of the great apostles of new history. He succeeded in integrating the long term, the evolution of structures, and the study of events into a single whole that attempted to explain the French Revolution of 1789. Thanks to his research on prices and revenues, he showed clearly the bourgeoisie moving up in the general prosperity of the eighteenth century, the rising class and the candidate for power. Still, he did not neglect studying the interconnections among economic crises that were essential for understanding all this social mobility. When he correlated the taking of the Bastille in mid-July and the law that fixed the "maximum" price of bread, he transcended the methodic school's traditional narrative history without underplaying events. If Labrousse did not at that time hold a central position in the *Annales*, it was because he located politics on the horizon of his economic approach and favored studying class antagonisms, whereas the *Annales* aspired to a society of consensus, although it was interested in social issues too. "My history leans principally toward the socioeconomic and the sociopolitical."[40]

By not renouncing the narrative of events, Labrousse did not move far enough away from traditional history in the eyes of Bloch and Febvre. He was in the end too "engagé" for the *Annales*. After having founded in 1910 at Barbezieux an autonomous group of young Socialists called the Jacobin Club and having launched a journal, *L'Avenir*, he established in 1911, again at Barbezieux, a group for social studies whose declaration of principles included these fighting slogans: "Complete freedom for the proletariat," "The abolition of misery," and "The universal social republic."[41] During the war, in 1916, he joined the Socialist party. In 1919, he was the editor of *L'Humanité*, later of *Populaire*, and finally of *L'Internationale*. But the Bolshevik leanings of the Section Française de l'Internationale Ouvrière (SFIO) chased him from *L'Humanité* in 1924 and he left the party in 1925. Unlike many others, including Febvre, who experienced a brief temptation to be accepted by those in power and to give up their political commitment, Labrousse returned to the Socialist party in 1938. He directed the *Revue socialiste* from its foundation in 1946 until he resigned in 1954 because the SFIO refused to accept a unified European defense. By emphasizing social antagonisms, he remained too close to Marxist historiography. He did not subscribe to the latter but nonetheless found himself marginalized. "In this sociocultural history, should not the history of class consciousness have its place? . . . One of the great tasks in the study of collective mentalities is the comparative social study of consciousness in these different classes, of its multifaceted progressions, of its extension within a class."[42] Still, he was extolled and almost canonized by a school that saw in him the initiator of an economic history founded on statistics, quantification, and cycles of long and short time periods. The *Annales* promoted this economic history, not simply to add another car to the train of history, but to include a major methodology for studying past and present societies. Economics belongs to a method that is larger than history narrowly defined and is part of the effort to understand society rationally.

The first time Marc Bloch was a candidate for the Collège de France, he claimed an affiliation with comparative history; the second time, in 1934, he refocused his teaching project on economics. Bloch wanted to be recognized as an economic historian when he wrote in his proposal: "In addition to ideas and sentiments, there are needs.... Through the economic substrata, studied with means appropriate to its own character, [I propose] to enrich the in-depth interpretation of social life in its entirety."[43] After having been rejected by the Collège de France, he succeeded Henri Hauser in 1936 at the Sorbonne, where he was named to the chair in economic history, which was the first ever of its kind in a liberal arts institution. As soon as he arrived in Paris, he and Maurice Halbwachs created the Institute of Economic and Social History at the Sorbonne. The history of prices became a favorite preoccupation of the journal. Febvre saluted the work of Earl Hamilton on the influx of precious metals from America and their impact on prices. This was the beginning of serial history integrated into a global social frame. Was the very quick rise in prices "due entirely, directly and solely, to the influx of precious metals from America? Evidently not.... There are general causes."[44] The word *serial* was still not mentioned, but the *Annales* did pick up what Simiand called "continuous phenomenoscope," that is, the continuous diachronic observation of a single phenomenon through a period of time. Thus the historian could appropriate the statistician's territory.

If the journal remained the principal tool for such takeovers, the editors of the *Annales* quickly understood that there would be no permanent overthrow of history writing without a radical change in the selection criteria used by the university. The lock to pick was the *agrégation* diploma. In 1935, the professor in charge of the history *agrégation* for women wrote indignantly about the candidates' indifference toward biography and their tendency to follow the "fashion" for the history of social groups.[45] In 1932, an open letter appeared in the *Bulletin de l'association des professeurs d'histoire-géographie* concerning the *agrégation* examination. It questioned the exam's results and thus the criteria of the traditional school. The letter was signed by Febvre,

Bloch, Georges Lefebvre, Charles-Edmond Perrin, and two geographers, Albert Demangeon and André Cholley. All were contributors to the *Annales* and four were from Strasbourg.[46] Twice, the editors of the journal returned to the question of the *agrégation*. In 1934, Febvre evoked the need to rethink the rules, the spirit, and the administration of the exam. He talked about it as the most anguishing problem of all. A new collective attack was written in 1937, but the *Annales* did not succeed in modifying the university that was resisting its plan. No influential voice picked up Febvre and Bloch's proposals. This is a striking contrast to the way in which the methodic school had slipped into the university and took it over. But now the pieces were in place, inflexibly committed since the end of the nineteenth century for a long haul, especially since the crisis of the thirties did not favor any great upheavals. Turning a weakness into a mobilizing strength, the *Annales* founders took from this failure the idea that they were pariahs and university outlaws. The argument was not really credible but it allowed them to win over the social sciences more easily and without the latter fearing they might be absorbed and dominated by a too-powerful neighbor.

This slide from politics toward economics presupposed an enlargement and a radical change in the very craft of historians, who could no longer limit themselves to written sources if they wanted to reach the foundations of society. Bloch was the first to write an agrarian history by stepping over the juridical borders that had defined ownership. He did not confine himself to working on the cartularies like Henri Sée, but melded into his history the transformation of the rural countryside, marking the differences between ribbonlike fields and compact squares, including population studies, demography, work tools, soil composition, variations in production, monetary fluctuations, and family relationships. Everything learned from geography and economics was included in this new body of history. In every issue of the *Annales* between the wars, a rubric devoted to surveys was intended to make readers more aware of social and economic history and of new materials that, unlike traditional archives, were unwitting documents. Increasing historians' interests did not, however, have to provoke a devaluing of man in favor of some technical or geographic determinism. Bloch showed simultaneously the need for technical innovation and its dependence upon social demand. The integration of the contributions of the social sciences did not mean the disintegration of history.

Another innovative aspect of the *Annales* is found in the importance it gave to history-through-problems, that is, through questions focused on problems. For Bloch and Febvre, historians should not be content to write under the dictation of documents; they should interrogate those documents and locate them within a frame of questioning. In contrast to Langlois and Seignobos, who practiced history as a narrative, they called for history as questioning, which was the theoretical matrix for the later conception of structural history. Historical periodization was no longer done along traditional time frames but rather with problems that were evoked and whose solution was sought. Advocating history-through-problems has been an essential element of the *Annales* program from 1929 to today. To Bernard Pivot's request for a definition of new history on the television show "Apostrophes," Jacques Le Goff answered: "New history is history-through-problems." Nonetheless, did the *Annales* really discover that any story is organized by a preestablished conceptual frame? Certainly not; there were many predecessors. Why then does the banner of "history-through-problems" continue to operate and to unite the group? "First for its strategic utility: it allows them to claim they are doing new history."[47] In the opening lecture that marked his reception into the Collège de France on 13 December 1933, Febvre emphasized the new look of historians who were breaking with the passivity that traditional history had encouraged: "To elaborate a fact is to construct it. . . . All history is a choice."[48] *Philippe II et la Franche-Comté*, the thesis Febvre defended in 1911, illustrated this approach, which, if not new, at least was a departure from the narrative history of that time. His thesis director was Gabriel Monod and his central hypothesis was still political. This was a pre-*Annales* work and predated the rejection of politics. When Febvre studied this province at a difficult, transitional moment after the death of Charles V, he was not content to add a supplement on local political conflicts. Rather, he attempted to read the underlying social conflicts and the province's resistance to the march of absolutism. "It is the struggle, it is the bitter conflict between two social classes, the nobility and the bourgeoisie. A struggle for power, for influence, for political domination."[49] Behind this major conflict that ravaged an entire region for the second half of the sixteenth century, Febvre also sought out the daily reality, the obscure and heretofore forgotten changes in popular life. As a result, he restored the vicissitudes and the dialectic interplay between provincial antagonism and central power. In this study Febvre did not avoid the political; he simply placed it at the heart of other conflicts. Thus, politics was no longer the exclusive component of social reality, but it did remain central. He described this intertwining of social and political tensions that exploded when the equilibrium established by Charles V was broken. He saw the province get entangled despite itself in the increasingly Spanish-oriented policies of Philip II. His history shows us, behind the struggle of the leaders, the region's misery, its overpopulation, the rise in prices, the devastation caused by the increasingly frequent passage of royal troops, not counting the natural calamities and the plague of 1584–86, which was more violent than in previous years. Febvre did not omit the consequences of both the decline of a feudal nobility and the rise of a bourgeoisie that made its fortune in commerce and usury: "Peasants were the victims of such forces. They who had already supported the nobles also created the wealth of the bourgeois."[50] Here Febvre presented a dynamic and complete picture of Franche-Comté society. It was also problem-oriented history in the sense that society was captured at a critical point in its social and political conflicts that produced permanent changes and altered its very nature.

The notion that history-through-problems provided a theoretical matrix for an eventual structural history is even more valid with Bloch, who wanted to reconstitute the structure of feudal society: "It is the analysis and the explanation of a social structure and all its connections that we propose to attempt here."[51] Already in his *Les Caractères originaux*, Bloch had opposed the overemphasis on the economic consequences of epidemics in explaining the crisis of the fourteenth and fifteenth centuries. In contrast, he brought out the decrease in feudal revenues and thus gave priority to the structural basis of a social system. Later in *La Société féodale* he captured a total reality that included the economic, social, and mental domains in one coherent overview. "The evolution of the economy brought in its wake a real modification of social values."[52] Adumbrating all future work on family relations, Bloch reflected on the connection between bloodlines and feudalism: "We see the vast kinship system of yesterday yield to groups that are much closer to our smaller families of today." But he continues: "Let us not imagine a regular emancipation of the individual continuing since the distant times of tribes."[53] He demonstrated that the vassal and the liege lord in fact were connected to each other with binds similar to those of kinship and with all they signified in terms of rights and obligations. In the feudal system, ownership of a fief was not automatically transferred upon the death of the holder. Nonetheless, inheritance always won out over law because the social reality always ended by mastering the judicial reality, just as the social historian would reconstitute a richer and more complex reality than the historian who did not go beyond the written law. Marking off the structural framework of a society did not mean for Bloch the death of historical movements, of evolution, of change. He clearly saw a rift beginning with what he called the second feudal age. What took place there was the opposite of the first period: centralization, concentration, and implantation of organizations with larger fields of action. Its basic structure upset, society saw the end of invasions, a rise in population, more clearing of land, urban development, the expanded use of money. As a result, what was precisely the basis of feudalism disappeared, and the state was weakened. Nonetheless, the nobility outlived feudalism. Bloch located his structural study within deep historical dynamics that modified feudalism both inside and outside.

Another particularly fertile field that also was captured and annexed to the historian's territory was geography. Transformed into geohistory, geography was a new and fecund paradigm that provided an obligatory framework for all the monographs published after World War II. This geohistory was born of the meeting of Vidalism and the *Annales*. Here Bloch and Febvre answered the challenge issued by geography in its heyday. Neither they nor their successors hesitated in invading the field of geography. They purely and simply annexed it when the geographic school lost its vitality. This marriage reflected the times, with a renewed emphasis on the regions and the provinces of a France whose overcentralization was noticed even before Jean-François Gravier. That contributed to the success of a geohistory that took the region as its framework and investigated its specificity: "Social groups expressing real man are natural geographical and economic units: the region and the profession."[54] Studies in demographics, economics, and social relations, which were the research topics the *Annales* favored, were better adapted to a restricted area where knowing the statistical givens and synthesizing them were easier than for a larger area. The historical perspective of the *Annales* was better adapted to smaller geographical units. To work in depth meant to choose areas on a human scale; that was the only way to realize the synthesis the leaders of the *Annales* were striving for. Febvre was particularly close to the Vidalian school: he had been a schoolmate of Jules Sion at the Ecole Normale and the friend of Albert Demangeon, another contributor to the *Annales* with whom he wrote a book on the Rhine in 1931. At the *Revue de synthèse historique* he was given responsibility for keeping tabs on the work of the French geographic school. In 1905 he wrote for the *Revue de synthèse historique,* as part of a series on the regions of France, a monograph on the Franche-Comté following the principles of synthesis enunciated by Henri Berr. Before seizing the field of geography for the historians, Febvre used his summaries of their work to open an interdisciplinary dialogue and to praise the merits of their work so that historians would be inspired by them. To connect historical writing with what was permanent and with the long duration in geography on one hand, and, on the other, to show how nature changed in the course of time was the twin aim of the *Annales* revolution that conceived the connection between historicity and geography in terms of complementarity and solidarity. In his reviews Febvre defended geographical work anchored in hypotheses and in central problems. In contrast, he criticized vehemently anything that smelled of compilation or of separate compartmentalized topics.[55] Just as he called for history-through-problems, he pleaded for geography-through-problems. In his study of the Franche-Comté, Febvre showed that the name of this region was not geographical in origin but historical, designating not the countryside but a state, and including a great diversity of geological strata, climates, products, and populations. This demonstration allowed him to set off the major role of man: "Man's portion remains preponderant. For it is he who, definitively, forged out of these disparate parts a single political unity, a state."[56] Bloch reached a similar conclusion in his study of the Ile-de-France for the same collection on the regions of France: "The Ile-de-France lacks any regional unity."[57] In *La Terre et l'évolution humaine* (1922) Febvre intervened in a debate between sociologists and geographers. He took up the geographers' cause and defended Vidalism, but only to better assimilate their territory. He challenged the attack of Durkheimian sociologists who wanted to absorb geography under the new term *social morphology:* sociology "cannot pretend to suppress human geography for its own advantage."[58] Febvre repeated the arguments of François Simiand against geography, but this time to gainsay them. Geographers could go no further than potential or simple causes; they could never reach definitive explanations. But that did not diminish geography's richness: "Geography does not want to be a science dealing with necessities."⁵⁹ According to Febvre, the objects and the methods of sociology and geography were quite different from each other. In contrast, the new history as the *Annales* understood it was made to get along with the geography of Vidal de la Blache. This twin revolution was supposed to lead to a symbiosis within the framework of observation and experimental research: "An immense expanse of work is opening up before us, historians and geographers, for an indefinite future."⁶⁰

Febvre also intervened in the debate between Ratzel's German geography and Vidal, and he vigorously took the latter's part. He equated Ratzel's political geography, which was organized around notions of position and space, with the political history that he condemned. Thus, he presented Vidal's break with Ratzel as a prefiguration in geography of what he intended to do with old-fashioned narrative history. Febvre also settled the score with geographic determinism; he chose the Vidalian notion of possibility. Nature was not a neutral force that conditioned human life; it was humanized right from the beginning and was already profoundly transformed by man: "Never do natural facts exert on the life of men an action that is purely mechanical, blind, or marked by fatalism."⁶¹ Here he got involved in an internal dispute among geographers in order to condemn traditional geographic studies based on the unavoidable determinism of natural conditions. Even if he went along with the tenets of the new human geographers, he received at best a critical welcome from them. They understood that Febvre was not intervening as a neutral umpire, but that he was planning to co-opt the Vidalian position in the name of new history. Camille Vallaux accused Febvre of trying to "break the back of human geography," and even Albert Demangeon, who would nonetheless contribute to the *Annales* later, denounced Febvre's "abusive critical spirit," his "more negative than positive effort," and his desire to "create a danger for the pleasure of denouncing it."⁶²

If Febvre laid the bases for an organic collaboration between geographers and historians, the price he demanded was the isolation of the geographers from the sociologists. If the result was an enrichment for historical discourse, it was also a loss of dynamism for geography that, by consecrating itself to historicity, surrendered any special epistemology it had formerly possessed. Thus, it lost the opportunity to bring to fruition a new social or political geography, it left to history the task of explaining the effect of natural conditions, along with other factors, and gave up at the same time its own sociological inspirations. The other great acquisition of geographical territory was made by Bloch. He studied a series of field maps as if they were documents and incorporated the history of the rural countryside into his *Les Caractères originaux de l'histoire rurale française* (1931). The symbiosis between history and geography found there its finest product. Geographers fell into line, enchanted.

One of the consequences of orienting the *Annales* discourse in the direction of economics, material life, and geography was the slowing down of time. Long duration replaced the short duration of regimes and reigns. Historians tended to favor what lasted and what was repeated so as to fix long cycles and century-long tendencies. On this point also new history broke with the narrative history that focused solely on events and that was still dominant at the turn of the century. The height of ridicule was reached in a thesis defended at the Sorbonne in 1906 by Albert Crémieux entitled "The Revolution of 1848: A Critical Study of the Days of February 21, 22, 23, and 24, 1848" and which became by 1911 an enormous doctoral thesis running to 535 pages. On the other hand, 45.9 percent of the articles in the *Annales* for the period 1929–39 deal with long duration as compared with 30.7 percent for *La Revue historique* and 25.3 percent for *La Revue d'histoire moderne et contemporaine*.[63]

Another direction taken by the *Annales* and especially by Marc Bloch answered the Durkheimian challenge: comparative history. Bloch proposed in Oslo in 1928 a program of comparative history for European societies. He formalized its purpose and methods. Sociologists considered their discipline a science to the extent that it was comparative. Bloch adopted this idea for historians: "This is perhaps what the future of our science will cost."[64] The conditions required for this undertaking to succeed were, according to Bloch, to compare what is comparable, that is, societies that shared certain similarities from the start. To avoid any nonhistorical procedures that would deal with extraspatial and chronological generalities in sweeping analogies, Bloch limited this comparativism to societies of the same type. He considered this procedure more scientific than studies of similarities between primitive societies and Western classical societies. It was important to have as a basis a close connection, either spatial or temporal. Comparative history would give historians access to the fundamental causes of the phenomena they observed and would show them true similarities and dissimilarities. The other principal interest of comparativism was to free history from the artificial limits its research was based on. Topographical compartmentalizations were just as anachronistic as the national boundaries of modern states when they were projected onto a map of the Middle Ages. Comparativism allowed Bloch to pick a wide horizon for testing his hypotheses. He never separated France's history from Europe's, not because he wanted to make some homogeneous entity, but rather to pick out what was different and original in it. Adopting a European point of view except for one reference to Japan in his study of feudal society, Bloch discovered a fault line in the common heritage of antiquity that separated western Europe from the rest of Europe. This was a remarkable intuition for a historian long before Yalta and it suggests a distinction that is much older than the one dating from 1945. Every inventor is a bit of a prophet in their own way.

■ HISTORIANS OF *MENTALITÉS*

In their efforts at aggrandizement, Bloch and Febvre took over another area of knowledge, one that is called the study of *mentalités* and that derives from disciplines foreign to history: ethnology and especially psychology. Febvre used the work of his friend and schoolmate from the Ecole Normale Charles Blondel. As early as 1926 Blondel had in fact employed the notion of primitive mentality, which can be found in Lucien Lévy-Bruhl earlier, in 1910.[65] This new disciplinary graft, which made psychohistory possible, happened only because a debilitated psychology was being torn between its clinical and theoretical vocations. It did not have much effect immediately, except perhaps on the direction of Bloch and Febvre's research. This turn toward *mentalités* nonetheless foretold subsequent developments and the irresistible blooming of the sixties. But in this first period of the *Annales*, the proportion of cultural history, in the large sense of that term, remained limited and even less than what it was in the *Revue historique*. Here there is a noticeable split between Febvre's preoccupations, which were more and more focused on *mentalités*, and the content of the journal, which retained its economic and social priorities. The work of the two leaders of the *Annales* was nonetheless heavily marked by the desire to decode the mental universe. This desire was fed by two impulses. The first was psychology, whose influence was particularly strong among historians who wanted to renovate their discipline: "In short, history is psychology: it is the birth and development of the psychic."[66] The second was Durkheimian sociology. These two inspirations marked the two leaders of the *Annales* differently.

Febvre was more attuned to what was properly psychological, to the confrontation between individuals and the mental universe in which each one lives. He opened an important breech in the traditional history of ideas by situating the historian's task at the point of articulation between a work and the social and mental conditions that created that work. Febvre's orientation was still strongly influenced by classical humanism and by his perception of man as an individual. He reacted against what he considered scientific excess, the diminishment of man. Febvre's historical horizon, the focal point of his research, was thus historical psychology. In order to investigate the mental and psychic universe, he more and more frequently took as his subject either an individual, e.g., Luther, Rabelais, Marguerite de Navarre, or an area of individual consciousness.

Bloch followed another path in his approach to *mentalités*. Starting in 1924 with *Les Rois thaumaturges,* he strove more to describe collective and symbolic practices, the unconscious mental representations of different social groups. In reaching these *mentalités* Bloch was aided more by Durkheimian sociology than by psychology. His approach was closer to structuralism and announced the methods of historical anthropology. In this regard, Febvre, who is often presented as the originator of the history of *mentalités,* is not the one who had the most heirs. "The theoretical orientation that dominated the social sciences in the fifties encouraged [everyone] to follow the path cleared by Bloch."[67] Historical psychology was quickly abandoned while, in contrast, fed by structuralism, research has flourished on the logic of daily routine; on collective, unconscious representations; on conditions of cultural production; on mental phenomena and their connection with social life and social groups. Thus, there was one interest in mental phenomena, but two different ways, two filiations within a single historical school. This duality can be seen when Febvre reviewed Bloch's *La Société féodale* for the *Annales* in 1940. Despite their friendship and the intellectual fraternity that linked the two men, Febvre was rather critical of Bloch's book: "I am not entirely satisfied. . . . What strikes me once I close the book is that the individual is almost entirely absent. . . . And I would say willingly, if I dared, that in

Bloch's book there is a return toward schematicism. Call it by its real name, toward sociology, which is a seductive form of the abstract."[68]

Psychology was then the great inspiration of Lucien Febvre, who called for a history of sentiment, of love, of death, of pity, of cruelty, of joy, of fear, etc. But he added also that such a history should blend into the global study of a civilization and not be isolated from its roots like an object cut off from its context by diachronic generalizations or by other sweeping conclusions on human nature. "When I say: we do not have a history of love, nor of joy, understand that I am not asking for a study on love or joy across all times, all ages, and all civilizations."[69] Psychology was selected as the material of history; it was supposed to fit into the analysis of civilizations from which it could not be separated. At the center of Febvre's questioning, the binary couple individual/society was presented thus: "The individual is nothing but what the time and the social milieu allow him to be."[70] In his *Luther,* Febvre juxtaposed the psychology of an individual, Luther, with the mental universe of sixteenth-century Germany.[71] The Reformation of the church and the break with Rome were born of this conjunction. In contrast to traditional history, the individual did not weigh more heavily because Febvre firmly rejected that concept. The mental universe prevailed as the point of conjunction between individual and collective aspirations. Nevertheless, in this psychohistory Febvre had a tendency to neglect social reality, which had been very present in his thesis on the Franche-Comté, to the advantage of mental phenomena. Retrospective psychology or historical psychology aimed to reconstitute the mental framework of the past, to break with the idea of a human nature that was atemporal and unchangeable as well as to break with all anachronisms, that is to say with the natural tendency to transpose our categories of thought, feeling, or language back to those societies where they have no meaning or a different one. That was the intent of *Rabelais,* published in 1942: "Avoid the sin of sins, the one unforgivable sin: anachronism."[72] In this book Febvre attacked A. Lefranc's thesis, which had made Rabelais a rationalist and a free thinker. He asked himself about the possibility of unbelief in the sixteenth century and for this purpose reconstructed the mental habits of that time. He concluded that Lefranc had committed the sin of anachronism, that he had read the texts of the sixteenth century with the eyes of the twentieth. In Febvre's eyes, the mental habits of the sixteenth century did not lend themselves to a logical thought process that was born later with the Cartesian seventeenth century, Galileo, and the Port-Royal grammar book. He showed the extent to which Christianity shaped both individual and collective life in the sixteenth century. "It was the very air they breathed."[73] If the discovery of the sixteenth century's structures of thought appears modern and announces Foucault's study of discursive categories, there are also a certain number of references to an outmoded Eurocentric evolutionism. Febvre suggested a "deficiency or lacunae of thought" in the sixteenth century because that period lacked a certain vocabulary or used syntax that gave "the impression of incoherence and jumping around."[74] Rabelais's religion could not be read in the context of future agnosticism but had to be referred to Erasmus and Renaissance thought, which affirmed the absolute value of nature and humanity. This would not be the method of Mikhail Bakhtin much later on the same topic.[75] Bakhtin gives us a reading of Rabelais as a symptomatic reproduction of an entire popular culture that is specific and peripheral in relation to the official high culture. Febvre's mental habits were split by this social dualism. Bakhtin presents Rabelais as a writer who had found the spontaneity and the purity of a culture repressed by the oppressive wheels of state. The importance accorded by Rabelais to physical activity and to material life merely continue the legacy of this culture, of this world apart, of this stronghold of resistance. This social horizon escaped Febvre, who was absorbed by the possibility of building a historical psychology.

The second instrument Febvre recommended in order to study mental phenomena went back to the origins of literary history, for which his *Rabelais* was a perfect illustration. There too it was an invasion directed against the most solid discipline in the university: literary studies. The first issue of Henri Berr's *Revue de synthèse historique* in 1900 included a manifesto by Gustave Lanson that revealed his ambition to shake up the rigidly inflexible world of literary study. He wanted to make the literary approach more historical, but his only partner was the traditional historical school that preferred to have revenge against the Germans rather than to study literature. If Lanson was in a sense deeply marked by the positions of Seignobos and Langlois, whose merits and methods he praised, he was no less an innovator when he discovered the neglected literatures of the provinces, of anonymous and forgotten authors. But he also laid the foundations for a sociology of literature and for a history of *mentalités* when he sought to uncover the conditions of production or of circulation in literature, the rapport that the reader establishes with a work, and the reasons for the success of one novel or another. He broke with the traditional monograph on great authors or great works that had been canonized in the name of eternal human nature: "Books exist for readers.... Who read and what did they read? These are two essential questions."[76] Although Lanson's project was not implemented by literary professors, it was nonetheless praised by Febvre. We see that his major preoccupation was the same as Lanson's. In 1941 Febvre was astonished that Lanson's project had been ignored. His own work on Luther and Rabelais demonstrated that historians were capable of doing it: "A historical literary history for a given epoch, including its connections with the social life of its time... to write it, it is necessary to reconstruct the milieu, to ask who was writing, and for whom; who was reading, and why."[77] He picked up Lanson's research project word for word. But this time it was to be undertaken by historians. Literature provided an efficient instrument for reconstructing the emotional life of the past, but it was only one piece in a much more complicated puzzle. Historians were supposed to take over other fields of study, like iconography, as well as a new science just hitting its full stride, linguistics. In this area, Febvre was influenced by Antoine Meillet, whose study of Greek was impregnated with history. "To do the history of Greek dialects means doing the history of Greek colonialization."[78] This osmosis between historical and linguistic hypotheses could confer on history a central position in a federalized discipline. If history could assimilate literature, linguistics, and iconography, it could aspire to a brilliant future in the area of cultural studies.

Bloch shared this interest with Febvre. He gave psychology a central position. He could not escape the influence of *mentalités* when he opined that historians should seek the antecedents of psychological facts in psychology. When Bloch talked up a history of food and eating,[79] he turned to the same inspiration as Febvre, who had directed an ethnological study on the contents of kitchen cabinets in different French regions. The history of material civilization would know a great success much later in the sixties.

Nonetheless, Bloch did not write the same history of *mentalités* as Febvre did. His principal inspiration was different. He was nourished more by the nascent historical anthropology, with which he had close contact, than by psychology. In fact, at the Ecole Normale he had been a schoolmate of Louis Gernet and Marcel Granet, whom he met again at the Foundation Thiers, where he was living from 1909 to 1912. Thanks to them, Bloch underwent the decisive influence of Durkheimism open to history. Louis Gernet, who later became a Greek scholar, collaborated with Simiand on the *Année sociologique*. He published his thesis in 1917 and his major work, *Le Génie grec dans la religion*, in 1932 in a collection edited by Henri Berr. He defended a global perspective for studying social and mental phenomena and mixed ethnology and history in the tradition of Marcel Mauss. Not only did Louis Gernet influence Bloch but he also adumbrated the brilliant French school of historical anthropology of classical Greece that included Jean-Pierre Vernant, Pierre Vidal-Naquet, Marcel Détienne, François Hartog, and Nicole Loraux. He worked with Bloch at the *Annales* and found him to be "more than the sociologists, the true heir of the Durkheimian tradition."[80]

Bloch was also influenced by Marcel Granet, a sinologist whose work after the war was quickly considered definitive.[81] Granet communicated to Bloch his interest in rites, myths, comparative collective psychology, and belief systems. All these themes would help bring forth Bloch's early major work, *Les Rois thaumaturges* (1924).[82] Bloch never limited his approach to conscious structured thought. He scrutinized the correlations between religious attitudes and social reality in order to understand the social implications of religious history and the religious implications of social history. In this kind of historiography the church belonged on the boundary between two worlds, the ideal and the material. Between these two orders Bloch did not search for causal relationships; rather, his synchronic studies sought interdependencies. Unlike Febvre, Bloch never strayed from the social substrata in his social psychology and always used its different categories. He was therefore close to what we would call historical anthropology. When he opened the way to the history of the body, the ages of life, and emotions, he enunciated the privileged topics that would be taken up one by one by the third *Annales* generation even as they forgot Bloch's desire to be comprehensive. Like Febvre, Bloch reacted against the concept of passive historians that was accepted by traditional history. He placed the accent on questioning, on hypotheses tested by the facts and not those dictated by facts. As for the history of *mentalités*, he opened a rich avenue by calling on historians to be more attentive to what documents did not say: "What the text specifically says has ceased today to be the preferred object of our attention."[83] Taking as his example the hagiography written in the high Middle Ages, he showed that the lives of the saints taught us nothing about the figures they pretended to resuscitate. In contrast, however, they were a mine of information for historians curious about the mental categories of those times. Bloch also included new sources, new objects in order to capture the *mentalité* of the Middle Ages. He did not limit himself to written documents, but added iconography and rituals. All these were additional ways to attain the unconscious level of social behaviors. Here we find the same procedures as in anthropology, both the subject matter and the interpretive methods.

One critical experience led Bloch down the road of studying deep structures and mental categories. That was the war of 1914–18 in which he participated as a soldier and as a historian who thought about what he was living: "The psychology of soldiers and of the men of 1914–18 will illuminate the attitude of the Middle Ages toward the royal miracle."[84] Thus, looking backward we see that his later book *Les Rois thaumaturges* (1924) was ripening during the war while he was at work on other projects centered on the rural history of the Ile-de-France. He confided to Charles Edmond Perrin in 1919: "When I've finished with the countryside, I will take up a study of the anointing and royal crowning at Rheims."[85] How could the war have inspired Bloch to ask himself about the ability of the king to cure scrofula? Through the intermediary of thinking about witnesses, rumor, calumny. Real, authentic history was not the only one to produce real effects: "Wrong information . . . has filled the life of humanity."[86] Bloch's aims were to seize the means of propagation and to describe the conditions favorable to it. He called for the development of a collective psychology, of a psychology of witnesses that was still at its beginnings. He told of the capture of a German sentinel by his infantry regiment in September 1917 just north of the town of Braisne, whose name was confused with Brême.[87] Immediately, the German was thought to be a spy posted in Braisne. This mutation did not take root either at the front nor in the rear, but between the two, in the closest rear lines where different regiments crisscrossed, where censure was omnipresent, and where the agony of death would ambush and completely fill the mind of the waiting soldiers. "The war was one immense experiment in social psychology."[88] Exploiting a method of backtracking that he proposed as a model, Bloch used this incident to question the collective belief in the king's power to cure; he concluded that it was "a gigantic bit of misinformation." Whenever he studied mental history, it was integrated within a global perspective, wide in the area covered, long in its duration, and encompassing all aspects of society, including politics, which was set, surprisingly, at the heart of the book: "What I wanted to do here is essentially a contribution to the political history of Europe, in the largest and truest sense of the word."[89] He asked about the force, vitality, and permanence of loyalist sentiment in favor of royal power. In the latter's supernatural character he saw a possible explanation. He was not content to note the royal cures; he asked how these miracles were perceived: "Here we are far removed from the history of traditional ideas in the positivistic or idealist tradition."[90]

Nonetheless, as was the case for Febvre's *Rabelais*, we find the residue of Bloch's rationalist judgment. He made his analyses in the name of reason and connected the miraculous cure of scrofula (a tubercular inflammation of the glands) to a "psychological system that we can for two reasons call primitive: first, because it carries the mark of thinking that has not evolved much and that is still plunged in the irrational; second, because we find it in its especially pure state in those societies we usually call primitive."[91] Bloch took his inspiration from anthropological work by Frazer and Lévy-Bruhl that was shot through with positivism. They contrasted the superior logic of the West with primitive *mentalités* and mythologies that were perceived as debilitated, an idea that Claude Lévi-Strauss laid to rest in 1962 with his *La Pensée Sauvage*. Bloch's mental equipment belonged then to an early anthropology that was still blinkered by its Eurocentric prejudices. He had a great deal of difficulty in overcoming the traditional explanations of the religious phenomena he rejected: the Voltairean explanation that accentuated the self-conscious, individual work of art, and the romantic explanation that favored the deep and obscure forces of society. Despite its shortcomings, this was a masterful examination of a power whose legitimacy was not limited to exercising its concrete, legal, and political prerogatives, but one that was based on the ideal and on magic. Bloch laid the foundation for a new history of ideas that would be fleshed out more by the facts of daily life than by theories. The rites of healing, of crowning, of the royal anointing were so many points of conflict between the church and the temporal princes. The conflict was sharp along this battle line, where the two dominant orders of medieval society, those who pray and those who fight, were struggling for primacy. The Gregorians, in their attempt to separate the sacred and the secular, did not succeed in uprooting the magical element in royal power. As it grew stronger in the sixteenth and seventeenth centuries, royal power leaned more and more on the divine nature of its leader. Louis XIV and the Stuarts on the other side of the channel became the object of an idolatry that was more and more widespread: "Absolutism is a kind of religion."[92] Political resistance against absolutism finally won out over this belief, in England with the Glorious Revolution as well as in France with the Enlightenment and the revolution of 1789. As rationalism progressed and absolutism collapsed, one conception of the universe disappeared and a new world was born. Bloch, whose principal aim was anthropological, was also fully a historian, not only by giving this belief its historical context, but also by placing it within the social fabric that gave it life. Similarly, when he later studied medieval society, he focused first and foremost on the medieval *mentalité*. Febvre's accusation of being too sociological does not hold for this work, which attempted to reconstruct a specific mental structure. Bloch's first book gave the lion's share to the "ways of feeling and thinking."[93] He showed that society's indifference to time was not due to faulty technology but rather was revealed through that imperfection. Underneath these general traits, the *mentalités* of the peasant, the cleric, and the noble were identified as different aspirations and modes of existence that nonetheless coexisted in the same society without crossing over the lines of separation and conflict that themselves changed in the course of social evolution. Bloch's attempt to construct a collective psychology was more closely connected than Febvre's to an anthropology in gestation, to a premature structuralism. It was one of the essential signposts in the history of the social sciences and one that would have a very rich prolongation.

■ THE INHERITANCE

When we read from the pen of Voltaire: "Only the history of kings has been written; the nation's history has not been done. It seems that for 1,400 years there have been in Gaul only kings, ministers, and generals; are our mores, our laws, our customs, our genius nothing then?"[94] We ask ourselves, what did the *Annales* really invent? Did it merely realize a project outlined as early as the eighteenth century? Voltaire took up this project in his *Nouvelles Considérations sur l'histoire* (1744) and applied it in his *Essai sur les moeurs de l'esprit des nations* (1740–56). Later, Chateaubriand in the preface to his *Etudes historiques* (1831) wrote what Jacques Le Goff has called the true manifesto of new history: "Now history is an encyclopedia. Everything has to fit into it, from astronomy to chemistry, from finance to manufacturing, from the art of the painter, the sculptor, and the architect to that of the economist."[95] But it is Jules Michelet whose conception of history was closest to the *Annales*, without the latter's statistics and with a dollop of romanticism. Michelet has only recently been canonized the pope of new history. He too distinguished himself from the dominant historical school of his time: "I perceived France. She had her annals, but no history."[96] He was critical of Guizot and Thierry. He reproached them, as Bloch and Febvre criticized Langlois, Lavisse, and Seignobos, with having favored an infinitesimally thin layer of history: "History . . . seems to me to be weak in both its methods. It is not material enough, taking account of race but not of soil, climate, food, and so many other physical and physiological circumstances. It is not spiritual enough, dealing with laws and legislation but not with the great progressive, internal movement of the national soul."[97] Michelet wanted to create a total history, gathering all aspects of reality in a single sweep. We can better understand why Michelet is being rehabilitated now when repressed phenomena are in vogue with new history. He is in fact the one who initiated interest in witches, the irrational, heresy, the marginalized, and popular culture. Was there truly an *Annales* revolution or is it simply the echo of a legacy whose origins go back to Voltaire and Michelet? We can answer that question by repeating what André Burguière said, that the *Annales* was more original in the manner of presenting its program than in the program itself. It is no less true that the program seemed innovative in comparison with the dominant methodic school; it is by this comparison that the epistemological break established by the *Annales* is measured.

Nonetheless, even in their desire to innovate, Bloch and Febvre remained faithful to certain orientations that fixed history as a specific discipline within the field of the social sciences. They did not situate history entirely on the turf of the neighboring disciplines. On the contrary, they succeeded in drawing the social sciences into history's orbit. We have to understand then to what extent they remained faithful to certain essential orientations and to what extent they innovated.

The *Annales*, as we have seen, did not contain a philosophy of history and refused all forms of dogmatism so as to rally the adjacent social sciences to its cause. As a result there were, within this artistic flux, a number of contradictions in what the two directors claimed global history covered. In a single article, Febvre held two mutually contradictory viewpoints when analyzing the links among the diverse incidences of reality: "In each historical period, it is society's economic structure that, by determining its political forms, determines also the social mores, and even the general direction of thought, and even the orientation of spiritual forces." This reads like Stalin's economic version of Marx, but further on, Febvre adjusted his sights: "The Reformation, the product of capitalism or the other way round, capitalism the fruit of the Reformation: no, a thousand times no. Let us substitute for such a simple and dogmatic interpretation something like the nascent notion of the interdependence of phenomena."[98] Neither Marx nor Jesus. Rather neither Marx nor Weber, against whom Febvre opposed the conception of a fluid totality in which everything depends on everything else and vice versa. Bloch described historical time as plasma: "History's time is the plasma in which phenomena are immersed and the locus of their intelligibility."[99] For Bloch, the deconstruction of reality was one way to apprehend it, a first step in the analysis but only on condition of having a global perspective: "The danger begins only when each projector claims to alone see everything; when each county of knowledge pretends to be a whole country."[100] Besides, historical knowledge cannot accumulate through the piling up of discrete bits of knowledge, each studied separately. Just as a crowd is not the sum of its individuals, history is not the sum of objects studied successively, one after the other; it can only exist in the recreation of the interactions among the various levels of reality. If Bloch's notion of plasma was very vague on the nature of the internal relations within the social system, the latter was not a simple juxtaposition of *homo economicus, homo religiosus, homo politicus*, etc., but rather a suggestion of the synthesis that can be reached from concepts like the agrarian regime in *Les Caractères originaux* or the feudal system and its unity in *La Société féodale*.

The historians at the *Annales* were not interested in discovering the laws of history. Their spontaneous empiricism induced them to concentrate on the *how* much more than on the *why*, despite their idea of history-through-problems. This trait linked the *Annales* to a continuing historical discourse. Bloch and Febvre remained committed to anthropocentrism: man was the sole preoccupation of historians, he was the meaning of their work. Of course, this man was not the same as the man of the methodic school, which favored the elite and the leaders of the state. Here he was rather the average man, in his work and daily life. But it is no less true that, despite this spatial displacement, history remained human history: "There is no history but man's history . . . history, the science of man, and then facts, of course; but human facts, that's the historian's task."[101] This was the leitmotif of the *Annales* discourse during its first period despite its pretensions to being a science. Bloch and Febvre would certainly not have appreciated the displacement of the historian's territory into zones where man is decentered or absent, as in the work of Emmanuel Le Roy Ladurie, who has presented his efforts as the end of a Copernican-Galilean revolution in the social sciences.[102] Bloch would have denied the epithet *historical* to such an enterprise: "It is men that history wants to catch. Whoever does not succeed in so doing will never be more than a stevedore of erudition, at best."[103] Man belonged at the center of the *Annales* discourse; he was the object of history just as, in Febvre's words, the rock was for the geologist, the animal for the biologist, the star for the astrophysicist: "Something to explain. To get someone to understand."[104] The man of the *Annales* was the average man, not eternal man; not human nature, but social man caught in the skein of his ambient society, for the *Annales* history of the thirties was not the slack water, the unchanging time that it later became.

History was therefore the science of change. This theme was repeated constantly in the writings of the directors of the *Annales*. A journal launched into a world in turmoil, its practice of history was to explain these changes and to make them comprehensible. In similar terms both Bloch and Febvre confirmed this as history's vocation: "History, the science of the perpetual changing of human societies."[105] "History is in its essence the science of change."[106] Bloch denounced the myth of the supposed immobility of rural life in *Les Caractères originaux*. What would he say about today's theses on the immobility of time for four or five centuries? Having seen the how, we can now better understand why the *Annales* succeeded. We found in the *Annales* discourse enough exhortations to rally the social sciences to their enterprise, but behind these innovations, the historical basis remained solid and resisted any attempt to dilute history's specificity. Bloch and Febvre owed their success as much to the innovations they made as to the inheritance they defended in their difficult confrontations with other methodologies and other concepts that were often linked to a more advanced scientific apparatus. To study a long period of time in its entirety, with man at its heart and concerned principally with changes: that was what the social sciences other than history could not claim.

The *Annales* discourse of today is, however, in flagrant contradiction with Bloch and Febvre's discourse. The current generation does not hesitate to get rid of the historical basis that the two founders of their school preserved. And it aligns itself with the other social sciences to such an extent that history risks losing its own identity.

By wanting to stay in power and have the upper hand over the other social sciences, the Annalists are on the point of killing history! What would their spiritual fathers say? To reduce these ghosts to silence, the Annalists venerate their memory, place flowers on their graves, and lavish praise upon them. But is it not just to hide their betrayal of the inheritance? There is a missing link in the chain that has to be examined before coming to the *Annales* of today. It is Braudel's epoch.

■ NOTES

1. L. Febvre, *Annales* (1956): 501.
2. R. Bonnaud, in an interview with the author, 16 Jan. 1986.
3. B. Geremek at the Eighth Conference on Marc Bloch, 17 June 1986. The text was read by J. Le Goff since Geremek was retained in Poland by the police.
4. M. Bloch, "Letter to L. Febvre," *Annales* 1 (1945): 22.
5. L. Febvre, "Letter to Bloch," *Annales* 1 (1945): 23.
6. M. Bloch, *Etrange Défaite* (Editions Franc-Tireurs, 1946), 191.
7. J. P. Lévy at the Eighth Conference on Marc Bloch, 17 June 1986.
8. G. Altman, *Annales* 1 (1945): 11–14.
9. L. Febvre, *Combats pour l'histoire*, 407.
10. M. Bloch, "Testament spirituel," *Annales* 1 (1945).
11. L. Febvre, *Combats pour l'histoire*, 402.
12. Quoted in A. Guerreau, *Le Féodalisme: Un Horizon théorique* (Le Sycomore, 1980), 122.
13. M. Bloch, *L'Etrange Défaite*, 188.
14. Ibid., 189.
15. Ibid.
16. T. Stoïanowich, *French Historical Method: The Annales Paradigm* (Ithaca: Cornell University Press, 1976), 237.

17. L. Febvre, *Annales* 3 (1948); reprinted in *Combats pour l'histoire*, 109.
18. L. Febvre, *Annales* (1930): 437–38; reprinted in *Pour une histoire à part entière* (Publications EHESS, 1982), 454–55.
19. M. Bloch, *L'Etrange Défaite*.
20. L. Febvre, *Foi et Vie* 57 (1934): 119–38; reprinted in *Pour une histoire à part entière*, 350–66.
21. L. Febvre, *Annales* (1935): 615–23; reprinted in *Pour une histoire à part entière*, 665–78.
22. L. Febvre, *Combats pour l'histoire*, 42.
23. Ibid., 117.
24. M. Bloch, *Apologie pour l'histoire* (A. Colin, 1974), 32.
25. Ibid., 48–49.
26. M. Bloch, "Seigneurie française et manoir anglais," *Cahiers des Annales* (1967). This was a course given at the Sorbonne in 1936.
27. M. Bloch, *Apologie pour l'histoire*, 48.
28. O. Dumoulin, seminar at the EHESS, 1980.
29. The editors, "Au bout d'un an," *Annales* (1930): 2.
30. Ibid., 3.
31. L. Febvre, *Annales* (1932): 281.
32. The editors, *Annales* 1 (1929): 1–2.
33. M. Ferro, *L'Histoire sous surveillance* (Calmann-Lévy, 1985), 125.
34. M. Bloch, *Annales* (1931): 1–3.
35. L. Febvre, *Annales* 4 (1932); reprinted in *Combats pour l'histoire*, 348–52.
36. Quoted by O. Dumoulin, "Profession historien: 1919–1939," 3d cycle diss. (EHESS, 1984), 326.
37. O. Dumoulin, *Dictionnaire des sciences historiques* (Presses Universitaires de France, 1986), 327.
38. L. Febvre, *Annales* (1930): 581–90.
39. E. Labrousse, *Esquisse du mouvement des prix et des revenus en France au XVIIIe siècle* (1932) and *Crise de l'économie française à la fin de l'Ancien Régime et au début de la Révolution* (1943).
40. E. Labrousse, interview, *Actes de la recherche en sciences sociales* (Apr. 1980): 115.
41. Ibid., 115.
42. Ibid., 114.
43. Quoted by G. Duby, "Préface," in Bloch, *Apologie pour l'histoire* (1974), 11.
44. L. Febvre, "Le Problème historique des prix," *Annales* (1930): 67–80; reprinted in *Pour une histoire à part entière*, 304.
45. *Bulletin de l'association des professeurs d'histoire-géographie* (1935), 130.
46. O. Dumoulin, *Revue d'histoire moderne et contemporaine* (1984), 24. Special issue: Cent Ans d'enseignement d'histoire.
47. H. Coutau-Bégarie, *Le Phénomène nouvelle histoire*, 52.
48. Reprinted in L. Febvre, *Combats pour l'histoire*, 7–8.
49. L. Febvre, *Philippe II et la Franche-Comté* (1912; rpt. Flammarion, 1970), 9.

50. Ibid., 149.
51. M. Bloch, *La Société féodale* (1939; rpt. A. Michel, 1986), 16.
52. Ibid., 114.
53. Ibid., 203, 206.
54. *Plans*, no. 1, p. 16.
55. L. Febvre, Review of Felice, *Basse Normandie, Revue de synthèse historique* (1907).
56. L. Febvre, *Philippe II et la Franche-Comté*, 30–31.
57. M. Bloch, *Ile-de-France* (1913), reprinted in S. Fleury, ed., *Mélanges M. Bloch* (EHESS, 1983), 2:692–787.
58. L. Febvre, *La Terre et l'évolution humaine* (1922; rpt. A. Michel, 1970), 78.
59. Ibid., 84.
60. Ibid., 398.
61. Ibid., 393.
62. Quoted by N. Broc in *Au Berceau des Annales* (Presses de l'Université de Toulouse, 1983), 258.
63. O. Dumoulin, "Profession historien: 1919–1939," 261.
64. M. Bloch, "Pour une histoire comparée des sociétés européenes," *Revue de synthèse historique* (Dec. 1928); reprinted in *Mélanges M. Bloch*, 16.
65. Lévy-Bruhl, *Les Fonctions mentales dans les sociétés inférieures* (1910).
66. H. Berr, *La Synthèse en histoire* (1911); quoted by J. Revel, *Dictionnaire des sciences historiques* (Presses Universitaires de France, 1986), 450–56.
67. A. Burguière in *Y a-t-il une nouvelle histoire?* (Institut Collégial Européen, 1980), 28.
68. L. Febvre, *Annales* (1940): 39–43 and (1941): 125–30; reprinted in *Pour une histoire à part entière*, 413–27.
69. L. Febvre, *Annales* (1941): 15–20; reprinted in *Combats pour l'histoire*, 221–38.
70. L. Febvre, "Histoire et psychologie," *Encyclopédie française* (1938), vol. 8; reprinted in *Combats pour l'histoire*, 211.
71. L. Febvre, *Un Destin: M. Luther* (1928; rpt. Presses Universitaires de France, 1968).
72. L. Febvre, *Rabelais ou le problème de l'incroyance au XVIe siècle* (1942; rpt. A. Michel, 1968), 15.
73. Ibid., 308.
74. Ibid., 328, 332.
75. M. Bakhtin, *L'Oeuvre de F. Rabelais et la culture populaire au Moyen Age et à la Renaissance* (Gallimard, 1970).
76. G. Lanson, "Programme d'études sur l'histoire provinciale de la vie littéraire en France," (1903), in *Essais de méthode et d'histoire littéraire* (rpt. Hachette, 1965), 83.
77. L. Febvre, "De Lanson à Mornet: un renoncement?" *Annales* (1941); reprinted in *Combats pour l'histoire*, 263–68.
78. A. Meillet, *Aperçu d'une histoire de la langue grecque* (1913), 174.
79. M. Bloch, "Technique et évolution sociale," *Europe* (1938): 23–32; reprinted in *Mélanges M. Bloch*, 833–38.

80. R. Di Donato, *Annales* (1982): 984–96.
81. M. Granet, *Fêtes et chansons anciennes de la Chine* (1919) and *La Religion des Chinois* (1922).
82. See J. Le Goff, "Préface," in Bloch, *Les Rois thaumaturges* (Gallimard, 1983).
83. M. Bloch, *Apologie pour l'histoire*, 62.
84. J. Le Goff, "Préface," in Bloch, *Les Rois thaumaturges*, vii.
85. Ch-E. Perrin, "Préface," *Mélanges M. Bloch*, x–xi.
86. M. Bloch, "Réflections d'un historian sur les fausses nouvelles de la guerre," *Revue de systhèse historique* (1921); reprinted in *Mélanges M. Bloch*, 43.
87. Brême is Bremen in English; in French, these two words are pronounced almost identically, which helps explain how and why there was so much confusion—Trans.
88. M. Bloch, "Réflections d'un historian," 57.
89. M. Bloch, *Les Rois thaumaturges* (1924; rpt. A. Colin, 1961), 21.
90. J. Le Goff, "Préface," xix.
91. M. Bloch, *Les Rois thaumaturges* (1924; rpt. Gallimard, 1983), 52.
92. Ibid., 345.
93. M. Bloch, *La Société féodale* (1968), vol. 1, book 1, chap. 2, p. 115.
94. Voltaire, "Lettre au Marquis d'Argenson," 26 Jan. 1740.
95. J. Le Goff in *La Nouvelle Histoire* (Retz, 1978), 223.
96. J. Michelet, "Préface," *Histoire de France* (1869).
97. Ibid.
98. L. Febvre, *Pour une histoire à part entière*, 364–65.
99. M. Bloch, *Apologie pour l'histoire*, 36.
100. Ibid., 126.
101. L. Febvre, *Combats pour l'histoire*, 12–13.
102. E. Le Roy Ladurie, *Histoire du climat depuis l'an 1000* (Flammarion, 1967).
103. M. Bloch, *Apologie pour l'histoire*, 35.
104. L. Febvre, *Combats pour l'histoire*, 117.
105. Ibid., 31.
106. M. Bloch, *L'Etrange Défaite*, 137.

PART 2

The Braudel Years

THREE

The Parry

■ THE EXPLOSION IN THE SOCIAL SCIENCES

After World War II ended, a new world grew up from its ruins. Once again history and its convulsions upset the historical consciousness of the West. The new situation was similar to what followed World War I, but every element was pushed to the extreme. Every single phenomenon seen in the twenties was amplified. The decline of western Europe was even more evident. The fate of the world, which was in the balance at Teheran, Yalta, and Potsdam, was decided principally by the Russians and the Americans. Henceforth the reconstruction of Europe passed either through New York and the Marshall Plan or through Moscow. Europe had become their vassal. The latter's preponderance, which had reached its apex between 1914 and 1918, disappeared in the middle of the twentieth century. The most obvious sign of this collapse was found in the process of decolonialization that shook the former imperial powers. Despite the fine term *Union* applied to it, the French empire was falling apart piece by piece as the peoples of Africa and Asia struggled for independence. The historical discourse founded on the nation-state and the European mission of spreading universal civilization did not withstand these changes in the contemporary world. The desire for a different history was therefore only more powerful. The barbarism unleashed during the world war exceeded the worst that could be imagined. As bulldozers piled up the bodies left by Nazi Germany, the horror of its atrocities, the extent of its crimes against humanity, its extermination of six million Jews came to light. The barbarity perpetrated by a nation as advanced as Germany rattled certitudes about the sense of history and humanity's forward march toward a civilization that was always evolving. The incredibly magnified power of destruction revealed in the bombing of Hiroshima and Nagasaki increased anxieties about the future. Would reason be able to win out over barbarity? Nothing was less sure in the wake of these disasters.

The other new postwar factor stemmed from a remarkable technological revolution. After a fast that lasted four long years, growth was at hand. Thirty "glorious" postwar years (1945–75) transformed the economy and the society not only of Europe and of the two superpowers but also of the Third World. For the economy became international. It branched out and crossed over the most diverse borders, peoples, and civilizations to impose its own way of thinking. Faced with this new situation, history felt the need for new analytic categories so as to better catch the changes taking place. The internationalization, not only of economics but also of communications among peoples from different continents, forced historical discourse to change and to adapt to a new awareness of historical time. The result of these transformations was a rejection of narrowly national history and an alignment with the other social sciences. This phenomenon can be seen everywhere, in the United States as well as in the Soviet Union. Given this situation, the epistemological revolution carried out by the *Annales* in 1929 was a foretaste of subsequent changes and it guaranteed success. The journal changed at the war's end under the impetus of new postwar stimuli. It took the title: "Annals: Economies, Societies, Civilizations." The disappearance of the term *history* hinted at the desire to go further in aligning with the social sciences. Febvre spoke of this necessary adaptation to current aspirations: "The *Annales* is changing because everything around it is changing: people, things, in a single word, the whole world. . . . Yesterday's world is over, finished forever. I tell you, let's get into the water and swim. . . . Let us explain the world to the world."[1] Starting from this moment the *Annales* could date its decisive victory over traditional history, which disappeared in the ruins of World War II. As Arnaldo Momigliano said in 1961, the *Annales* school "was in the process of taking the place formerly occupied in Europe by the German historical school as the nursery of historians."[2] This harmony between the postwar spirit and *Annales* themes assured the international expansion of the journal. For this postwar growth society in which the themes of modernization, equipment, investment, and inflation dominated national life, economics covered the entire social spectrum and shaped its thinking even more than in the thirties. The second *Annales* generation, with Febvre still at its head, picked and chose in this inheritance. It favored economics to the detriment of the other possible paths: cultural history, the study of *mentalités*, psychohistory. All these fields were rejected during this period to the advantage of economic studies. Favoring economics explains why a researcher like Philippe Ariès, a pioneer in the study of *mentalités*, remained solitary and isolated. His *Histoire des populations françaises et de leurs attitudes devant la vie*, published in 1948, was pointedly ignored. A study in the *Revue historique* showed that work in social and economic history represented 41 percent of the total number of doctoral theses and 40 percent of other advanced degrees in 1961 for the field of modern, contemporary history.[3] Such a preponderance of economics demonstrates the success of the prewar *Annales* positions.

Nonetheless, the focus moved from the study of crises, which was the consequence of the crash of 1929 as seen in the work of Ernest Labrousse, toward economic growth and the impact of production. *Annales* history concentrated on the modern period, the sixteenth to the eighteenth century, and abandoned both contemporary society and antiquity as fields of study because they did not lend themselves to quantitative methods and statistical studies applied over a long period. It relinquished a field that had been claimed vociferously by the first generation, the generation of the contemporary world. As the banner of the heroic period of the *Annales*, economic history had its moment of glory up until the sixties thanks to statistics and quantification. Economics was, at this time, closely related to another expanding discipline, demography. In the journal *Population* in 1946, Jean Meuvret correlated food and population crises under the *ancien régime*. In addition, Louis Henry equipped demography with a new and efficient methodology.[4] An entire generation of *Annales* historians would swarm over church registers and legal documents containing prices, counting and fixing curves and cycles. Serial studies on population and prices became the credo of the *Annales* discourse in the fifties. That was the heyday of regional monographs. Robert Boutruche defended his thesis on Bordeaux society during the Hundred Years' War in 1947; Georges Duby defended his on the Macon region in the eleventh and twelfth centuries in 1953; Pierre Goubert on the Beauvaisis from 1600 to 1730 as well as Paul Bois on the peasants of the Sarthe in 1960; Pierre Vilar presented his Catalonia in modern Spain in 1962, Emmanuel Le Roy Ladurie his peasants of Languedoc in 1966. History at this time mixed demographics, economic curves, and the analysis of social relations. Synthesis, which was so dear to the creators of the *Annales*, took place in regional groupings. Teams were organized in provincial universities to enhance their ability to scrutinize the facts. In Caen, Pierre Chaunu founded a center for quantitative studies; teams gathered around André Armengaud in Toulouse and Jean-Pierre Poussou in Bordeaux. Demography's importance reflected its ability to integrate facts into massive quantifications; it corresponded to a new conceptual framework made possible by a new technology, the computer. Number crunching over long periods of time favored the prestatistical era of the Middle Ages and modern times (i.e., sixteenth-eighteenth centuries) and diminished antiquity and the contemporary period. Politics was just as neglected as in the period between the wars. Triumphant economics accentuated the role of mechanisms and weakened the role of human beings as well as their capacity either to make history or to be its active and conscious subject: "The history we suffer through is invading our world; we have just our head out of the water, and then barely.... The factor of human liberty is very weak; that is the conclusion from my long life as a historian."[5] Bloch and Febvre's humanism disappeared in the face of the inexorable interplay of economic forces. Humanity found itself displaced from the center of historical studies.

This reorientation of historical discourse was fed by the spectacular development of the social sciences. This growth was based on the information furnished by new organizations that were powerfully equipped. They became the new and indispensable organizers of good social order. The Institut National de la Statistique et des Etudes Economiques was created in 1946. The Institut National des Etudes Démographiques, founded in 1945 under the authority of the Ministry of Health, had its own journal, *Population,* edited by Alfred Sauvy. Statistics and demographics became, then, the auxiliaries of political power. Sociology advanced when the National Center for Scientific Research (CNRS) created the Center for Sociological Studies (CES) in 1946 under Georges Gurvitch. This was necessary because sociology had failed to enter the university curriculum and was confined to a single degree option within the field of philosophy. Georges Gurvitch launched in 1946 the *Cahiers internationaux de la sociologie.* In 1947, psychology became an independent university discipline when it secured its own separate diploma. In 1948, Gurvitch, who had been up to then a professor at Strasbourg, which had been a successful launching pad, was elected professor at the Sorbonne. This was one sign of the recognition and validation of sociology.

State and international organizations connected to UNESCO gave an impetus to research by commissioning social surveys, which helps to explain the explosion in the social sciences. Febvre represented the social sciences on an advisory commission in 1945–46 and proposed that UNESCO "draw up a list of questions that would interest the social sciences."[6] UNESCO increased its publications and its initiatives. It founded in 1949 the International Associations of Sociology and Comparative Law as well as the French Association of Political Science. Those in charge emphasized the time lost by France in the social sciences. "It is time to make up for lost time by combining the efforts of sociologists and demographers."[7] The will to transform society and to think social was based on the economic growth of this period.

Expansion in the social sciences was not limited to the forties. It continued and even accelerated into the sixties. The number of researchers in sociology at the CNRS increased from fifty-six in 1960 to ninety in 1964. We can then speak of a real "social science policy"[8] on the part of organizations as different as the state, businesses, and unions. Everywhere social need meant an increased number of undertakings, studies, new institutions. Society in the fifties and sixties wanted to be more rational. It turned to the social sciences to achieve its ambition of dominating social and economic facts through state planning. "Planners asked sociologists to add what was missing to their economic plans."[9] Sociologists were expected to have technical competence. They became experts and specialists whose knowledge could be immediately operational in society's functioning. They were expected to have useful, concrete information for business executives, government administrators, planners. This enchantment with the social sciences led to their institutionalization in the university at the end of the fifties. Professors of sociology, social psychology, and psychology were named to the Sorbonne. In 1958 a *licence* [roughly equivalent to an American M.A. degree] and a doctoral program in sociology were created. In the same year the colleges of liberal arts became colleges of liberal arts and social sciences. In 1959, the law schools became schools of law and economic sciences; a master's in economic science was created in 1957. France, which had only about twenty centers for research in the social sciences in 1955, counted more than three hundred ten years later. The pressure exerted on history became very great. The social sciences were about to influence historical discourse decisively, especially *Annales* discourse, which had always been most responsive to any suits brought by neighboring disciplines. Historians lived this peril even in their relationship with the public at large because the social sciences took over the best-seller list and monopolized the most important intellectual events. This was the moment when Ferdinand de Saussure's *Cours de linguistique* became famous. It was published in 1928 but in thirty years it had not sold more than 15,000 copies. During the sixties it sold 10,000 a year. The same explosion for Freud's *Introduction to Psychoanalysis*, which topped the figure of 165,000 copies sold from 1962 to 1967 while it only reached 30,000 in the previous thirty years. In 1955, the public was conquered by an anthropologist, Claude Lévi-Strauss, who became an instant celebrity with *Tristes Tropiques*.

The other moving force behind the social sciences was located beyond the Atlantic. The United States was blinding Europe with its modern lights. In postwar Europe, not only did dollars from the Marshall Plan abound but so did the methods and the investigative techniques of the American social sciences. Pragmatic American sociology found in France a field of application thanks to Jean Stoetzel, head of the CES, who created in 1945 the Institut Français d'Opinion Publique after a period of study in the United States at the Gallop Institute.[10] Research in the social sciences was reworked and realigned around notions of profitability and rationality in order to acquire American efficiency. Psychology and sociology were called upon to produce the kinds of knowledge that would be effective in business within the framework of the new religion of the fifties, modernity. Like music, they were supposed to soothe the mores and to eliminate conflict from the workplace while simultaneously maximizing the rate of production. This nascent techno society needed the new knowledge furnished by the social sciences and spread by management schools that were then proliferating.[11] The social sciences were better placed than history to answer this demand. History was running the risk of watching the train of change pull out of the station while it stood on the platform. The pressure exerted on history from within the university can be quantified. Roger Chartier has calculated the rates of growth for the number of instructors between 1963 and 1967 in liberal arts colleges.[12] He took into account the professors of named chairs as well as associate and assistant professors. Here we notice the differences among the traditional disciplines including history that dominate the top half of table 1, as well as the pressure that was exerted by the newer disciplines at the bottom. Growing more quickly, the latter threatened to knock over the chessboard, reverse the fixed order, and set up a new hierarchy. This was a risk *Annales* historians wanted to avoid, one that provoked a sharp reaction both within institutions as well as in the definition of history. The advancing social sciences no longer tolerated the domination of "legitimate" disciplines. Sociology hoped to get free of its dependence on philosophy. History saw itself once again challenged as the major science of all things social. The reaction of the social sciences was even more extreme than that of François Simiand or of the Durkheimians in the twenties and thirties. A school that would dominate the humanities, including literature, was aborning. Structuralism defined itself by its antihistoricism and found in the ethnologist Claude Lévi-Strauss a leader who took careful aim at history.

Fernand Braudel had met the anthropologist Lévi-Strauss before the war when he was the ambassador of the *Annales* at the University of Sao Paulo. He had been able to gauge the feelings of rivalry and theoretical confrontation, and he did not hesitate to wax ironic about the scientific pretensions of ethnologists who could not solve a simple algebraic equation.[13] At the University of Sao Paulo each man emphasized the superiority of his own discipline and kept an eagle eye on the other's successes. Already by 1934 Braudel had finished large parts of his thesis on the Mediterranean, according to Jean Maugüe, who rode with him to campus in his noisy Chevrolet. Braudel never left the boxes of cards and microfilms that he consulted in an extra room

Table 1. 1963–67

Subject	Number of Instructors	Percent Increase
Literature	675	200
Classical languages	300	168
Philosophy	227	183
History	527	170
Psychology	221	325
Linguistics	250	250
Sociology	98	288

Source: R. Chartier, seminar on the history of the *Annales,* EHESS, 1980.

he had to rent in the Terminus Hotel, later at the Esplanade, before moving into a large house with a cook and chauffeur. He helped Lévi-Strauss return to France at the end of the forties. When Lévi-Strauss defined social anthropology in 1949, he gave it a hegemonic position not only in the field of the social sciences but also well beyond. Social anthropology was supposed to extend its territory to the very heart of the natural sciences, all the way to the boundary between nature and culture.[14]

According to Lévi-Strauss, historians remain at the level of the empirical and the observable, incapable of creating models and thus of gaining access to society's deep structures. They are condemned to stay blind in their caves unless they get light from ethnologists, for conscious models intervene as obstacles between the observers and their subjects. History and ethnology are doubly close by their institutional placement and by their methods. Both have the *other* as field of study, either in space or in time. Lévi-Strauss believes that these two disciplines have the same object, the same aim, which is to understand human societies, and the same methods. The key distinction would be empirical science on one side, theoretical research on the other: "They differ primarily by the choice of complementary perspectives: history organizes its facts according to conscious expressions, ethnologists according to the unconscious expressions of social life."[15] By moving toward these unconscious structures, ethnology has progressed from the particular to the general, from the contingent to the necessary, from the idiographic to the nomographic. Lévi-Strauss quoted Karl Marx's famous saying "Men make their own history, but they don't know what they are doing" and applied the first part of the sentence to history, the second to ethnography.

Lévi-Strauss's ambition, which was closely related to his attempt at dehistoricization, lay in discovering how the human mind functioned. That was the real invariable and the human characteristic that would be permanent through any diversity of time or space. The anthropologist's task was to map the mental boundaries according to the invariables already located. What myths mean, in the last analysis after all the variations and modulations have been inventoried, is the human mind that elaborated them. Lévi-Strauss brought back one of the oldest ideas, one that was thought to have been long forgotten, with his rich and new methodology: the idea of a *human nature*, an ahistorical fact, unavoidable, atemporal, and caught revealing the existence of universal, underlying, unconscious structures. This he did rather than study institutions and their functioning, or the conditions of production and power. Whether he studied kinship systems or mythological symbols, he discovered the immanent necessities behind illusions of liberty and followed them into the domain that seemed to owe the least to material contingencies like mythology: "In allowing myself to be guided by the search for the constraining structures of the mind, I am proceeding in the manner of Kantian philosophy."[16] Dialectic reasoning disappeared as a logic of content and was replaced by a neo-Aristotelianism or, in Paul Ricoeur's terms, a Kantism without a transcendental subject in which the unconscious was more a categorical unconscious than a Freudian unconscious. Rather than reveal a confrontation between the social realm and the unconscious psyche, myths would, when seen from such a perspective, bring to light the fundamental immobility of the human mind despite its diverse manifestations. Antihistoricism and invariability regularly reappeared in Lévi-Strauss, who imagined mythology and music as "instruments for the obliteration of time."[17] This radical accusation characterized history as mere foundation work, as a contingency, as a chancy, unreliable material, a discipline that resisted every modernization. Fernand Braudel answered this challenge by reorienting historical research and giving it a structuralist character.

■ THE PLURALISM OF TIME

Braudel set the legacy of Bloch and Febvre against Lévi-Strauss but he modified its orientation so as to slow down the structuralist offensive. *Annales* history found in Braudel a man who would revitalize its strategy and make history the central, unifying discipline by stealing the social sciences' program. "Fernand Braudel had to push his thinking forward about the connection between history and the social sciences."[18] In addition Braudel recognized a direct affiliation with the social sciences in his manner of writing history. He took up their methods the better to strangle them.

First there was the influence of the French geographic school of Demangeon and de Martonne. From their teaching Braudel drew his attempt to slow down the rhythm of history as much as possible.[19] Marcel Mauss inspired him to enlarge his historical focus from the social to the study of civilization, which was a distinctive postwar trait.

"I was one of the rare historians who knew Marcel Mauss."[20] Braudel remembered from the revolution in the social sciences, which he judged to be even more essential than the revolution in history, the need to open up the borders between the disciplines and to knock down the walls erected by each one of them. He was in favor of a free exchange of ideas and of personnel among disciplines. Whenever he mentioned the social sciences, Braudel called them imperialistic and said that history should not shirk confronting them. History could only be enhanced by such conflicts, for Braudel never doubted history's ability to absorb, assimilate, and subdue according to a blueprint that had become automatic. In his inaugural lecture at the Collège de France to which he was appointed in 1950, he referred to his rivals: "We have seen, for fifty years, a series of imperialistic disciplines be born, reborn, and flourish."[21] He called upon history, in the preface to his thesis on *La Méditerranée*, to maintain its connection with "the young but imperialistic sciences of man."[22] The tone struck was full of paternal condescension on the part of one who was sure to have the long duration on his side and who was defending a deeply rooted discipline like history and the continuity of a school that claimed dominance over ephemeral comings and goings, over those young upstarts that were the other social sciences. Nonetheless, vigilance was needed in face of their pretensions. There was a double language in Braudel's strategy to tame these young ambitions. On one hand, he acknowledged the affinity of those social sciences that were not really different from history: "Sociology and history are one and the same adventure of the human spirit, not the inside and the outside of one piece of cloth, but the cloth itself in the thickness of its fibers."[23] However, should a partner rebel, try to escape from the *Annales* embrace, and claim his independence, Braudel would drop his condescending tone and cross swords with him. Such was the case of sociology that resisted annexation. He denounced its theoretical weakness: "It fails to define its object. What is society?"[24] "Sociologists' time cannot be our time; the deep structure of our profession finds it repugnant."[25] He mocked Georges Gurvitch's concept of global society: "It appears to be a kind of general envelope for the social, as thin as a fragile and transparent glass bell."[26] The polemic edge was sharpened in order to limit sociology's advances. Yet Georges Gurvitch intended to transcend the opposition between stasis and social dynamics by reintroducing social dynamics as an ongoing process of destructuring and restructuring: "the duration of a social structure is then never at rest, but rather it is a struggle, a movement across winding paths opened up by the multiplicity of social times."[27] By reintroducing movement, the sociological approach became more dangerous for history. Today, facing the success of Pierre Bourdieu, his colleague and rival at the Ecole des Hautes Etudes en Sciences Sociales (EHESS), Braudel denounces sociology's immoderate taste for general ideas and its lack of historical sense. He rejoins Febvre in rejecting the work of Max Weber: "You are the victim of a fluttering present.... What I would like is sociologists who work for me."[28] The territories of historians and sociologists are too close to avoid such conflicts. And Braudel is exasperated by their vitality because it is free from the *Annales*.

Braudel wanted history to be first and foremost synthesis, like anthropology, but with the advantage of thinking in space and time. He took up the legacy of the first *Annales* generation. Duration permeated all the social sciences and conferred a central role on history: "Time, duration, history assert themselves in fact, or should assert themselves in all the social sciences."[29] History's ambition was to reconstitute the global nature of human phenomena. History alone could assign a place and measure the efficiency of all the partial disciplines. Braudelian history's great ambition was to capture the totality of the social realm in a single swoop. It alone had access to what he called the "ensemble of the ensembles."[30] In Braudelian discourse, this globality was characterized by its close dependence on concrete, observable reality. It was, therefore, far removed from the quasi-mathematical systems used by structural anthropology: "We prefer observing concrete experiences to pursuing abstract definitions."[31] The ideal, which as defined by Braudel would be impossible to realize, was to present everything on one single level and in one single sweep. But his concept of globality meant simply adding different levels of reality without producing a conceptual instrument that was capable of catching the dominant and determining forces in play. He did not then go beyond descriptive narration, which was ambitious by what it tried to capture but limited in its capacity to explain: "Is it not good that history is first of all description, simple observation, classification without too many preconceived ideas?"[32] The totality that is defended here should not be related to a causal conception of history. No system of causality is at work, and most frequently we reach only a simple accumulation of different stages. Observing, classifying, comparing, isolating are the principal surgical operations that Braudel practiced. Like Linnaeus, he increased the systematic classifications of the phenomena that were observed. He inventoried and then arranged them in a logical order. Behind Braudel's concept of total history lay a conception of history as magma, the famous plasma that Bloch had talked about. The key word in Braudelian discourse is "reciprocally": everything influences everything else and reciprocally. We understand why Braudel had difficulty in moving from description to analysis with this handling of time: "One could write the following equations in any direction one wished: economics is politics, culture, society; culture is economics, politics, society, etc."[33] Braudelian history was of necessity worldwide; its vision was extensive and presupposed mastery of the comparative method across the longest time periods and the widest spaces.

The specific reply to the challenge thrown at history by Lévi-Strauss in his article "Histoire et ethnologie"[34] was given by Braudel in an essay-manifesto that appeared in the *Annales* in 1958, the same year that *Anthropologie structurale* was published.[35] Braudel admitted having had long discussions in 1958 with Lévi-Strauss, whom he admired and of whom he was jealous. While he showed nothing but scorn for sociology, Braudel did not engage in direct polemics with Lévi-Strauss. He never attacked him despite their increasingly sharp theoretical differences. In contrast to the way he treated Georges Gurvitch, Braudel spoke of Lévi-Strauss's "mastery" in decrypting the language underlying kinship systems, myths, and economic exchanges.[36] Braudel the orchestra conductor, who usually looked down on these young imperialistic sciences, for once left his podium and even spoke of Lévi-Strauss as "our guide." But he did not relinquish his baton. Here was a clear indication that he understood the force and the attraction of this anthropological discourse. Anthropology gave signs of being total, it was supported by mathematics and models that gave it access to the unconscious element in social behavior and that allowed it to acquire quickly within the social sciences a superiority that annulled history's.

To regain the initiative, Braudel borrowed directly from Lévi-Strauss. He played the historian's trump card: not the short duration of the traditional pair event/date, but the long duration that treated the most immutable structures anthropologists could find: "The prohibition against incest is a phenomenon that belongs to the long duration."[37] He recognized that François Simiand's criticism of the singular event and its futility for the social sciences was accurate: "Social science abhors the event. Rightly so: the short time period is the most capricious and the most deceptive of durations."[38] He proposed reorganizing all the social sciences around a common program that would have as its main reference point the notion of long duration. All should defer to the latter, which, dealing with time and periodization, would make history king again. Braudel presented this change of direction as a Copernican revolution in history and as a hint of the radical change in perspective that would allow all the social sciences to speak the same language. In the course of his own life he abandoned the short period for the long duration: "As time passed, from 1960 to 1985, he tended to identify more and more with long history."[39]

The social sciences had two tactics for escaping from history's grasp and both had to be countered. The first was an infratemporal view that cut reality off from any chronological depth. This was, for Braudel, sociology, whose method was too limited to disturb historians. The second was the supratemporal view that tried to construct a science of communications around timeless structures. Here we recognize structuralism, which called on historians and called them into question. Braudel responded by pushing long duration: "I have tried to show, I don't dare say I have shown, that all the new research done by Lévi-Strauss is successful only when his models sail on the waters of long duration."[40] He reappropriated the concept of structure that he had borrowed from Lévi-Strauss but it meant something very different in Braudelian discourse. For Braudel and in contrast to Lévi-Strauss, structure was architecture and construction, but it had to be observable and located in concrete reality. His concept remained basically descriptive and thus faithful to a traditional way of writing history. However, in reappropriating the notion of structure, he did give it a temporal dimension: "These historical structures can be uncovered and in a certain sense measured: their duration is a measure."[41] So, in his book *La Méditerranée*, the structures he uncovered were the sum of a network of relationships, the routes, the commercial exchanges, all the connections that animated the area that he knowingly described and whose relative weights he measured. But he did not inquire into the internal logic of these relations. He concluded his book with a profession of faith in a specific historical structuralism: "I am a structuralist by temperament, not much interested by events, only somewhat by the interconnection and regrouping of events of the same type. But the historian's structuralism has nothing to do with the questioning that torments the other social sciences under that same name. Historians do not push toward mathematical abstractions and connections that are expressed in formulas. Rather they push toward the sources of life and what is most concrete, ordinary, indestructible, and anonymously human in life."[42] Braudelian structures were visible and immediately accessible. They ordered other facts, which gave primacy to the long duration over other temporal rhythms and especially over single events. Braudel's behavior was deliberately welcoming. It melded all positions together to give everyone room in the great laboratory of the social sciences that would transcend all borders and realize, around the historians who were specialists in duration, the unification of all research.

Braudel's reply to Lévi-Strauss and to the social sciences in general was not limited to confronting them with the long duration as a structure. It also consisted in pluralizing time. Already put into practice in his 1949 thesis, this pluralization became a theoretical model in 1958. Time was decomposed into several different rhythms that would break the unity of the duration. Time became qualitative and acquired new meaning at several levels. The Braudelian architecture was articulated around three different time levels: the event, cyclical or conjunctural time, and long duration. One could then distinguish different levels of time and the distances between them. This approach helped to overthrow narrative history, but it was not as new as it pretended. If Braudel pluralized duration, he remained committed to a historical vision whose ambition was to restore a dialectic among these time frames and to refer them back to a single time. Events, conjunctures, and long duration remained complementary. Even if the temporal unit could be divided into several levels, those levels remained linked to a global time that reunited them in a single ensemble. He thus distanced himself from the sociologists' idea of time as multiple and without depth.

We should now give some flesh to the three-part Braudelian skeleton of fleeting time. Duration no longer appeared as a free given, but as a construct. The new commandments according to Braudel were in three parts. They were deliberately constructed without reference to any theory and were located solely at the level of empirical observation. In his book he attributed to each duration a specific domain: "Distinguish, in historical time, between geographical time, social time, individual time."[43] *La Méditerranée* can be cut into three parts, three time frames, three domains. It began with a "nearly immobile history," the story of man's connections with his geographical milieu.[44] At this point Braudel's personal innovation appeared, the integration of space and time. Then came slow history, the history of economics and society. Here Braudel modified the history of economic cycles that had grown out of the new social and economic history of Ernest Labrousse. Finally, the history of events, on an individual scale with the brief and dramatic oscillations of traditional history. This three-part chronological separation into different domains was, in fact, arbitrary since politics, relegated to short history, could have taken form in an institution belonging to the long duration. In contrast, geography showed, often dramatically, that changes did not always take place on the geological scale. The sequence of three time frames did not mean that Braudel gave each equal weight. Without question, there was a temporal causality that was the foundation for the evolution of men and things; that was long duration. Since long duration referred to nature, nature played the determining role. His historical discourse was located, then, at the outer limit of nature and culture. If Lévi-Strauss's ambition was to uncover the mysteries of human nature in the in-between area that connected biology and psychology, Braudel emphasized the irreducibility of physical nature and the slowness of geological time. Neurons or geology? Events per se were relegated to insignificance even if they represented a third of Braudel's thesis about the Mediterranean. He only talked about the "agitation of the waves," "sand storms," "the fireworks of lightning bugs," "a decor." Braudel was steadfast against traditional history in the proper *Annales* spirit, showing an antipathy to events that Jack Hexter calls "passionate and sometimes unreasonable."[45] He justified the social sciences' rejection of individual events and aligned himself both with François Simiand's criticisms of 1903 and with those of Lévi-Strauss in 1962. Instead of placing events in the dynamics of the situation that created them, Braudel preferred to consider events superficial and mere appearances so as to move the historian's focus to slow evolution and to what was permanent. Long duration had certain advantages over other durations. It determined the rhythm of events and their conjunctions; it outlined what was possible or impossible by controlling variations beyond certain limits. If the event was marginal, the conjunction was cyclical. Only structures belonging to long duration were irreversible. This long-range chronology had an advantage: it could be cut up into a series of phenomena that repeated themselves, into permanent features that revealed an equilibrium or general order underlying the apparent disorder of the surface facts. In seeking what was permanent, Braudel gave special importance to space, which seemed to adapt itself best to the notion of slow time: "There is, even slower than the history of civilizations, a nearly immobile history of men and their close connections with the earth that bears them and nourishes them."[46] In this context, man's freedom is infinitesimal, he is caught unrelentingly in the contingencies of a natural milieu, of habits, and of repeated gestures that escape from his consciousness and his control.

Lévi-Strauss's challenge forced Braudel to conceptualize a structural history based on almost immobile time. Febvre did not totally appreciate the concept of structure: "Structures? It's a fashionable term, I know. It's spread out all over the *Annales,* too much so for my taste."[47] But Febvre was in the twilight of his life and Braudel knew what was at stake. Even before structural anthropology, the *Annales* historians had constructed stable and definable totalities. All that was needed was to conceptualize this method in order to resist anthropology's hegemony. Historical movement was thought of as repetition; what was permanent took precedence over what changed. At the end of this transformation, Lévi-Strauss recognized the metamorphosis that had brought history into the same field of inquiry as anthropology: "The idea of structural history contains nothing that can shock historians."[48] Writing history that dove into the depths of what made the ecosystem had, as its first effect, diminished the role of humanity as a collective force. Displaced and relegated to the margins, human beings were caught struggling and powerless: "What I am doing goes against human freedom," Braudel once said.[49] Human beings could do nothing against the world and the long duration of economic cycles that impinged upon them. There was no escape from the spider's web in which humans were caught: "You cannot struggle against a record high tide. . . . Nothing can be done with the weight of the past, except to be conscious of it."[50] Underlying this decentering of humanity was a profoundly pessimistic conception of destiny: "It crushes individuals."[51] "Therefore I am always tempted to see man enclosed within a destiny that he has scarcely made for himself."[52] Humans have lost any mastery over their own history; they are caught in it, and like spectators, the objects of their own temporal nature, they suffer it. Their freedom is reduced to the tragic image of a Colombian girl caught forever in the mud of a volcanic eruption, from which she will be freed only to die.

Beyond our consciousness, our infinitely repeated habits create a voluntary prison and provoke phony decisions lost in the labyrinth of unchanging daily life: "The history we suffer through is invading our world; we have just our head out of the water, and then barely."[53] We are not far from the "man is dead" of structuralism. This decentering, which is paradoxical for historians, was the result of decomposing chronological time into three heterogenous rhythms according to their nature and their time frame: geographical time, social time, and individual time. Braudel himself recognized the consequences of breaking history into such blocks and "decomposing man into a line-up of personages."[54] Long duration acted like a vanishing point for humans by introducing an order outside their control. Braudelian rhetoric remained, however, humanistic to the extent that humanity was only moved off center and not absent from the chronological construction. In this he was faithful to the anthropocentric heritage of Bloch and Febvre, an organic humanism that did not imagine human reality as a finality but rather as a plurality of its organs.

Like Lévi-Strauss, Braudel reversed the linear conception of time that was progressing toward perfection. He substituted for it a stationary time in which past, present, and future were no longer different and reproduced each other without discontinuity. Only the sequence of repetition is possible; it favored the invariables and made the notion of event illusory. "In the historical explanation that I see, it is always the long time frame that wins out. It negates a crowd of events."[55] The social hierarchy was the major permanent feature highlighted by Braudel, whose central concern had always been human society. Society was unavoidably unequal and therefore any egalitarian attempt was bound to fail because of its illusory nature. He forgot his own relativism when he emphasized this invariable, which was found in many different epochs and places: "Every observation reveals this visceral inequality that is the unbroken law of societies."[56] He saw there a structural law that brooked no exception like the prohibition against incest in Lévi-Strauss's work. We realize to what extent this notion of invariability negated history and any possibility of change. Every social fact was put on the same level of hierarchy and inequality. Only variations in this immutable law could change and produce a society founded on slavery, serfdom, or salaried workers. But these solutions referred back to the same reductive phenomenon of mass obedience. For Braudel, it was good that this was the way it was: "Societies are only worthwhile when they are ruled by an elite."[57] Long duration negated historicity. Furthermore, Braudel did not think there was much progress between slave societies and modern democracies. The top of the social pyramid has always been narrowly limited. What good is it to change the form of exploitation if the exploitation continues? Nonetheless, history is made up of changes in the elites in power. But, "nine times out of ten, [the change only] replicates the former state of things, or pretty close to it."[58] The task of every society is to reproduce its structures, as in the "cold societies" of Lévi-Strauss. The power in place perpetuates itself, making man's efforts at transformation vain. Wanting to transcend these facts of life is a waste of time. If the social hierarchy represents a border that cannot be crossed under any latitude, Braudel did not stop at a single invariable: "The state, capitalism, civilization, society have existed forever."[59] Long duration sticks and the paradox appears, obvious but never spotlighted: Braudel has emptied history. The self-regulation at work within society's structures allows repetition of the same phenomenon and forestalls any attempt to change, to break off, or to transform. Any historical break is doomed to failure; what remains behind is illusory. It was thus, according to Braudel, that China kept its mandarins, India its castes, and even Europe, the most mobile society in the world, evolved in slow motion.[60]

In the Mediterranean of the sixteenth century, social agitation was in evidence, but it was nothing but "accidents along the road," "the dust of news reports."[61] The movements mentioned were far from being conscious revolutions; they were merely the actions of bandits in Catalonia, Calabria, or Abruzzi. The desire for social revolution was simply reduced to a kind of murderous delinquency. The class struggle was only recognized by Braudel in the guise of family vengeances wreaked by passersby, vagabonds, criminals; all such revolts were, of course, condemned to failure. It was no more than a question of the interplay of cops and robbers. The impoverishment that struck the whole working class in the sixteenth century provoked "incessant plundering, a long, useless, true social revolution."[62] Revolutions, like wounds, heal quickly. The organism itself produces antibodies that fight the attempt to revolt. The two great cultural breaks in modern

Europe, the Renaissance and the Reformation, were reintroduced into the process of repetition: "Everything builds up and gets incorporated in the existing orders."[63] The Renaissance spelled the success of Machiavelli's Prince and the Reformation led to the temporal power of the German princes. Only the window was broken in the course of these cultural revolutions; society and its power structure remained intact. It was the same for contemporary history. The events of 1968 were "reclaimed by a patient society."[64] In addition, this recuperation of the new by the old was positive for Braudel, who recently criticized the movement of 1968, which had, according to him, devalued the notion of work, undermined moral values, and led to misfortune, for "no one can be happy if they are not under the protection of established values."[65] Braudelian long duration and its various invariables clearly were what they seemed to be: one reading of our history that exorcised any possibility of change, for in function of their connection with the present, historians used one prism or another to reconstitute the past.

Braudel successfully parried anthropology's challenge to the extent that history remained the centerpiece of the social sciences, although it paid the price for changing that is inherent in any radical metamorphosis. Having failed to destabilize the historians as an institution, Lévi-Strauss recently returned to their turf to pick up their used and discarded trappings: "While new history judged that we were right in getting interested in a number of things that they should account for, *we* began to get interested in areas that new history had ignored, like dynastic alliances, kinship in extended families, which became the choice topics for young ethnologists. There is, then, a real back-and-forth exchange."[66] History became anthropological, anthropology became historical. Braudel thus prepared the twists and turns in the historical discourse of the third generation of the *Annales*. He was the unavoidable link in the evolution who opened wide the field of vision and of research for historians. But we can ask ourselves if in fact it was not anthropology that completely took over historical discourse from the inside. Like the Trojan horse, Lévi-Strauss's *L'Homme nu* might have stripped Clio naked.

■ BRAUDEL THE BUILDER

Fernand Braudel was first and foremost a builder of empires, a skilled worker in organizing whose primary concern was to consolidate and to enlarge the historian's territory. Thanks to him, the *Annales* was able to resist the structuralist onslaught because it was supported by an institutional base that was becoming more and more solid. He answered the antihistory challenge as regards both research options and positions of power. Thus, "the war between history and structuralism will not take place."[67] Like a feudal lord, Braudel knighted his vassals and gave them power over the numerous bits of the territory of which he was master. His charisma was recognized by his closest disciples like Marc Ferro: "He ran [his business] like a lord, like a head of state."[68] Right after the war in 1946, the journal changed its name and gave up the reference to history in its former title to become *Annales, économies, sociétés, civilisations*. This change signaled a desire to facilitate the osmosis among the diverse social sciences. While historians were supposed to be the linchpin of this synthesis, the change also disguised their participation so that their organizing role would not be so obvious. The editorial staff was reorganized to take into account the losses due to the war and the rise of new stars. There was only one director, Lucien Febvre, but he was surrounded by Braudel, who would take over from him in 1947, Charles Morazé, Georges Friedmann, and Paul Leuilliot. This new team included collaborators from diverse points in the social sciences. To the historians Pierre Chaunu, Pierre Goubert, Maurice Crouzet, Claude Folhen, Maurice Lombart, and Yves Renouart were added geographers like Pierre Gourou, Dion, and Menier as well as economists like Bettelheim and Fourastié. The postwar journal kept, then, its federal character. Nonetheless, victory was not won for the *Annales* historians since, in their long march toward hegemony, they still faced a rival that stubbornly resisted annexation because it had long coveted its own place in the sun: Durkheimian sociology.

Of course the sociological school was largely leaderless in 1945. Célestin Bouglé died in 1940. Maurice Halbwachs had been deported to Buchenwald, where he died in 1945. Marcel Mauss retired from the Collège de France in 1942. But Georges Gurvitch, fleeing the Nazis, had founded the Institute of Sociology in New York in 1942 at a French-language university, the Free School of Higher Studies. Gurvitch's intention was similar to that of the *Annales*, that is, to promote interaction among the social sciences. However, he wanted to promote them in sociology's favor. A rival network of economists, sociologists, and ethnologists, including Lévi-Strauss, who had learned to work together on the other side of the Atlantic was able, then, to fight the historians for leadership at the very moment when the Rockefeller Foundation proposed, in 1945, to fund research in the social sciences in Europe. In addition, Gurvitch beat the historians to the punch by creating the Center for Sociological Studies (CES) in March 1946. He wanted to create another unit, which eventually would be section six, for the social sciences at the Ecole Pratique des Hautes Etudes (EPHE). This was not the first time the sociologists conceived such an ambition. Mauss had drawn up a project to start an institute of social sciences at the University of Paris and submitted it to the Rockefeller Foundation in 1929. The idea of another section at EPHE seemed, then, to be a fallback position, a passing phase in a much larger program.[69] The project failed because the Americans thought the French situation was not conducive to the project, while Mauss's socialist leanings frightened the donors. Gurvitch seemed to be positioned much better at the beginning of the cold war. The director of the Social Sciences Division at the Rockefeller Foundation, J. H. Willit, clearly understood what was at stake and wrote in October 1946: "A new France, a new society is about to rise from the ruins of the occupation. The best of these efforts are magnificent, but the problems are daunting. In France, the outcome of the conflict and the choice between communism and Western democracy appears in its most accused form. It is a field of battle or a laboratory."[70] The situation was, therefore, conducive to creating section six. The sociologists seemed the most likely to succeed with their project.

But the directorship escaped from them and fell to the *Annales* historians. Lucien Febvre was a member of the executive committee for the Center for Sociological Studies (CES) along with first-class scholars like Louis Gernet, Gabriel Le Bras, Maurice Leenhardt, and L. Lévy-Bruhl, all of whom were associated with Gurvitch. The director for higher education at that time, Pierre Auger, was influenced, however, by Charles Morazé, who was a member of the editorial board of the *Annales*. These two men complemented each other. Pierre Auger wanted to create a new section devoted to the social sciences at EPHE but there was no money since the French government had no funds to contribute. Morazé, secretary for the International Committee for Historical Sciences, had already received large grants from the Rockefeller Foundation. Together they drew up the first list of research directors that was submitted to the foundation in 1947. "In one stroke the historians became the majority."[71] This modification in the project for section six favored the *Annales*, whose principal collaborators were involved, and hinged on Charles Morazé. The latter was not only on the staff of the journal but he founded in 1947 an association for the friends of the *Annales* that later took the name Association Marc Bloch. But Febvre did not immediately catch on to the value of getting involved in this adventure. He was only convinced by Morazé in the fall of 1947 when the latter explained that if the *Annales* did not take the initiative, Gurvitch would turn his Center for Sociological Studies into section six: "The institutional leadership of the social sciences risks, then, falling into the hands of the sociologists."[72] Febvre was elected president of the first executive committee of section six in 1948. At the same time Braudel was designated as the organizer of the *Annales* hegemony because he held the position of secretary charged with running section six. He was also made director of the Center for Historical Research. Febvre had clearly seen Braudel's skills as leader and organizer and his ability to win confidence across the Atlantic. For Braudel, section six was a decisive tool in history's vast project of ingesting the other social sciences. For there was cannibalism in his strategy: "We must understand what the lesson of the *Annales* and the *Annales* school really is. . . . It is that all the social sciences are incorporated within history and are becoming its auxiliaries."[73] Braudel, a power broker, took over the apparatus that produced the alignments desired by the first generation and gave it an institutional basis. He was not, as he himself admitted, at his best as a journalist; rather, he excelled as a builder, constructing a school. What is more, he satisfied the Americans that he belonged to an Atlantic world that was breaking away from the Soviet continental sphere. The conclusion of his thesis, written in December 1948, gave the necessary guarantees: "It seems, for example, that the Atlantic is the center of the current world, but for how much longer? . . . Perhaps we will no longer talk about it until the day when—let us hope it comes as late as possible—that ocean's decline will have created the success of other liquid spaces or—monstrous possibility—the success of other lands."[74] We see the Soviet Union behind the monster. Paris was not, however, New York, and Braudel was not Marshall. If he gave some guarantees to the Americans, he did not submit to them completely. Seeking economists for section six, he backed Charles Bettelheim and made him the first research director in March 1948. A specialist in the Russian economy and a Marxist, Bettelheim was not a typical postwar Atlanticist. His nomination revealed independent thinking and crafty politics at section six. Braudel never allowed himself to be manipulated even in the depths of the cold war when the Americans exerted maximum pressure. He refused to part with Jean Chesneaux and forced the Americans to accept Annie Kriegel, Claude Frioux, and Georges Haupt, among others.[75]

At the end of 1951, Febvre and Braudel solicited another grant from the Rockefeller Foundation. The monies advanced up to that point had in fact been modest, only one-fourth of the amount given to Charles Rist's Economics Institute. It was an attempt, then, to give a leg up to the still-impoverished section six. The justification this time was made openly in the name of the priority accorded to history. A grant of $13,500 (4,500,000 old francs) was to support, for a period of two and a half years beginning 1 July 1952,[76] interdisciplinary colloquia and the ongoing program of the Center for Historical Research, where Braudel had already initiated a series of studies on ports, traffic, routes, and international economic exchanges at the end of the fifteenth and the beginning of the sixteenth century.

During the fifties Braudel did not neglect teaching history within those traditional university structures that the *Annales* wanted to transform radically. We remember the failed effort to overhaul the *agrégation* examination that the two founding fathers had attempted in 1934. Braudel took up this legacy from a better vantage point since he was named president of the jury for the *agrégation* from 1950 to 1955. Of course the exam was not fundamentally changed by that, but the president did use his position for five years to speak out in favor of new criteria, which were those of the *Annales* school. Michel Vovelle has recounted that he knew many candidates who took the exam when Braudel presided over the jury.[77] Braudel is supposed to have told them with a hint of disdain that their presentation did not smell enough of dung, in the same way that Febvre had criticized Bloch's *La Société féodale* by claiming that it did not smell enough of the earth. Changes in tone and outlook were obvious from the ritual reports about the examination. Instead of the eternal complaint about lower grades, Braudel called for the transformation of higher education, for opening up to economic history, for a better training in scientific techniques, and for breaking down disciplinary barriers: "More and more history implies, almost structurally, a knowledge of the methods and the results of the neighboring social sciences, and not only geography."[78]

But the principal project that bore Braudel's own personal stamp turned up at the end of his tenure as president of the examination jury for 1956. He proposed a program that would grant section six a long-term scientific objective and assure its vigor. This project was rooted in the experience of American universities with area studies and consisted in organizing research around cultural spaces along the American model. These cultural spaces would allow the interplay of historical, economic, and sociological methods. Braudel had made a long trip through the United States at the end of 1955 to investigate the impact of area studies. He returned skeptical about the ability of the Americans to implement their project. For him, they fell short in three fundamental dimensions: philosophy, history, and geography, which they had abandoned to study current topics. On the other hand, however, their experiment could be repeated successfully by section six at EPHE.[79] This program of area studies was conceived in collaboration with Clemens Heller, who had been involved in the development of section six with Braudel since 1952. Heller, a Harvard graduate living in Paris since 1949, had the idea of adapting the American model of area studies to France. This program was not only supposed to facilitate the organic collaboration of several disciplines but also to help understand the contemporary world and the past thanks to a temporal thickness that French historians could supply more easily than the Americans since the French were orchestrating the social sciences. The project was accepted by the Rockefeller Foundation after a year of difficult negotiations. In 1955 the foundation informed Braudel and Heller of the conditions for funding. Among other restrictions, it refused to fund the work of Etienne Balazs on Chinese medieval history or the research of Jean Chesneaux, both of which were picked up by the Ministry of National Education. The area studies program was born, however, and was granted $60,000 in December 1955 for two years, to which the foundation added $80,000 in 1958 for three years.[80] The area studies program gave a decisive quantitative vigor to section six. Between 1954 and 1957 the section added about forty new positions, about half of them in area studies. In 1959 Braudel obtained from the Ministry of National Education sixty research positions for his 1960 budget, another sign of section six's success in becoming part of the institution. This program might have prepared the terrain for a victorious anthropology. In 1960, section six made another leap forward. It had sixty-seven professors in 1958; in 1960 it had eighty, benefiting from a real political commitment to the social sciences on the part of the state as well as different social organizations, which also showed strong support. Section six seemed to be the most appropriate unit for responding to any strong social demand not covered by traditional university institutions.

But Braudel did not limit himself to domestic expansion, he also played the international card. The fact that the *Annales* was more worldwide in its concerns becomes obvious when we compare the geographic distribution of the papers presented in a collection honoring Lucien Febvre that was published in 1953 with the *Mélanges* that appeared twenty years later in honor of Braudel.[81] For Febvre, the area of influence was very French: seventy French articles compared with fifteen from foreign historians, of whom nine were Italian. In contrast, for Braudel, the *Annales* space branched out: forty articles from France and fifty from foreign historians. During the 1950s, important publications from section six appeared under Braudel's aegis: ports, routes, traffic; monies, prices, conjunctions; business and businessmen; men and the land; societies and civilizations. "Simiand's dream . . . of a social science laboratory in which a director would supervise research" became a reality.[82] Looking at these advances, we can measure how little the structuralist attempt to destabilize history succeeded despite the vogue of structuralism in intellectual circles. Solidly defended, the *Annales* resisted the new attack launched against history at the end of the fifties as it had at the beginning of the century. Braudel did more than bring section six to life. He helped draft the Longchambon plan in 1958, which was supported by Gaston Berger, Director of Higher Education. In it he proposed a new university separate from the Sorbonne and the law schools that would be reserved for the social sciences. But he ran into a wall of resistance on every side. The law schools and colleges of liberal arts denounced Braudel's imperialistic undertaking. Legal and literary scholars aligned themselves for once, ignoring internal quarrels, to oppose together this attempt by Braudel, who was called by some another Louis XIV. Resisted on the left and the right, accused of being the valet of American imperialism and the Marshall Plan by the French Communist party, he was a revolutionary figure for conservative historians who were still attached to traditional history: Pierre Renouvin denounced the

"Braudel plan." He floundered especially on the reef of resistance that was the university establishment. Nonetheless, he was not stopped by this failure and solicited funding from the government and the Ford Foundation to create a museum of the sciences of man. He obtained funding and founded in 1962 a new research laboratory on the site of the old Cherche-Midi prison. Its installation was particularly laborious, punctuated by a seventeen-year-long dispute between the Ministries of Justice and National Education. Its creation owed a lot to Braudel's stubbornness: "I am in a museum that would never have been built without me."[83] Known principally for his writings, Braudel was nonetheless principally a builder, more effective in the solidity of institutions that he ran than by the originality of his theories. More a man of action than a theoretician, he changed the course set by the first generation of the *Annales*. He is, for this reason, an essential link in the school's progression toward its triumphant moment.

▪ NOTES

1. L. Febvre, "Face au vent," *Annales* (Jan. 1946).
2. Quoted by G. Barraclough, *Tendances actuelles de l'histoire* (Flammarion, 1980), 66.
3. J. Schneider and Ph. Vigier, *Revue historique* (1961): 403.
4. L. Henry, *Une Richesse démographique en friche: les registres paroissiaux* (1953); *Des Registres paroissiaux à l'histoire de la population* (Presses Universitaires de France, 1956).
5. F. Braudel, "Y a-t-il une nouvelle histoire?" debate at the FNAC organized by *Les Nouvelles littéraires*, 7 Mar. 1980.
6. Quoted by A. Drouard, *Revue française de sociologie* (Jan. 1982): 58.
7. J. Stoetzel, "Sociologie et démographie," *Population* 1 (Jan. 1946).
8. A. Drouard, *Revue française de sociologie* (Jan. 1982): 70.
9. C. Gruson, "Planification économique et recherche sociologique," *Revue française de sociologie* (1964).
10. M. Pollak, "La Planification des sciences sociales," *Actes de la recherche* (June 1976): 105–21.
11. L. Boltanski, "America, America: Le Plan Marshall et l'importation du management," *Actes de la recherche* (May 1981): 19–41.
12. R. Chartier, seminar on the history of the *Annales*, EHESS, 1980.
13. J. Maugüe, *Les Dents agacées* (1982), 118.
14. F. Dosse, "Les Habits neufs du président Braudel," *Espaces-Temps* 34–35 (Dec. 1986).
15. Cl. Lévi-Strauss, *Anthropologie structurale* (1958), 25.
16. Cl. Lévi-Strauss, *Le Cru et le Cuit* (Plon, 1964), 18.
17. Ibid., 22.

18. J. Hexter, "Braudel and the monde braudélien," *Journal of Modern History* (1972): 499.
19. "Lundis de l'histoire," France Culture, 3 Jan. 1977.
20. Ibid., 21 Jan. 1977.
21. F. Braudel, *Ecrits sur l'histoire* (Flammarion, 1969), 31.
22. Ibid., 13.
23. Ibid., 105.
24. F. Braudel, *Civilisation matérielle, économie et capitalisme* (A. Colin, 1979), 2:408.
25. F. Braudel, *Ecrits sur l'histoire*, 77.
26. F. Braudel, *Civilisation matérielle*, 408.
27. G. Gurvitch, "Le Concept de structure sociale," *Cahiers internationaux de sociologie* 19 (7 Dec. 1955): 3–44.
28. "Apostrophes," Antenne 2, 21 Feb. 1979.
29. F. Braudel, "Histoire et sociologie," in *Ecrits sur l'histoire*, 105.
30. F. Braudel, *Civilisation matérielle*, 408.
31. Ibid., 3:199.
32. F. Braudel, *La Dynamique du capitalisme* (Arthaud, 1985), 25.
33. F. Braudel, *Civilisation matérielle*, 3:34.
34. Cl. Lévi-Strauss, "Histoire et ethnologie," *Revue de métaphysique et de morale* (1949); reprinted in *Anthropologie structurale*, 3–33.
35. F. Braudel, "Histoire et sciences sociales: la longue durée," *Annales* (Dec. 1958): 725–53.
36. Ibid.; reprinted in *Ecrits sur l'histoire*, 70.
37. Ibid., 73.
38. Ibid., 46.
39. M. Ferro, *Espaces-Temps* 34-35 (Dec. 1986).
40. F. Braudel, "Histoire et sociologie," in *Ecrits sur l'histoire*, 114.
41. F. Braudel, *Civilisation matérielle*, 2:410.
42. F. Braudel, *La Méditerranée et le monde méditerranéen à l'époque de Philippe II* (A. Colin, 1966), 2:520.
43. Ibid., 1:17; preface to the first edition.
44. Ibid., 16.
45. J. Hexter, "Braudel and the monde braudélien," *Journal of Modern History* (1972): 507.
46. F. Braudel, "Leçon inaugurale au Collège de France (1950)," in *Ecrits sur l'histoire*, 24.
47. L. Febvre, "Préface," in P. Chaunu, *Séville et l'Atlantique* (SEVPEN, 1975), xi.
48. Cl. Lévi-Strauss, "L'Anthropologie sociale devant l'histoire," *Annales* (July-Aug. 1960): 634.
49. TF1, 22 Aug. 1984.
50. Ibid.
51. Ibid.
52. F. Braudel, *La Méditerranée*, 2:520.
53. "Y a-t-il une nouvelle histoire?" debate at the FNAC, 7 Mar. 1980.

54. F. Braudel, *La Méditerranée*, 1:17.
55. Ibid., 2:520.
56. F. Braudel, *Civilization matérielle*, 2:415.
57. TF1, 22 Aug. 1984.
58. F. Braudel, *Civilization matérielle*, 2:422.
59. Interview, *Magazine littéraire* (Nov. 1984): 20.
60. F. Braudel, *Civilisation matérielle*, 3:48.
61. F. Braudel, *La Méditerranée*, 2:76–77.
62. Ibid., 1:417.
63. F. Braudel, *Civilisation matérielle*, 3:542.
64. Ibid.
65. TF1, 22 Aug. 1984.
66. Personal interview with Claude Lévi-Strauss, 26 Feb. 1985.
67. A. Burguière, *Annales* (1971), special issue entitled "Histoire et structure." The allusion is to Giraudoux's play, "The Trojan War Will Not Take Place." The English title "Lion at the Gates" does not capture the word play—Trans.
68. M. Ferro, "Le Laboratoire des *Annales*," *Magazine littéraire* (Nov. 1984): 25.
69. B. Mazon, "Fondations américaines et sciences sociales en France: 1920–1960," 3d cycle diss. (EHESS 1985), 54–56.
70. Ibid, 103.
71. Ibid., 128.
72. Ibid., 123.
73. F. Braudel, *Une Leçon d'histoire* (Arthaud-Flammarion, 1986), 222.
74. F. Braudel, *La Méditerranée*, 1095.
75. O. Dumoulin, "Un Entrepreneur des sciences de l'homme," *Espaces-Temps* 34-35 (Dec. 1986).
76. B. Mazon, "Fondations américaines," 154.
77. M. Vovelle, *Espace-Temps* 34-35 (Dec. 1986).
78. F. Braudel, "Rapport du concours 1953," *Bulletin de l'Association des professeurs d'histoire-géographie* (1954): 226–84.
79. F. Braudel, "Rapport préliminaire sur les sciences humaines au ministère de l'Education nationale" (1956); quoted by B. Mazon, "Fondations américaines," 167.
80. B. Mazon, "Fondations américaines," 172.
81. J. Hexter, "Braudel and the monde braudélien," 495–96.
82. Georg G. Iggers, *New Directions in European Historiography* (1975), 61.
83. Interview, *L'Histoire* (Sept. 1982).

FOUR

The Paradigm

■ GEOHISTORY

At the fiftieth birthday celebration of the *Annales* at Strasbourg in 1979, Fernand Braudel defined the difference between the roles of its founding fathers thus: Marc Bloch was the chief executive officer and Lucien Febvre the minister for foreign affairs. What he did not add was that he himself was both, having taken on this double paternity, this double legacy in order to bring the *Annales* to the largest audience and to consolidate its theoretical and institutional positions. He is first of all the heir of Febvre, who was his spiritual father and whose faithful disciple he was, taking over the *Annales* in 1947, the same year he defended his thesis. He replaced Febvre in 1949 as the chair of modern history at the Collège de France where he taught for twenty-three years, up until 1972; in 1956, upon Febvre's death, he succeeded him as president of section six at the Ecole Pratique des Hautes Etudes (EPHE).

Fernand Braudel saw Lucien Febvre for the first time in 1934 at Henri Berr's Center for Historical Synthesis, but their real meeting, the decisive one, took place later. It was in 1937, during a crossing of the Atlantic. Both historians were returning from Latin America. The dialogue that started then between two men who had so much in common was never interrupted. "Once I entered into Lucien Febvre's life, I occupied a place that gradually grew, like a child of the house."[1] Like his predecessors, Braudel came from the frontier region of eastern France: he was born at the beginning of this century, in 1902 in Lunéville in the Barois, on the border between Champagne and Lorraine. He was born along with this century just as Victor Hugo was born along with the nineteenth in 1802; curiously, their lives ended in 1885 and 1985! The son of a schoolteacher, Braudel became an *agrégé* in history three years after his baccalaureate degree, at the age of 21! From 1924 to 1932 he taught in the lycée in Constantine (Algeria) and then in Algiers. A man of the northeast, he discovered ecstatically the charms of the Mediterranean, to which he devoted a good part of his life. "I loved the Mediterranean passionately."[2] In 1923 he decided upon his thesis topic, which seemed quite traditional: his aim was to study Philip II's diplomatic policies in the Mediterranean. Quite naturally he wrote to the author of another thesis on Philip II, Lucien Febvre, who admitted being interested by the subject and ready to direct it. But he suggested a major modification that became a historiographic revolution: "Philip II and the Mediterranean is a fine subject. But why not the Mediterranean and Philip II? Isn't that an equally fine but different subject? For between these two protagonists, Philip and the interior ocean, the match is not equal."[3] Thus history changed its subject, no longer Philip II but the Mediterranean, a geographical subject for a historian. It was a decisive maneuver that Braudel skillfully mastered as he took up the suggestion and the legacy of Febvre. Writing that thesis has become one of the legends of the century, thanks principally to Febvre, who claimed to have received 1,100 pages from Braudel, who was a prisoner in Germany for the whole war, first at Mayence, then at Lübeck. They were written from memory in grade-school copy books. Certainly a remarkable performance. However, according to Jean Maugüe, a colleague and friend of Braudel's in Sao Paulo from 1935 to 1937, the main part had already been written. Braudel himself noted for the second edition of his thesis in 1963: "The main arguments had been fixed, even if not written down, by 1939, at the end of the stunning, youthful period of Bloch and Levbre's *Annales,* of which it is the direct fruit."[4] It is thus certain that while a good part of *La Méditerranée* was written in a German prison camp, all the research preceded World War II. This fact disproves the hypothesis according to which the book's structure was conceived as an antidote to the German news about the war, as if it were a form of escape into long duration in contrast to the daily events broadcast over Nazi radio.

Right from the beginning Braudel took up Febvre's legacy by constructing a geohistory in the footsteps of his master. He was no less the heir of Marc Bloch, and we find in his work this double paternity. This synthesis was forged during an intellectual journey that led from geohistory to the study of economic structures, concepts of world economy, reflections upon capitalism and the market economy. These themes are more sociological and economic, and thus closer to Bloch's *La Société féodale*. We note, then, a curve that led Braudel from Febvre to Bloch and, in the twilight of his life, back to his first love with *L'Identité de la France*. This last work belongs within Febvre's sphere since he also projected a book on the history of France that he could not complete, unless we consider *Honneur et Patrie*, which has disappeared, as a preliminary sketch for it. Braudel is, therefore, the pivotal figure, the man astride two *Annales* paths, a position that has contributed to his aura throughout the entire school. He claimed this double paternity when he entered the Académie Française: "First and foremost, I recognize with pleasure Marc Bloch and Lucien Febvre, the greatest historians of this century. If I have innovated, it was by following them."[5]

It was by constructing geohistory that Braudel followed Febvre's legacy to its culmination. After having been in 1920–23 a student of the leaders of the Vidalian school, Braudel naturalized history by picking up the axioms of Vidal de la Blache: "Some of the richest work for history, perhaps the richest, was Vidal de la Blache's."[6] During the twenties Braudel also discovered Febvre's book *La Terre et l'évolution humaine* (1922). It was a "thunderbolt."[7] Space or milieu, synonyms for Braudel as for Vidal de la Blache, became the key to his writing and the basis for a civilization's evolution. Moreover, Braudel, countermanding his own refusal of causal systems, used space as an explanation for the diverse aspects of civilization: "Any civilization is at bottom a space worked by men and history."[8] This phrase catches the lens that illuminates human reality with the rays of a new reading: geohistory. Time almost disappears into space, and we should not be astonished that history, in this process of naturalization, is fixed on the earth. Civilization is defined by and often reduced to space: "What is civilization if not the timeworn placement of a certain humanity in a certain space."[9] Geohistory judges, determines, and establishes an inviolate horizon. It cannot be enclosed within any strata of human reality; it includes phenomena like climate as well as culture. Geohistory absorbed everything and prepared the total history that Braudel so ardently desired. The vegetable kingdom, that in-between world, caught between soil studies and the human condition, was the ideal terrain that Braudel worked. He saw in it an example of the "determinism in civilization" that Pierre Gourou spoke about.[10] One by one he followed the growth and the itinerary of those civilizing plants, wheat, rice, and corn, that have dominated material life from one end of the globe to the other. These plants became the principal characters in the saga told in the first volume of *Civilisation matérielle*. They imposed their intangible laws upon human societies that had to produce or disintegrate. They were capable of moving mountains or of pushing back the limits of the impossible. Such was the case of corn, that miraculous plant: "Without corn, nothing would have been possible, not the giant pyramids of the Mayans or the Aztecs, nor the cyclopean walls of Cuzco, nor the impressive marvels of Machu Pichu."[11] A view that was more spatial than temporal, Braudel's geohistory made geography an interpretation of society, a solid rock men could anchor on.

Geohistory held another interest for Braudel even though he claimed to have understood it only in 1941, eighteen years after his work began. Geography allowed him to emphasize long duration and to minimize the weight of man as an actor in history by replacing him with a spatial subject, in this case the Mediterranean raised up to the level of historical subject: "Geography was the best means of slowing down history."[12] Braudel's three-part temporal construction rested upon the nearly immobile history that he considered primary in an arrangement where geohistory was synonymous with long duration. There had been, before him, systematic study of long-term phenomena and repetitions using Labrousse's model. These were essentially economic matters, the cyclical changes in prices and production. With Braudel and geohistory, the study of cycles was expanded to all phenomena whose changes were often hidden from view and not spectacular. It was appropriate, then, to uncover this underlying level of history that could be studied as space or material life, the privileged sites of resistance to change. Observing and classifying the slow swings of geohistory would determine those periodic rhythms, the very writing of history.

The other dimension of geohistory consisted in identifying what Braudel called the structures of history. Thus, geohistory took a central position as an explanation of human phenomena. For Braudel, structure belonged to the order of the visible; it was related to what is possible and to the constraints that make human beings prisoners and whose forms time can erode only slowly. Accessible to historians, this structure was nothing but the geographical frame whose diverse components, whether climatic, vegetable, or animal, established a near-permanent equilibrium. Causality existed, then, at the level of natural conditions and fixed the limits that human beings could not escape: "Let us remember the congenital fragility of man in the face of the colossal forces of nature."[13] Of course Vidalian potentiality allowed Braudel to reintroduce change into the unchangeable and to bypass certain obstacles. Impelled by necessity, human beings had sometimes transcended what appeared to be an immutable horizon. That did not stop Braudel from assigning a privileged status to geography as a constraint: "Geography first," he said about commercial activities.[14] The primacy given to nature led to an esthetic regression in Braudel's historical discourse, the loss of dialectics and movement, for the relationship is no longer contradictory but complementary: "A countryside is always full, centered on itself, without any affinity or relation to other countrysides save that of coexistence or juxtaposition."[15] Braudel's spatialization of time and economics neutralized the internal contradictions breaking down change. Different ways of cutting up space localized the subsets of this coexistence. Space constrained man and described the shape of what was permanent in civilization. Beyond the changes attributed to what was not essential, we can usually find the signs of the great articulations that divide space, the unchanging points on which civilizations stick. Thus, Braudel evoked "an essential articulation of the Mediterranean world"[16] located along the Rhine and the Danube, that old wound where we find not only the European boundaries of classical Rome but also the sphere of influence of the Reformation, which also crashed into this borderline. Similarly, between West and East, there was an unmoving barrier that ran through Zagreb and Belgrade, "the most astounding wound."[17] In this complementary space Braudel used many organic images. They reveal the Vidalian legacy of a geography whose concepts are based on biology. This organic tendency is more than metaphor: "The weakness of Genoa is hereditary."[18] "Western Europe, small and overcharged."[19] "The Lowlands and England are more muscled, more easily unified."[20] "That's one reason why Spain's heart beats slower than others."[21] Vitalism functioned as a model in Braudel's writing. France and England, like other countries, were pictured as organic beings with their blood circulating, their heart, their limbs, but also with their conscience: "England, without being conscious of it at the time, became an island."[22] France avoided an imperial adventure in the sixteenth century thanks to its temperament, its wisdom, its taste for real values. The function of the geographic milieu was to collect the scattered parts of the organism and to keep them together. It produced and defined a common life.

If Bloch and Febvre had used the teachings of Vidal de la Blache for their own purposes, Braudel can be read as entirely faithful to the Vidalian legacy. His last work, *L'Identité de la France* (1986), is a remarkable example of this: "For a contemporary geographer, reading *L'Identité de la France* in 1986 has the charm of an old attic where you might discover [an old atlas like] the *Tableau géographique de la France.*"[23] Belonging more to his father's generation, Braudel ignored the changes that had taken place in geography, changes that bothered him more than they pleased him. The opportunity to think of geography as the science of societal space rather than as the science of natural space and of countrysides did not affect Braudelian discourse. A debate at Châteauvallon in the autumn of 1985 between the geographer Etienne Juillard and Braudel points to this epistemological generation gap. Braudel acted like the heir of a geographic determinism that Febvre had violently rejected in 1922: "If there is no geographic determinism, what can geographic science be?"[24] He accused geographers of eliminating space from history by making physical constraints relative and by relocating them historically. For Braudel, constraints play the role of last resort, the most essential basis for deep history. He admitted that he was attached to an old-fashioned and deterministic geography. Natural constraints were the first part of a process that seasoned diverse civilizations. Their way of adapting was closely related to the environment and the ecosystem. The geomorphology and the different climates on both sides of the Mediterranean basin determined mechanically the existence of two diametrically opposed civilizations. If the Byzantine Empire outlived the Ottoman Empire, that was because it "was on the good side of the Mediterranean."[25] The Turkish Empire's first trump card, which allowed it to be autonomous, was its spatial dimension, its vast surface area. As a subject, the Mediterranean seemed animated by the will to resist any enclosure. Overwhelmed by its natural poverty, the Mediterranean sought to overcome its weaknesses by exploiting distant worlds through imperialistic expansion that was "almost instinctive."[26] Of course, awareness of the milieu's constraints was necessary and even enlightening, as when Braudel divided the Mediterranean year into two seasons. The fine weather allowed a period of war whereas the winter led to peace since the stormy sea prevented large military convoys from traveling from one point to another inside the Mediterranean space. That was the time for crazy rumors but also for negotiations and peace initiatives. Peace treaties were discussed in winter, signed in spring, and broken in summer. Thus was time closely linked to changes in climate.

Too often, however, the spatial argument functioned as an absolute determinant. The Mediterranean was crisscrossed by trading routes that connected commercial cities. Braudel emphasized these exchanges and insisted upon this spatial overdetermination in his analytic schema. Unified by their climate, and therefore as agricultural civilizations, the Mediterranean countries comprised a single reality despite their differences: "Nature and man have worked together."[27] Often spatial determinism was used in contradictory ways without any explanation. Thus, the prosperity of the Italian cities in the fourteenth through sixteenth centuries was due to the homogeneity of the restricted space around them, which allowed them to win new routes. These small urban states were conquerors to the extent that they could rapidly mobilize their resources. In contrast, vast states moved with difficulty, mired in their rural nature, caught in their own giantism. Nonetheless, this spatial determinism turned around in the sixteenth century and signaled the decline of the commercial cities, which were eclipsed by vast spread-out states like Spain, England, or France. In Braudel's spatial atlas, the port of Genoa owed its glory to a restrictive geography that obliged it to be adventurous: on one side, a sterile mountain barrier; on the other, a dangerous coastline where Barbary pirates cruised. The Genoese transformed this site into an advantage, which explained "the suppleness, the agility, the availability, the weightlessness of Genoese businessman."[28] Yet is being hemmed in by a mountain enough to produce the Genoese glory? The failure of Genoese capitalism stemmed also from geography and from the geographic revolution that promoted the Atlantic space and doomed the nerve centers of Mediterranean capitalism. The British hegemony of the pound sterling was essentially a geographic phenomenon, the "aggressive tension of a country constrained by being an island."[29] People and organizations change, the Mediterranean remains. Attica was poor and therefore condemned to outdo itself; whence was born the Greek miracle. Geohistory excited the factors of civilization without intermediary. The backwardness of modern France was attributed to its giantism: "In the case of France, is not the very immensity of its territory the major source of its inertia?"[30] As the sole rational factor, a dialectic of space articulated the hierarchy of the world. If France is too vast, it goes without saying that Russia, Asia, and Africa don't even count. Retrospective geography, therefore, implied a schematic reading that was too often mechanical. In any case it remained the method favored by Braudel, who considered it more reliable than "an aberrant retrospective sociology."[31] The definition he gave of France's identity emphasized its natural phenomena. The Massif Central was thus raised, not in altitude, but in importance as a factor of national unity because it was a mountain range: "Finally, more than we might think, France can be explained by its high central elevations."[32] The examples he cited to support his argument about France are so many proofs of his mechanical analysis. He did not hesitate to claim, when talking about Besançon and its location, that "geographic determinism here is surely not an idle word."[33] This determinism allowed him to discover the crushing forces that weighed man down and that had their origin in nature and the earth, his milieu. Furthermore, Braudel insisted upon giving a lesson to the geographers of today with the geography of yesterday: "Geographers gave up a long time ago."[34] No, the decisive element was not history, not humanity, despite what Febvre thought. Braudel picked up on the main route of French commerce marked in Vidal de la Blache's atlas of France. Although it was on the borders and not in the heartland, this French isthmus, which displays a "remarkable permanence,"[35] was the axis of the Rhone.

As the cause of the rise and fall in population we find the same geographic determinism with climatic variations: "The age of Louis XIV was a small glacial period."[36] Geographical coincidences are like economic ones, and they have an influence on large spaces. For Braudel, only one reason was plausible in explaining the general rise in population in Europe as well as in other parts of the globe during the eighteenth century: the change in climate, the warming that followed the glaciation of the seventeenth century. Long duration was then inseparable from the space that subtended it: "The easiest way to understand long duration is to think of geographical constraints."[37] Without recourse to theory, Braudel floated along, pushed by the description of different instances of reality in which the only thing that can be affirmed is that social classes and social groups play only an insignificant role. For everything else Braudel applied a mechanical determinism to natural conditions (climate, earth, geomorphology) or to technology. Everything became a cause in his retelling. This echoes the positivistic history that was so decried and mocked by the *Annales* because its collecting, classifying, and arranging facts functioned like a causal system. The difference is only that the perspective is not the same. In Vidal's tradition of space, politics was avoided as a subject. Pierre Chaunu explained that depoliticized space excited him as he read Braudel's thesis: "It was a marvelous discovery, space freed from the state, real space, I mean the countryside, the dialogue of man with the earth, and climate, that age-old struggle between man and things, without the filter of the state."[38] Political history was thus relegated to the role of decor, bit actor, or tag-along, while the countryside took on the role of the star. Commenting on his division of the sixteenth-century Mediterranean into a Turkish empire in the east and a Spanish empire in the west, Braudel mechanically juxtaposed the duality of climate with the duality of civilization: "Politics did no more than to trace an underlying reality."[39]

■ "HISTOR-IST" OR "ECONOM-IAN"?

After the Mediterranean, Braudel's second favorite topic was capitalism in the modern era (fifteenth to eighteenth centuries). As the inspiration behind this turn toward economic history we find his mentor Lucien Febvre, who asked him in 1952 to write a volume in the series "Destins du monde" on preindustrial Europe. The subject was "amicably imposed."[40] Febvre himself intended to write a complementary volume on Western thoughts and beliefs in the same period. Braudel's task consisted in presenting the theories then in vogue about the European economy. *Mentalités* decoded by Febvre, economics by Braudel: such was the division of labor that marked for a long time Braudel's research. In 1967 he published *La Civilisation matérielle* in the collection "Destins du monde" but did not stop there. Economic history kept his attention until 1979 when he published his three-volume work. To a reworked first volume he added two more. Meanwhile, he made economics and economic history his specialty: even the economists quoted him with respect. They recognized the failure of their crisis interventions. Often lost in sophisticated mathematical models that were still incapable of explaining economic fluctuations, they started turning to Clio and discovered Braudel.

We can distinguish two ways the economists used Braudel's work. On one hand were those who found in him a historical guaranty and a temporal thickness for their analysis of the present. They were "more Braudelian than Braudel"[41] in that, pushing his logic to the extreme, they made him say what he did not say. Here we can mention Alain Minc, for whom the future of capitalism resided in the basement of Braudel's three-part construction, i.e., in daily structures and in barter, the primary exchange. Also Jacques Attali, who nominated Braudel for a Nobel prize in economics in 1979. He continued Braudel's schema of the chronological sequence of world economies and foresaw the displacement of those centers toward the Pacific. On the other hand, Braudel has become an obligatory point of reference for regulatory economists, like Michel Aglietta, Robert Boyer, and Alain Lipietz, who found in his work the spatial and temporal roots of capitalism's unequal growth in a long-term worldwide perspective.[42]

Braudel has then dealt with different interpretations about the genesis of capitalism. He has mentioned and discussed the prevalent theories without adopting any single one. Resolutely nontheoretical, he shunned any conceptual limitation and preferred to observe and classify economic phenomena. He refuted theoretical arguments by comparing them with irreducible facts. Faithful to his own bias, he emphasized equilibrium over long duration. In condemning causal, global explanations, he often practiced a factual pointillism that stemmed from his definition of structure as any empirical, observable entity. As we have seen, economics was only accidentally Braudel's field of research because for him history was always global. When he reviewed Pierre Chaunu's thesis, he congratulated the author but denied him the direct affiliation the latter had claimed with the aims of *La Méditerranée*.[43] Chaunu was wrong to restrict himself to serial, economic history while historical reality overflowed any limited selection. Similarly, he admonished his disciple Emmanuel Le Roy Ladurie, representing the aims of the third *Annales* generation, who was fascinated by cliometrics, or statistical history: "I am afraid, and I'll quibble with Emmanuel Le Roy Ladurie about it, that it is an illusion or an excuse to claim, speaking of statistical history, that the future historian will have to be a computer programmer or not be a historian. What interests me is the programmer's program. Right now, he should aim at unifying all the social sciences."[44] If more than twenty-five years of Braudel's life have had economics as their horizon, we should not, therefore, forget his continually proclaimed desire for a total history. His approach to economics always leaned more on the juxtapositioning of facts than on any explanation by one dominant factor or another, i.e., a morphogenesis that accommodates the economic facts. This economic horizon energized the three-part chronology of his global approach. He could not, in fact, be satisfied as a historian with his immutable geography as last resort nor with the froth of common events. *Homo economicus* gave him a middle point in time that was conjunctural and cyclic. This point was indispensable for breathing life into those significant movements that exist between the unsearchable depths and the frothy play of surfaces. Braudel's version of what is historically possible is then "the product of geographical determinism and economic necessity," and it risks winding up in the dead end of "social paralysis."[45] Economic history was useful for Braudel only when movement and historical dynamics were introduced. This position illuminates the very sharp criticism that he made about Pierre Goubert's thesis on the Beauvaisis, which he called "a needle in a haystack."[46] He did not like this thesis because he found the area studied too narrow. In addition, by limiting itself to the tragic seventeenth century, which was a period of recession, it gave a static view of the economy, whereas historians should be interested in growth: "In a third part, I would have attempted to mark a growth in the Beauvaisis."[47] That is what René Baehrel did a year later for Basse-Provence from the end of the sixteenth century up to 1789.

Nonetheless, Braudel was confronted by theoretical analyses of the modern economy and had to discuss those different theses. He especially had to position himself in relation to Marx's analysis of capital. He parted company with Marx in that he conceived capitalism as an external phenomenon in the development of the market. He dated the genesis of the capitalistic era much earlier than Marx, for whom the qualitative break only occurred with the mass production of goods based on exploiting salaried workers who were cut off from owning the means of production. In contrast, Braudel located capitalism within the sphere of capital circulation and thus could push the origins of this economic system much further back. The theory Braudel used and discussed the most was Werner Sombart's.[48] Sombart introduced the concept of capitalism after Marx's concept of capital. Braudel criticized Sombart's idealistic concept by refuting the privilege it accorded to the capitalist "spirit." He saw in this overemphasis on *mentalités*, which he found both in Sombart and in Max Weber, a mistaken effort to escape from Marx's schema. Braudel replaced it with his own long-range three-stage rocket. In his opinion Sombart was the victim of the conceptual habits of the turn of the century, which had a tendency to consider Western history as the natural and logical end point for world history because of its high-performance economic system: "We have lost that self-assurance."[49] The history of the world could have turned out differently, Braudel told us, if Chinese junks had rounded the Cape of Good Hope in 1419. With world capitalism in full crisis and Europe out of sync with the key motors of the international market, we lost our superiority complex. As for Joseph Schumpeter's theory that capitalistic development goes through four successive phases and is based on innovation and credit, Braudel criticized its underestimation of the state and its institutions. Max Weber's thesis that the Reformation freed capitalism's energy seemed accurate in its correlation between Protestant countries and the areas where capitalism flourished.[50] But its systematic sociology did not sit well with Braudel, who, while acknowledging its richness, claimed "to be as allergic to it as Lucien Febvre himself."[51] Finally, the anthropologist Karl Polanyi theorized that the market did not exist before 1834, when it became autonomous and self-regulating, but only for a short period that ended in 1929. Before and after there was only regulated commerce. Braudel found this theory unconvincing because he rejected the idea of including in a single explanation such diverse realities as ancient Babylonia, the Trobriand Islands, and medieval Europe. Surely history should use the other social sciences to reconstitute the history of exchanges and accept their insights. But, in the end, historians alone were in charge and the concepts from the neighboring sciences were all deceptive: "Sociologists and economists yesterday, anthropologists today, all have unfortunately accustomed us to their nearly perfect misunderstanding of history."[52]

If the economists worried little about history, Braudel for his part abandoned their conceptual apparatus. His recent success hides, in fact, what Serge Christophe Kölhm called a "missed opportunity."[53] Even the economists who shared Braudel's concerns (like the search for irreversible phenomena and the beginnings of capitalism) found in him not the concepts they needed but only notions too vague to be useful. For example, the notion of unequal exchange, a key concept in economics, has two distinct meanings. It indicates the transfer of surplus value from the periphery to the center for Arghiri Emmanuel. But it refers to the deterioration of the exchange itself when the countries that produce the primary products suffer, according to the analyses of Pierre Jalée or Gunther Franck. Braudel used this notion without ever defining it and therefore disappointed the economists concerned with theory. When Kölhm studied the Venetian economy in the sixteenth century and the practice of lending in the Rialto, he did not find any helpful material in Braudel, who had given great importance to Venice, but did in Frédéric Lane, whose historical study was based on economic concepts.[54]

Unlike most economists, Braudel limited capitalism to exchange and circulation and not to production or labor. Yet in capitalism there is capital, that is to say, the means of production. We note the overemphasis on exchange to the detriment of production. For example, trading over long distances, which seems to regulate conjunctural cycles, represents for Immanuel Wallerstein an infinitely small portion of European consumption, since 95 percent of what is consumed comes from a distance of less than five kilometers. That did not stop Braudel from claiming that "it is primarily through exchange and circulation that capitalism exists."[55] Two paths of Braudel's inquiry correspond to this fetish about exchange. For one, he does not define capitalism by the social relations of production; for the other, he favors what can be observed and measured in the archives. But, in contrast to production, "circulation has the advantage of being easily observable."[56] Braudelian empiricism leads, then, to an interpretation of capitalism that is restricted to what is visible. It limits its observations to one major parameter, the changes in prices, but not to the mechanism that changes them; it does not focus on the correlation with production but simply records price fluctuations in diverse markets in different time periods. Of course it is true that before the industrial era speculation and the most advanced capitalistic techniques were found in long-distance trading. From that to limiting capitalism to exchanges is only one step, which Braudel did not hesitate to take. He saw only poverty, precariousness, and tradition in the preindustrial eighteenth century. Then people aspired to become merchants while they became artisans or skilled workers out of necessity: "The whole problem of the matrix value of production is put in doubt."[57] The most common system, piecework, or working at home, put merchants in a dominating position in relation to artisans, who were mere executors. Stimulation and capital came from exchanges that dominated production. Of course there were mines that required significant capital investments and transformed artisans into unskilled workers, but attempts by great merchants like the Fuggers to monopolize this productive sector failed and led to the active participation of the state. Industrial profits were crushed by the merchants' take: "The bottom line of preindustrial capitalism is in the red."[58] The great capitalist domain was the sea, where the stakes were enormous because the real profit was in distributing goods. The outline of Braudel's work on exchanges is clear.[59] He distinguished inside capitalism (the mercantile upper classes, the commercial enterprises) from outside capitalism (land, preindustry, transportation). Behind this masking of the productive sector lies another shadowy area, where we find exploitation and the extortion of surplus value. Under the decorations of the ducal palaces in Venice, under the splendor of a prosperous city that connected East and West, Braudel did not mention the efficient exploitations by the city that used slaves to build and to row its galleys. He picked up the traditional theory of Paul Mantoux and Henri Pirenne, who claimed that commerce guided and inspired all economic initiatives. He proceeded to inventory the whole hierarchy of the trading society, from the wretched small-time dealers in cloth, wheat, and vegetables through the crowd of resellers, shopkeepers, and peddlers to the rich speculators. This exchange society set up house in privileged sites like marketplaces that became permanent and multiplied in the larger cities, and like fairs that declined in the eighteenth century to the benefit of depots and stores. Stock markets increased the possibilities for speculators and made business transactions quick and public. A horde of peddlers filled the cracks in this business institution by traveling from place to place and thereby sustaining the commercial momentum. But Braudel chose to recreate these newly formed axes of exchange in their local color and the "thickness" of their daily life. He did not discuss their underlying system of production, the value they added to every item exchanged, or even the division of labor in those areas involved in exchanges. In this modern circulation of wealth, he gave a key place to money. A permanent feature of human history, monetary instruments appeared in Braudelian discourse as things, supports, and were identified most often with precious metals. He detailed at length the duel between the two great precious metals, gold and silver. He seemed fascinated by this duel and overestimated its importance because it coincided with his global schema that emphasized circulation. Just as production was neglected to the advantage of exchange, monetary practices were eclipsed by the description of money as a support in an analysis that was predominately functional or instrumental. Thus, there was no money before the widespread use of metals, and money only appeared "where and when people needed it."[60] Here again the importance accorded to money confused, on one hand, its visibility, its representations, and its coding of an epoch's *mentalités*, and, on the other, what it really was: "The role of precious metals never seemed more important than in the sixteenth century. Without hesitation, contemporaries assigned them first place."[61] The cyclical rhythms of the European economy depended on the production of precious metals. A noticeable decrease in the production of silver from South American mines provoked an initial slowdown at the beginning of the seventeenth century and later, when things started functioning again in the Potosi minefields, a boom at the end of the century. Braudel succumbed, then, to the magic of that precious metal, which was the prime item in the circulation of rare goods in modern times. However, he was well aware that this exchange was not sufficient. He saw that the Iberian Peninsula, the lucky place where these treasures landed, remained desperately poor because it did not know how to make this money grow. Failing to produce an economic takeoff, Spain stagnated as the storehouse for precious metals that would be distributed throughout all of Europe and beyond: "The observation of fluctuations and stockpiles postulates an adequacy between monetary functions and relations, and it reduces the monetary act to the transfer of the precious metal as an object."[62]

The schema that Braudel proposed is a three-part construction. Just as there are three time frames, there are three stages of economic activity. "At ground level, material life,"[63] the level of inertia, the structures of daily life that exist outside collective consciousness, a history made up of repetitive habits. This is the demographic stage, the works and days that correspond to the elementary needs of the population. Primitive exchange and barter fit into this murky area that eludes the marketplace. It is a chain of realities composed of micro-events. This stage was conceived like a Freudian unconscious, like the foundation that motivates essential behaviors. Unlike the unconscious, however, the structure of daily life is accessible, it is a concrete object that historians can recuperate if they go beyond the exploits recorded in chronicles and seek out a life-style that is more passive than active, the life of the nameless in the world of routine.

Located above this stage is what we usually mean by economy, the marketplace understood as a natural economy: "It is a liberation, an opening, an access to another world. It is like coming to the surface."[64] The interplay of exchange takes place on two levels within this stage. On the first level, the authentic market economy consists of a network of local exchanges and of trading over short distances, a transparent location whose best example is the small town. Its law is competition without restrictions or intermediaries since the connection is direct between producer and consumer. Its physical extension is necessarily limited, however. At a second, upper level, this market economy contains a network of circulation that is assured by itinerant merchants who go beyond the direct connection between producer and consumer. At this point we touch the borders of the third stage, capitalism. The latter comes into its own with long-distance trading and is a sophisticated countermarket that takes root at the top of the exchange's interplay. Capitalism did not, however, appear as a prolongation of the market economy and its accumulations, but rather as the negation of the market, a kind of countermarket whose key mechanism is a monopoly that breaks all the rules of free competition. Braudel's concept ends in paradox.[65] A true market can be nothing but the direct exchange between producer and consumer. Any go-between disturbs the natural laws of the market. A true market could exist only in the absence of traders. This concept is based on two opaque extremes. One is the infra-economy, barter, daily material life; the other large companies, monopolies, and international speculation. In between, a transparent area, the market, enjoys a special status. Confronting the notion of exchange and attempting to explain its equalities and inequalities, Braudel praised the transparent marketplace and rejected a capitalism that he envisioned as a malignant tumor foreign to the marketplace, a superstructure responsible for unequal exchanges. The foreign graft that is capitalism is a timeless figure that existed in the period of the Fuggers and the Welsers of the sixteenth century as well as in today's multinationals. On one hand there is "a normal exchange economy" and on the other, "an area of shadow and glare, of insider activities, and of social parasites."[66] Rich traders know sophisticated techniques; they benefit from the complicity of social and political authorities. Thus, they pervert the free play of the natural exchange just as the state does.

This schema was presented as an alternative both to Marx and to the liberal visions of Léon Walras or Adam Smith, who saw capitalism as the logical extension of the market economy. Contrasting the singularity of capitalism with the substance of the marketplace, Braudel overestimated the extent of mercantilism in modern preindustrial Europe. We read in his conception of a transparent market that is above suspicion a moral judgment that favors a disembodied but normal exchange, without any middleman to upset the natural interplay of small businesses. Without reducing Braudel's theory to old-fashioned neo-Poujadism [or Thatcherism], we can read it as an ode to small shopkeepers or, like Alain Lipietz, as an echo of Prudhon. This is plausible because it would situate Braudel directly in line with the initial positions of his mentor Febvre. Braudel has nonetheless asked economic science a central question by distinguishing market economy and capitalism. He has been able to distinguish two forces at work within exchanges. One is an international capitalism dedicated to profit making and the other is a more local desire just to remain solvent.[67]

Immanuel Wallerstein considers the Braudelian construction to be quite rich. It can transcend the traditional analysis based on a sequence of carefully delimited steps: feudalism is followed by capitalism, which is overtaken by socialism. Wallerstein thinks that such an approach is no longer viable today because we know the critical role the marketplace played before capitalism in the heart of the feudal system, which was much less autarchic than is generally thought, and afterwards when it seemed that socialistic countries had reintroduced marketplace laws, like Liberman in the Soviet Union or Deng Xiao Ping in China.

Another advantage of splitting market economy and capitalism, according to Wallerstein, is that it obviates the false problem of distinguishing among different kinds of capitalists, traders, industrial figures, financiers, etc. The richest capitalists try to do everything; those whose means are limited have to restrict themselves to a single field of investment. The distinction should be made, then, between specialists and nonspecialists. The meaning of the split between capitalism and market economy was clearly revealed by Braudel himself in the conclusion to his trilogy when he completed the description of his three stages: "Finally, should not admitting without hesitation the distinction between capitalism and market economy spare us the all or nothing alternative that our politicians continually propose?"[68] The message is clear. We should preserve our system, but modify it, improve it. But what does this split allow us to understand? Above the infra-economic level, there is a market economy that is characterized first as a conscious reality. The criterion that Braudel adopted to test for a market economy was simultaneous change in prices: "Historically, we have to speak, I think, of a market economy once there are concerted changes in prices across the markets in a given area."[69] This factor is not conclusive for the epoch Braudel studied because the variations among regions were too significant to permit any reference to a single economic unit. The only moment when the economic reality corresponded even slightly to Braudel's market economy dates back to the Middle Ages, to a period when the merchant class succeeded in winning its autonomy in production. Still, as Alain Caillé has shown, "creating a market is also creating capitalism."[70] The continuing growth of both market and capitalism and their necessary interrelations contradict Braudel's theory that claims that capitalism emerged as an artificial excrescence, foreign to the market. Rather, capitalism appears to be the necessary end point of the market economy. Ricardo had already noted this unbreakable link in stating that all markets tend toward monopoly. However, Braudel's schema isolates the capitalistic forces that tend toward monopoly and that cut themselves off from both nature and competition in good faith, as if monopoly were not the end point of the inexorable laws of the market.

The third volume that completes the trilogy on modern economy was devoted to the sequence of world economies. Braudel got this notion from the difficulty he had translating the word *Weltwirtschaft*, which he rendered by the term *world economy* and not *worldwide economy*.[71] He took this concept from Immanuel Wallerstein, who is considered his disciple.[72] This concept held several advantages for Braudel and allowed him to remain faithful to the historical approach he had practiced ever since his thesis. First, world economy belongs in a space; it is an autonomous fragment of the planet. Economy is conceived as beginning with geography. This space constitutes an organic, articulated, and functional unit. It is characterized by three areas (always the magic figure three): a narrow center, a middle area concentrated around the center, and, finally, a periphery. Geographic transformations play a major role in the evolution of the world according to this schema. Centers change over time, new hierarchies appear and redefine space depending on how things are recentered or decentered. These world economies reconstitute new centers of gravity indefinitely. These organisms cannot live without the decisive beating of a heart. Thus, along with his world economy Braudel returned to his concepts of immutable long duration and the search for invariables: "There have always been world economies."[73] He parted company here with Wallerstein, for whom there was only one world economy, the European capitalism that emerged in the sixteenth century. He considered all other preceding ensembles as world empires whose division of labor and whose network of exchanges corresponded to a system of political domination. In contrast, a world economy is spread over an exploded political space.

We also find all of Braudel's organic inspiration in his idea that a world economy functions just as "the arterial system distributes blood to a living body."[74] All the Braudelian themes can be found in the notion of world economy: emphasis on exchange within an articulated space, unchanging duration, organicism. This theory allowed him, moreover, to refine his model in opposition to the Marxist explanation that different kinds of productive modes follow each other. In contrast, world economy evokes interlacing, simultaneity, and synchronization more than temporal sequence. In his third volume Braudel enumerated, one by one, the centers of world economy from the sixteenth to the eighteenth century. Preponderance passed from Genoa to Venice, Holland, and England, each time modifying the center and the periphery. This sequence recalls a very simple and event-oriented chronology. The historian Michel Morineau commented ironically: "As a caricature, we could ask if this does not look like Halphen and Sagnac [a traditional history text], with economics replacing politics."[75] The narrative of diplomatic events in the third part of *La Méditerranée* seems to correspond to the succession of world economy centers in the third part of *La Civilisation matérielle*. This differential geography articulated by the world economies that concentrate wealth and exploit their periphery offers an interpretive reading that is viable for any epoch. Thus, the cultural rift that separates developed and underdeveloped countries was already a reality from the fifteenth to the eighteenth century. Just as the Roman Empire recruited its slaves on the periphery of its empire, the centers of world economy recruit their unskilled labor on their periphery. This conclusion is apparently correct and leaves a promise of comparative history. But there are anachronisms, since it denies historical evolution and the emergence of new modes of production whose functioning might be different. This schema in fact erases from European history the singularity of capitalism and imperialism as historic moments. Braudel replaces them with an implacable geographical law that is unchanging and ahistorical.

■ THE MAN IN THE MIDDLE

"The miracle of the historian is that all the people we touch are extraordinarily alive. It is a victory over death."[76] Death, which he tried to exorcise, surprised the uncontested leader of the *Annales* in full stride and tore him from the Promethean task of writing a history of France that he undertook at eighty-three years of age! His disappearance provided the occasion to note the importance he had won in the intellectual circles that accorded him such a warm testimony. "A prince of history," wrote Pierre Goubert on the first page of *Le Monde*. "An epicurean scholar," according to *Libération*. "The first of historians," wrote Pierre Chaunu in *Le Figaro*. For *Le Matin*, "the man who reinvented history." "The man who changed the course of history," according to *Le Quotidien de Paris*. "The epic poem of King Braudel" from *Le Nouvel Observateur*. "Braudel the innovator," wrote Emmanuel Le Roy Ladurie in *L'Express*. We can measure from these few headlines a "Braudel effect" that won a massive following in the eighties, a following that is underlined by the rising curve of the sale of his work since 1979. This is the triumph of a historian who has assured the success of the *Annales* school, who left it an intellectual and institutional legacy without precedent. Thanks to the powerful positions in the media that the present generation now holds, Braudel was able to cut through a wall of misunderstanding that had separated historical scholarship from the public. When he handed on the torch in 1968 to a younger team, Braudel retired a bit from the French intellectual scene, at least in appearance, for his reputation did not stop growing abroad. How can we explain that he managed an impressive return to favor in the eighties? We have seen him on television retelling his life with gusto; he orchestrated a series of twelve hour-long programs on the Mediterranean; the public buys his books more to give as gifts than to read because they are so long, except for one little work, *La Dynamique du capitalisme*, which was advantageously displayed next to the cash registers. Any book lover can own a pocket-sized Braudel. This favor with the grand public, which he won in the last hours of his life, corresponded surely to a social need and cannot be attributed solely to the fact that he recently entered the Académie Française. At eighty-three he cut the figure of a patriarch among his epigones who, carried away by an often incongruous cacophony, attempted to stuff him alive. His fame goes beyond the borders of the hexagon where the public at large still cannot quite place the master. Braudelism sells well in all climates, and some have advanced the idea that his current success is due to an echo that bounced back from America. His ambition was to catch in a single vision the widely stretched horizons of the Mediterranean and more recently of the entire world. He intended thereby to capture the fate of the world in a totalizing process that carefully avoided any philosophical a priori. Beyond all fragmentary knowledge and all the specialists, he felt he was the master of that chaotic world he wanted to recreate for us. Without a doubt there was something gigantic in his ambition. He recognized no equal in his generation; he had only modest students who "do not understand him."[77] An exception proves the rule, as always. One man had the audacity to be more famous than he and to incarnate his time better. Jean-Paul Sartre was the only one Braudel accepted as his superior. Of course, he conceded, "He was completely wrong as far as I am concerned, but he was engaged more brilliantly in French life."[78] Sartre was the conscience of a generation, something Braudel never was because he was not involved in public life and because he was a worker entirely devoted to building that impregnable fortress, the empire of French historians. Braudel's fame has a good chance of being more solid because, in addition to the man and his works, the institutions that he ran, or reoriented, or created out of nothing will remain. Despite his positions so contrary to Sartre's, he recognized the latter's advantage. In the conclusion to his trilogy he discussed Sartre's position: "J-P Sartre can dream of a society where inequality will disappear and where no one will dominate over another. But no society in the real world has yet renounced that tradition or given up that privilege."[79] For Braudel, there can be no society without hierarchy; that is an invariable. Hierarchy can change forms and evolve from slavery to serfdom to salary, but it remains the domination of some over others. In contrast to Sartre, he tried to demonstrate that human liberty is a narrow gate that gets narrower and narrower.

To explain his success, we should not forget first of all that Braudel has only apparently left the stage; he remains omnipresent for the new historians who will reap the ripened fruit of their master and uncontested leader's triumph. Marc Ferro, former student and codirector of the *Annales*, recounts that whenever a choice is made for the journal, everyone asks anxiously: "What will Fernand think?"[80] It was enough to see him happily enthroned during the three days devoted to him at Châteauvallon to comprehend the dimensions of his power: "I only have friends and I try to show them that I am right."[81] There was a lot of humor and complicity in all these games, but underneath the seductive smile of the old master with the mane of white hair, the conviction of a charismatic leader shone through. At that moment when the historiographical discourse of the *Annales* bent back on itself and everyone retreated into their own fragmentary knowledge, he appeared as the only emblematic figure capable of rallying and unifying the most antagonistic personalities. He could without difficulty invite to his side historians as different as Georges Duby and Pierre Chaunu, who share nothing but their acknowledgment of Braudel as their master. The Braudel effect has won a massive following and a recognition that today works to the advantage of the whole French historical school. He was especially the king of that middle kingdom, the critical link in the chain and pivot point between the generations of the *Annales:* the generation of the founding fathers in the thirties, Bloch and Febvre, and the current generation of their heirs. Braudel is, in this sense, a direct heir and an innovator, the one who initiated a series of gradual slides that ended in the current explosion of the historical disciplines. By favoring naturalized history and long duration, he opened the way to immobile history. By assimilating a number of subjects from the social sciences, he announced their alignment behind history. By breaking down time, he introduced the study of heterogenous objects, the decomposition of time, and the crumbling of history. Nonetheless, he remained faithful to the historical basis that his successors rejected. Global awareness, the singleness of the temporal referent, the interaction of different levels of reality, the place of social history in his research, all these make him the faithful heir of his spiritual fathers, Bloch and Febvre. He was the man in the middle between the first and third *Annales* generations and therefore the obligatory reference point.

The second fact that explains his success in the eighties can be found in our long-standing economic crisis. The failure of economics and the bankruptcy of their cures, whether Keynesian or liberal, led to a questioning of our distant economic past so as to understand and to better read the current state of the crisis. Braudel the economic historian thus became the reference for economists. One particular aspect of the crisis explains this turn toward Braudel: his fatalism or pessimism that impacted on the effectiveness of human actions that depend on ungovernable phenomena they cannot control. Governments do not govern their national economies; the dysfunctioning of the world economy increases. One historian, Braudel, thinks that the only acceptable attitude is to wait: "We live through a Kondratieff cycle the way we live through the rotation of the earth."[82] The Braudelian man is powerless, at the mercy of economic and geographical phenomena that displace him from the center: "What I do goes against human freedom."[83] The weight of long duration lies heavy on humanity, which moves about like a rat in its confining cage. Braudel reassures us then by showing that our current powerlessness echoes the same weakness as yesterday. Measured by long duration, human willpower becomes insignificant.

His triumph is simultaneously that of party chief and that of a unique individual. If he has bequeathed a flourishing patrimony, he does not have any disciples able to pick up his worldwide and total designs as their own. In this respect Braudel, the last example of encyclopedism, has no heir. He sees himself as a solitary man. At Châteauvallon he sketched a self-portrait that made him look like a martyr. We had the impression that this much-honored man identified with a mendicant friar in giving new life to the *Annales:* he saw himself as Don Fernando evangelizing the crowds, marginalized by the official church, understood by no one, but certain of the last judgment. To Theodore Zeldin's question about who understood him, he answered: "One historian, a Russian Argentine Jew, because of his mixed background perhaps." "I spent my life being misunderstood."[84] Don't misunderstand, this is not a crowned head expressing resentment but rather affirming his de Gaulle–like grandeur beyond any allegiance to a school. He wanted to incarnate history the same way the general incarnated France. Going over each stage in his intellectual life, he only saw the unfolding of a plot against himself. From the generation of his mentors he kept the militant, anti-institutional spirit even when he was at the summit of the institution and enjoyed its veneration: "I had a very difficult life."[85] He remembered the moment when, after his return from Brazil, he attempted his innovations at the

Sorbonne and was pushed aside. He presented his nomination to that venerable institution, the Collège de France, as an exile, his Colombey-les-deux-Eglises. Trying to create a college of social sciences, he watched literary scholars and jurists unite against him and create colleges of liberal arts and sciences and schools of law and economics. As a consolation, he retreated and created a "house of social sciences." But it was only a "parking space"[86] like section six at EPHE during that period when his academic credentials were not recognized officially. It was then a real way of the cross, and our martyr for the social sciences had a desert to traverse. Surely there is quite a distance between this apocalyptic vision and the reality of the master, adored and canonized during his lifetime. But his hagiography is ready.

Of course, Braudel preached in the tradition of Febvre even as he hoped to go beyond his teaching and to conquer more territory for historians: "Lucien Febvre used to say: history is man. As for myself, I say: history is man and all the rest. Everything is history, the earth, the climate, the geological movements."[87] We witness here the decentering of humanity that, for Braudel, was his personal contribution to the history writing of the first generation. He waxed nostalgic, however, about that first heroic phase of the *Annales*, that militant period before it reached its dominating position in French historiography. The *Annales* of today "is a stranger to me,"[88] he confided in an interview with the journal *L'Histoire*, regretting the time when the journal was marginal, when it questioned and upset people whereas now success has institutionalized it and made it orthodox like other journals. This vision of a school that had been beyond the pale harks back, of course, to a mythic interpretation of the past that Braudel cultivated since he was one of the heroes of that myth. At Châteauvallon he distinguished between his own concept of new history and that of today's third generation, which, according to Braudel, has constructed a different history "for these disciples have not followed my precepts. ... There has been an enormous break between me and my successors."[89] He criticized his disciples for renouncing the ambition to do total history and for restricting themselves to *mentalités* without connecting history to a larger whole. History lost, thereby, its main vocation, which, according to him, is to be the unifying center for all the social sciences. History has in fact contributed to its own breakdown by allowing the objects it studies to define how they are to be divided up. Such a breakup can only displease Braudel, the historian of the total picture. As the heir of Bloch and Febvre, his thinking about long duration and different time frames prepared the way for the current generation's research, from which Braudel has kept his distance.

As the man in the middle, his median position stems also from the fact that he stands at the juncture between idiography and nomography without ever having chosen one or the other. If, to counter the attack of the social sciences, he sought the unconscious in social behavior, in structures, and in the depths of history, he nonetheless advocated narrative history of the most traditional sort even when it was not related to the rest of his story. The third part of *La Méditerranée* contains only events in the most traditional sense. We must understand that this event-oriented section remained like a residue from the initial project for his very traditional thesis, and it was later shifted to the end portion of the book as insignificant. This narrative is nothing but the froth of daily life in which authentic history shows its true face. Events are not captured like symptoms of deeper phenomena in a dialectics of long and short durations, which is missing. On the contrary, it is nothing but an appendix without any logical connection to the rest of the work; at best, there is a chronological coexistence between them. Besides, Braudel did not hide this break in rhythm and purpose: "This third part ... belongs to a frankly traditional vision. Leopold von Ranke would recognize there his own advice, his way of writing and thinking."[90] If he retained this old-fashioned narrative, worthy of the set pieces and battle descriptions of the traditional history that the *Annales* detested, it was because he understood that limiting himself to immobile history was tantamount to denying history itself. He had to recapture history somehow or other. Lacking a dialectics that could link short and long durations, he could only present a picture of the "dust" of events. Even if such a picture was illusory, it was at least an illusion shared by the contemporaries of the events narrated. Here we find the Capouan delights of traditional historians. Braudel spares us no detail of diplomatic history, year by year, up to Lepanto. Necessity yields to chance and the imponderable. The peace that reigned in the Mediterranean from 1545 to 1550 was due to financial necessities, but "also to some powerful coincidences: the great fighters of the first half of the century disappeared one after the other."[91] We enter a history in which the temperaments of the grandees of this world and their dynastic unions constitute the principal material. This connection, which began with the psychology of Philip II, highlights the most obvious dangers of narrative history. In such history there were battles, and Braudel did not hesitate to show his admiration for them. Concerning a combat that took place on Malta in 1564: "The grand master, Jean de la Valette Parisot, and his knights defended themselves admirably. Their courage saved the day."[92] Just as traditional history did, Braudel dated the decadence of the Ottoman Empire from the death of Suliman the Magnificent (5 September 1566) because he was succeeded by a weakling, Selim II, who liked Cyprian wine. We can appreciate the extent to which Braudel was enthralled by a history that assigned to individuals a significant role in the destiny of civilizations. This is the history that the *Annales* struggled against. But Braudel makes us feel the responsibility that weighed upon the Duke of Alba. He had not understood that the danger for the Spanish Netherlands came more from England than from Germany: "Narrow-minded, this phony great man was politically myopic and struck only at close range. He allowed the Queen of Scotland to escape to England and Scotland to become Protestant."[93] In contrast, great figures force destiny, like Pius V who, having made the decision that led in 1571 to the holy alliance between Venice, Rome, and Spain, succeeded thanks to his overwhelming personality. Without Pius V, no holy alliance, no battle of Lepanto in 1571. We can then judge the importance of the pope's character. As for the battle of Lepanto itself, that great run-in between Christians and Moslems, who deserves the credit for the Christian victory? "The leader, Don Juan? Without any doubt."[94] This event is far from being as insignificant as Voltaire believed when he waxed ironic about its consequences. The immediate impact of this victory was enormous. We have to await the death of our hero Philip II in 1598 before Braudel mentions the few connections between his initial subject and the book he actually wrote. The disappearance of this prudent king was not a real event for Mediterranean history since Philip II never really truly occupied that inland sea and his policies never crossed the Spanish borders.

Each stage of the Braudelian construction seems to close upon itself. From the unmoving horizon of spatial time to the rapid horizon of diplomatic history, humanity as a collective force remained absent, caught between military events that touched only the nobles and the weight of an ecosystem and the habits of daily life that constituted an inescapable world.

Braudel's middle position allowed him to be appreciated both by specialists for his erudition and by the public at large or specialists from other disciplines for his writing: "I like Braudel's works not only for their scientific contribution but also for their esthetic worth."[95] Braudel also cultivated this pivotal position as man in the middle in politics. Never engaged, he remained enigmatic between the Right and the Left, never alienating either one. In this he initiated the disengagement of the future generation. In the fifties and sixties Pierre Renouvin was on his right and Ernest Labrousse on his left. Everyone knows that the best position is in the middle, where Braudel sat as president of the jury for the *agrégation*. Bitterly attacked by the French Communist party in 1951[96] as the source of imperialist Yankee doctrines against the workers and the Soviet Union, he was equally maligned by traditional historians as a purveyor of Marxist history. We know how many advantages such a position can have, demonstrating great independence of spirit. Furthermore, his position as the martyr of the center allowed him to rule without rival and be the necessary reference for historians of the Left or the Right. He labored for a catch-all school that, with its third generation, ruled without ever drawing the sword that Braudel wielded like a warrior before sheathing it like an academician at the height of his fame.

■ NOTES

1. F. Braudel, "Présence de L. Febvre," *Eventail de l'histoire vivante* (A. Colin, 1953), 5.
2. F. Braudel, preface to the first edition, *La Méditerranée* (1949; rpt. A. Colin, 1976), 13.
3. L. Febvre, "La Méditerranée et le monde méditerranéen," *Revue historique* (1950): 216–24; reprinted in *Pour une histoire à part entière*, 167–79.
4. F. Braudel, preface to the second edition, *La Méditerranée* (1963; rpt. A. Colin, 1976), 1:11.
5. F. Braudel, acceptance speech, *Le Monde*, 2 June 1985.
6. F. Braudel, *Ecrits sur l'histoire*, 31.
7. Interview, *Magazine littéraire* (Nov. 1984).
8. F. Braudel, *La Méditerranée*, 2:107.
9. F. Braudel, *Civilisation matérielle*, 1:495.
10. P. Gourou, "La Civilisation du végétal," *Indonésie*, no. 5, 385–96.
11. F. Braudel, *Civilisation matérielle*, 1:133.
12. Interview, *Magazine littéraire* (Nov. 1984): 18.
13. F. Braudel, *Civilisation matérielle*, 1:33.
14. Ibid., 2:394.
15. B. Barret-Kriegel, "Histoire et politique," *Annales* (Nov. 1973): 1444.
16. F. Braudel, *La Méditerranée*, 1:107.

17. Ibid.
18. F. Braudel, *Civilisation matérielle*, 3:134.
19. Ibid., 332.
20. Ibid., 269.
21. F. Braudel, *La Méditerranée*, 1:343.
22. F. Braudel, *Civilisation matérielle*, 3:302.
23. C. Grataloup, "L'Appel des grands espaces," *Espaces-Temps* 34–35 (Dec. 1986).
24. F. Braudel, *Une Leçon d'histoire*, 175.
25. F. Braudel, debate at Châteauvallon, 18 Oct. 1985.
26. F. Braudel, *La Méditerranée*, 1:224.
27. Ibid., 215.
28. F. Braudel, *Civilisation matérielle*, 3:134.
29. Ibid., 312.
30. Ibid., 269.
31. Ibid., 2:507.
32. F. Braudel, *L'Identité de la France* (Flammarion, 1986), 49.
33. Ibid., 169.
34. Ibid., 237.
35. Ibid., 241.
36. F. Braudel, *Civilisation matérielle*, 1:30.
37. Interview, *L'Express*, 22 Nov. 1971.
38. P. Chaunu, *Histoire, science sociale* (SEDES, 1974).
39. F. Braudel, *La Méditerranée*, 1:125.
40. F. Braudel, *La Dynamique du capitalisme* (Arthaud, 1985), 9.
41. J. M. Goursolas, "Les Jeux de l'échange entre l'histoire braudélienne et l'analyse économique," *Espaces-Temps* 34–35 (Dec. 1986).
42. Ibid.
43. F. Braudel, "Séville et l'Atlantique: 1504–1650," *Annales* (1963); reprinted in *Ecrits sur l'histoire*, 137.
44. F. Braudel, "Préface," *Ecrits sur l'histoire*.
45. C. Grataloup, "L'Appel des grands espaces," *Espaces-Temps* 34-35 (Dec. 1986).
46. F. Braudel, review of Goubert, *Beauvais et le Beauvaisis de 1600 à 1730*, *Annales* (July-Aug. 1963): 767–78.
47. Ibid.
48. W. Sombart, *Der modern Kapitalismus* (1902).
49. F. Braudel, *Civilisation matérielle*, 2:517.
50. Dosse gives the French title of this reference: M. Weber, *L'Eglise protestante et l'esprit du capitalisme* (1904).
51. F. Braudel, *Civilisation matérielle*, 2:506.
52. Ibid, 193.
53. S. C. Kölhm, *Espaces-Temps* 34-35 (Dec. 1986).
54. F. Lane, *Venise, une république maritime* (Flammarion, 1985).
55. F. Braudel, *Civilisation matérielle*, 2:200.
56. Ibid., 12.

57. Ibid., 272.
58. Ibid., 327.
59. Ibid., vol. 2, "Les Jeux de l'échange."
60. Ibid., 1:386.
61. F. Braudel, *La Méditerranée*, 1:420.
62. J. M. Baldner, "La Monnaie et l'historien," *Espaces-Temps* 34-35 (Dec. 1986).
63. F. Braudel, *Civilisation matérielle*, 1:8.
64. Ibid., 2:12.
65. A. Caillé, "Comment on écrit l'histoire du marché," in *Splendeurs et misères des sciences sociales* (Droz, 1986).
66. F. Braudel, *Civilisation matérielle*, 2:18.
67. J. M. Goursolas, "Les Jeux de l'échange."
68. F. Braudel, *Civilisation matérielle*, 3:547.
69. Ibid., 2:195.
70. A. Caillé, "Comment on écrit l'histoire du marché."
71. "Economie-monde" and "économie mondiale" respectively. The use of one noun to modify another is unnatural in French, which prefers an adjective to the apposition of two nouns. English has no problem with the double noun construction, so the distinction between the two phrases is easily lost—Trans.
72. I. Wallerstein, *Le Système du monde du XVe siècle à nos jours*. Vol. 1: *Capitalisme et économie-monde: 1450–1640* (Flammarion, 1980); vol. 2: *Le Mercantilisme et la consolidation de l'économie-monde européenne: 1600–1750* (Flammarion, 1985).
73. F. Braudel, *Civilisation matérielle*, 3:14.
74. Ibid., 66.
75. M. Morineau, *Revue d'histoire moderne et contemporaine* (Oct. 1981): 665.
76. F. Braudel, "Les Méthodes de l'histoire," France-Culture, 30 July 1970.
77. Interview at Châteauvallon, 20 Oct. 1985.
78. Ibid.
79. F. Braudel, *Civilisation matérielle*, 3:544.
80. M. Ferro, *Magazine littéraire* (Nov. 1984): 26.
81. Interview at Châteauvallon, 19 Oct. 1985.
82. TF1, 22 Aug. 1984.
83. Ibid.
84. Interview at Châteauvallon, 20 Oct. 1985.
85. Ibid.
86. Ibid.
87. Interview, *Magazine littéraire* (Nov. 1984): 22.
88. *L'Histoire* (Sept. 1982).
89. Interview at Châteauvallon, 20 Oct. 1985.
90. F. Braudel, *La Méditerranée*, 2:223.
91. Ibid., 226.
92. Ibid., 322.
93. Ibid., 355.

94. Ibid., 395.
95. A. Lipietz, *Espaces-Temps* 34-35 (Dec. 1986).
96. J. Blot (J. Chambaz), "Le Révisionnisme en histoire ou l'école des *Annales*," *La Nouvelle Critique* 30 (Nov. 1951).

PART 3

The Crumbling of History

FIVE

Historical Anthropology

Despite the Braudelian counterattack, structuralism had an advantage, which was the favorable context of decolonialization. Ethnological consciousness discovered the interest that *other* civilizations can have. Studies focused on what enabled these societies to resist, on the permanence of their structures and their values, which seemed incompatible with the West. Here was the discovery of the other, in real space, held up as an example, the discovery also of a human truth that put Eurocentrism into perspective. The West began to realize that there was no longer human history, but the history of humanity. Just as the Third World resisted history often through radical struggle, Western intellectuals were tempted to throw overboard the history of their own society and to look at the world more spatially than chronologically. Such a reversal favored anthropology, ethnology, and structuralism. When ethnologists returned to the mother country, they discovered colonies inside the Western world, like geological formations resisting change. Passivity leads to silence and powerlessness. At this rate the past is dying and is remembered only to be buried again or to provoke vague nostalgia.

Thus, historians seek the traces of a past that is always visible in space, in the present. We discovered the exotic at home, among ourselves, as was shown by André Burguière's survey in Plozévet, where the Breton locals were pursued by diverse social scientists who fought over whatever they left behind. Here is the impetus for the popularity of folk memory, that unreal marriage between Mme. Denis and her washing machine.[1] The anthropological discourse on the replication of structures and the invariables at work in "cold" societies has adapted to the temperate climate of the West; it no longer has to remain in the tropics. Research on blockages and on phases of equilibrium increased after the seventies when the economic boom ran out of steam and gave way to a severe global crisis that plunged the industrial world into inflation, unemployment, and recession. The West began to appreciate the discreet charms of another time, of a lost golden age, of the "Belle Epoque" it wanted to rediscover. It is this paradise regained that historians try to resuscitate by borrowing the tools and the codes of ethnographers. What was suppressed now has meaning. Everything is an object of curiosity for historians who examine the margins, the underside of accepted values, the insane, witches, and deviants. The historian's horizon stops at an immobile present; there is no more future: "There is a sign that I find encouraging ... it is the end of progressivism."[2]

This crisis in the idea of progress has accentuated the renewed interest in cultures that preceded industrialization. New history has jumped on the bandwagon seeking tradition, emphasizing repetitive time, the turns and the returns of individuals. Lacking any collective purpose, this research has become more local, more personal. Crucial moments when changes were made have been abandoned for memories of the forgotten life of little people. That has bred a neo-romanticism that echos the esthetic values of the beginning of the nineteenth century when Chateaubriand, Prosper Mérimée, and Augustin Thierry were bringing the medieval period and the troubadour style back into favor. Today, the Middle Ages are a gold mine, and efforts are increasing to restore period texts in authentic versions. Similarly, a new esthetic topography snaps into place when one speaks of villages, women, immigrants, and all who are marginalized. The third generation of the *Annales*, sensitive like the other generations to interest in the present, has shifted its discourse toward historical anthropology. Answering the challenge of structural anthropology, *Annales* historians have once again dressed up in the clothes of their most serious rivals in order to confirm their own hegemony. The price paid for this reconversion was abandoning Braudel's economic spaces and rejecting social concerns in favor of symbolic and cultural ones. A new history that Daniel Roche called "sociocultural history"[3] was born.

The internal organization of the *Annales* underwent a significant change in 1969 when the single leadership that had characterized the journal since its beginning was replaced by a collegial team. The leaders of the second generation, Braudel and Charles Morazé, remained on the editorial staff but left the executive power to a group composed of André Burguière, Marc Ferro, Jacques Le Goff, Emmanuel Le Roy

Ladurie, and Jacques Revel. Not only was Braudel's discourse marginalized but he himself was shunted to the side despite the unanimous veneration all felt for him. This sociocultural history is nothing but history wearing an ethnologist's clothes, which inspired Claude Lévi-Strauss to say: "I feel that we are doing the same thing. The great book of history is an ethnographic essay on past societies."[4] This ethnographic history or historical anthropology has accentuated the slowing down of duration that Braudel initiated for spatial time. Here time is fully human, but it is just as unmoving as geological evolution. The ethnological approach has discarded the breakthrough event in favor of permanence and the repetitive calendar filled with the daily gestures of a humanity whose movements are reduced to the biological or familial evidence of its existence: birth, baptism, marriage, death. *Annales* historians have become specialists of an immobile time in a fixed present, frozen with fear in face of uncertain change. They are the vestal virgins of an anxious society that, seeking certitudes, is slouching toward the past as if it were a new religion.

We see in this turn toward ethnography in the historical discourse of the seventies a response to May 1968, a desire to exorcise the risk of that momentous split that has, perhaps, caused all our subsequent problems. It is also a desire to relive those rallying cries against a consumer society whose concrete materialism was put in question. As Jacques Le Goff wrote: "The success [of history with students] is due, it seems to me, to a rebound from disenchantment after 1968. Some, in 1968 and after, tried to make history and failed to a certain extent. Consequently they felt the need to better understand how this history came into being. In order to find out how they could change the course of events. Understand in order to change. Do history because of the failure to make history."[5] And thus a date with Clio, the muse who looked like a phantom haunting the modern world.

Another historical factor also helped alter historical discourse. The seventies were marked by a post–de Gaulle attitude, incarnated in Georges Pompidou and then Valéry Giscard d'Estaing, which sought the appearance of change without really wanting change. Those in power managing and preserving the system allowed a few transformations to take place in daily life, customs, and marriage. They responded to the deeper aspirations articulated by, for example, the women's movement, which was also a product of 1968. Legislation touched on the rights of husband and wife, on contraception and abortion, on voting at eighteen years of age. Historians responded to real changes in society and gave a temporal "thickness" to these precise issues by questioning how the family functioned, the role and image of the child, the place of discipline, the contraceptive practices of the past. Little people, displaced as a potential political force and lacking the power to flip the dominant social order over into a new society, reappeared in this anthropological discourse as a worthy subject in their daily activities and routines. They were reappraised for their singularity, like a separate world, but always within the inescapable framework of those in power. History's turn toward ethnology seemed to integrate other factors, other values into the technocratic society by restoring people's rights. It gave society a dual character that was much closer to reality and more solid in its bases. The omnipresence of the media in modern society played a role in modifying the *Annales* discourse. The media's oral nature enhanced the value of the nonwritten historiography of old-fashioned customs and oral traditions. The *Annales* underwent these diverse influences and in the seventies opened itself up to new fields of study, like material civilization or the history of feeling. *Annales* historians pulled on their ethnographers' boots and abandoned change, economics, and social concerns.

Economic crisis modified these perspectives. Just as in the fifties everyone looked at the basis of growth, technical advances, and the opening up of space, in the seventies attention was fixed on blockages, inertia, and what was permanent in social systems. Thus, a special number of the *Annales* for 1948 accented growth in Brazil, Argentina, and Mexico, and ignored the Andes region. We see there an Atlantic vision of Latin American that led to more intense relations with Europe based on increased production and trade. This 1948 issue of the *Annales* was profoundly Eurocentric. Its articles concentrated on trade, harbors, traffic, and the shoreline of the American continent that was thought to be the key to European vigor. This vision of the world found its counterpart on the other side of the Atlantic in Europe in the work of Pierre Chaunu on Seville and of Pierre Vilar on Catalonia, both of whom emphasized areas and examples of growth. The present time is quite different and the outlook on the same South America has substantially changed. The *Annales* devoted another special number to that continent in 1978. The studies supervised by Nathan Wachtel concentrated on the permanent features of the Inca Empire during colonialization, on acculturation, on the inland Andes region, on the symbolic representation of native Indian societies and their transformations. The approach had become anthropological. We catch a similar evolution for Italy. After having favored in the fifties the Italian merchant cities, growth, trade, and capitalism, in the middle of the sixties the *Annales* turned toward the Mezzogiorno and what hindered development. Emphasis fell on the land, the countryside. The economic viewpoint, when it existed at all, retreated to study blockages.

In general social and economic history gave way to cultural history, which made spectacular progress in this period. Jean-Louis Oosterhoof's survey of the content of the *Annales* demonstrates this advance: cultural history included 22.4 percent of the articles in 1957–69 and increased to 32.8 percent in 1969–76.[6] Similarly, economic history decreased from 39 percent in the first period to 25.7 percent in the second. The EHESS, the *Annales* laboratory because it houses a historical research center, reflected this movement away from economics toward historical anthropology. Jack Hexter's survey done in 1972–73 already had concluded that history was growing and economics declining.[7] History's share rose to 35 percent of the total of the eleven disciplines at EHESS. That tendency has quickened since history had about 40 percent of the seminars for 1985–86. While economics boasted eighteen seminars in 1972 in contrast to thirty-four in history, it leveled off in 1986 at nineteen against seventy-five in history. Economics is shrinking as historical anthropology grows. A noteworthy symbol of this deep change was the election of an anthropologist as president of EHESS on 29 June 1985. Marc Augé succeeded François Furet for a term of five years. Even if the new president did not consider his election a radical turning point after the dynasty of *Annales* historians, he did nonetheless admit: "I do seem to be something of a Polish pope."[8] As economics disappears in one sense, it also reappears within anthropological discourse. To think economics from the anthropological point of view seemed to be the aim of the new leadership at the school: "You can say that we ask ourselves more about meaning, about what is cultural, and that corresponds to something. But whether economics is an integral part of that meaning or that cultural order, that is what we are in the process of finding out."[9]

The capture of ethnography by the historians of the *Annales* was made possible by formulating it in terms that were used by social and economic history. The notions of *mentalités* and behaviors profited from the quantitative methods already used in demography or in the serial analysis of prices and revenues. Anthropology always preferred to qualify its subject matter. Now it was tamed by quantifiable methods that structured that subject matter and gave priority, as in demography, to long duration. The history of *mentalités* makes the ideal contrast with Lévi-Strauss because of its integrative nature. A blurry concept, it covers many different dimensions. For those who relegated history to the simple description of conscious phenomena, the *Annales* countered with a history of *mentalités* that was based on the unconscious level of social behaviors, the automatic and collective thought of an epoch or social group. The *Annales* concept of *mentalités* is closer to psychology (the triple legacy of Durkheim, Lévy-Bruhl, and Jean Piaget) than to conscious intellect, contrary to the ideology that it both contains and transcends. The history of collective or social psychology that characterized the first *Annales* generation took the name history of *mentalités* in 1962 from two manifestoes by Georges Duby and Robert Mandrou.[10] Subsequently it would slide toward historical anthropology. After being the noun, history became the adjective. Researchers ask how things happen rather than why they change. The accent falls on what continues. The French medieval school adopted this new way of looking at history under the joint influence of the Germans and the Anglo-Saxons.[11] As a result, splits were deemphasized and social issues were replaced by cultural ones. Some abandoned the hazy concept of *mentalité* and adopted the schemas and the models of anthropology. Such was the case of medievalists like Jean-Claude Schmitt, who began his study of suicide with an anthropology article by Marcel Mauss on the idea of death.[12] In the same way, anthropology inspired Michel Sot to start his study of the post-Carolingian episcopacy with the *gesta episcoporum:* "What was in the end going to inform my approach and what had informed it for the past several years? The presence of anthropology."[13]

History's ethnographical method had as its consequence "the advancement of material or cultural civilization."[14] The *Annales* took all of French society as its subject just as Lévi-Strauss had taken primitive societies for his subject in *La Pensée sauvage*. The only difference was that it was the past. The concepts of historical anthropology or of material culture often represented a descriptive process that left out a dimension that the *Annales* had in its beginning: history based on problems. At the center of the *Annales* discourse we find a description of both the physical and mental daily life of ordinary people of past societies. This description is closely related to positivistic history in its factual aspect; it simply leaves out whatever is political. Repetition and habit form its essential basis, "the physical, nutritional, affective, and gesticular habits, the mental habits."[15] The history of material culture had the advantage of bringing to life people who had disappeared under the debris of demography's interlacing cycles and the economic curves of long duration: "By dint of studying the price of grain, we sometimes forgot those who ate it."[16] Now the focus was on man the consumer of material and cultural objects and not the producer of these objects, not the man acting on his environment. The descriptive side of this history was championed by its authors: "We still remain on the descriptive level when we are collecting facts."[17] There is then really no question of a connection with other levels of reality. Jean-Michel Pesez even demanded more autonomy for studying the evidence of material culture in relation to the underlying social facts, which had often concealed that evidence. His call has been answered by Jean-Louis Flandrin, a pioneer in new topics who argued for a history of taste. Following the lead of Jean-Jacques Hemardinquer,[18] he proposed in the journal *L'Histoire* a history of taste.[19] Table manners thus move from the ethnologist's field of observation to that of anthropological historians. This produces some interesting conclusions about the evolution of criteria for social distinctions that were founded on speaking well in the sixteenth century and moved to the distinction between good and bad taste in the seventeenth. Taste in food became part of the conflict between an old aristocracy and a new upstart class emerging from the bourgeoisie.

The initiator and precursor in exploiting material culture is Norbert Elias, described as an Annalist before the fact. His book on the evolution of customs and mores appeared in 1939.[20] His descriptions turn around a central thesis. He wanted to show the progress made since the Middle Ages in the increased control that Westerners exerted over their bodies. The interest of the *Annales* focused on Elias's descriptions of customs, of techniques, and of life-styles. The gradations from top to bottom of society in matters of shame, self-discipline, refusing bodily functions, and distancing the body from the self were just those aspects of daily life that corresponded to the spirit of today's *Annales*. When Emmanuel Le Roy Ladurie wrote *Montaillou,* he recounted the daily life of an ordinary sixteenth-century shepherd in an isolated village of the Haut-Ariège and thus resuscitated the average man, that silent figure so long absent from history. He was able to locate ordinary behaviors within the symbolism of their time. Discursive breaks were apparent in different periods: sickness was, in Molière's time, represented as an evil body that had infiltrated a healthy body. Doctors aimed to extirpate the evil by bloodletting. Meals were an opportunity to counterbalance the risk of illness by absorbing good food in quantity, even to the point of stuffing oneself.

The microhistory that Carlo Ginzburg defined was limited to the field of ethnohistory: "We intend to define microhistory, and history in general, as the science of what has been lived."[21] Material culture tended to cover those other levels of society that disappeared as it advanced. This was a new and interesting opening onto history provided that it historicize its discoveries, which was not always done, especially when description was considered enough. This historicization of ethnographic material was done by Jean-Paul Aron, who showed how the art of the table and conspicuous consumption in restaurants became a privileged site of investment for the bourgeoisie, who imitated the aristocracy by the delicacy of their food and thereby highlighted their distance from the lower classes.[22] The bourgeoisie confirmed its identity in this physical accumulation of perishables. The history of material culture is surely rich in discoveries, but only when it is the site of "crisscrossing"[23] social, economic, and cultural history. At that level it takes on real interest, but today too often it serves as a blanket that stifles reality. Society is supposed to reveal itself transparently through its material culture according to an out-of-date empirical belief that is returning to fashion.

The progressive disappearance of events, the lack of any historical motivation, the ethnographic monographs about an unchanging society, all obliged *Annales* historians to rediscover a dynamic approach to reality in order to distinguish the historical method from the other social sciences. The cultural domain that was favored and omnipresent in the *Annales* of the seventies was articulated around the split between high and low culture: "It is especially when the opposition between high and low culture becomes the definitional axis that the historian becomes an anthropologist."[24] The social and political conflict between those who dominate and those who are dominated reappears in the cultural domain, where modern evolution and progress come only from the dominators, and from the high culture that entraps the whole of society. From the historian's perspective, this rift reintroduced a certain internal dialectic into duration, but only for the benefit of social elites. Besides, this opposition is only nominal since the two cultures are not foreign to each other in most *Annales* research. Emphasis on the cultural level at first permitted its liberation from other kinds of reality to such an extent that culture was reputed to have its own chronology and its own dynamics that differed from other social patterns. The cultural was even supposed to create the social. This shift in the *Annales* discourse was not limited to widening the social field to include culture, but substituted one for the other. Culture, as the creator of social concerns, became the site of contradictions, the stakes in dispute, the intelligible kernel of society.

The new *Annales* dialectic contrasted (1) time, the culture of the unchanging people who could not rid themselves of customs; repetitive, ethnological time with (2) time, the elite culture that was dynamic, creative, and the source of innovations and thus history. The ability to change was no longer located in political or social concerns, but in culture where history could be reborn and escape from ethnographic descriptions of endless repetitions: "Change is essentially in culture. One fine day, culture tips everything over."[25] The high/low culture split has thus become the means of resuscitating past societies. With his peasants from Languedoc, Emmanuel Le Roy Ladurie contrasted the urban world in which literacy increases, violence decreases, and religion loses its importance, to the countryside imbued with an oral culture marked by "primitive violence or religious fanaticism with neurotic symptoms."[26] There must be, then, an atemporal culture, close to nature and to animals, and alongside it, a high culture. As culture creates society, movement belongs to the elite, inertia to the lower classes. The split seems irreconcilable between these two worlds, these two cultures that are foreign despite their proximity in time and place.

We find two temperaments behind this single split. One is based on the elite culture that initiates progress; this is Le Roy Ladurie's interpretation. The other sifts through the rubbish of a lost popular culture; this is Philippe Ariès's nostalgic look at the past. This split does not fit, however, the historical reality because what is uncovered as part of popular culture often began as high culture. Equating a certain culture with the people is false, for this culture was usually proposed or imposed by the dominating class in degraded forms that were destined for the people but that did not take root in the lower classes. It is not logical to have two cultures function as if they were entirely separate from each other. Any such separation is too simpleminded given that the notions of "people" and "elite" cover much more complex realities. Robert Mandrou and Georges Duby warned against the new rigidity coming from such a flawed premise: "I am not convinced that they [the lower classes] possess the means of producing a culture."[27] For Duby, a society's culture is one: it functions like a dominant ideology secreted by the instruments of power and is diffused by the attraction and adhesion it elicits through all social levels. The culture that erupts spontaneously from popular feeling and that wells up from the bottom of the social universe without mediation is, therefore, a myth that exists in the historian's discourse today. Many hesitate to use this schema. Philippe Joutard has shown that the Camisard legends, although based on oral tradition, were nonetheless created and diffused by professional tale-tellers and were inspired by written sources.[28] Pierre Bourdieu analyzed the hierarchical process that flows from the legitimate to the popular culture, the latter being a foil, a degraded reproduction of the former. He rightly affirmed: "The only arena where a counterculture can take shape is the political arena. The tradition of struggle belongs to popular culture."[29] Real popular culture was in fact completely masked by the *Annales* because the political dimension had been missing from its discourse since the thirties and the social since the seventies. In contrast, when Marc Soriano studied Perrault's fairy tales, it was not to find in them an expression of popular culture. He demonstrated the myth of the archetype that was transmitted unchanged from generation to generation. His approach to the fairy tales was first of all historical. He made them historical objects by showing how each change in a fairy tale corresponded to something in the social life of the time.[30] Two procedures exist, then, for dealing with popular literature. Envisaging its production as Soriano did shows that it is not popular. Examining only its effect upon its consumers leads to the opposite result, that it was indeed destined for a popular audience and is therefore popular. But this avoids the real historical analysis that relates the text to a precise social and geographical place so as to determine how it was made.

We find this same debate and these same procedures in studies by Geneviève Bollème and Robert Mandrou on the "Bibliothèque Bleue de Troyes," which have the same aim but pursue it differently.[31] Mandrou thinks that this popular literature enslaves and alienates the masses. This collection, or "library," composed of little books covered in the same blue paper used to wrap sugar loaves, was in fact destined for the people: "These works were written for the lower classes."[32] But the construction, the themes, and the purpose of these writings are not at all popular. Printers drew on sixteenth-century publications they found in the old holdings of the publishing houses in Troyes. They exhumed a high culture intended for the medieval aristocracy and out of date: religious books, stories about knights, treatises on the occult. Religious works make up one fourth of the "Bibliothèque bleue." Society is absent from its pages except as a social vision in three parts: those outside the law (robbers, vagabonds, soldiers, witches, Jews), the people of the towns and countrysides, and the rich, especially those of noble birth. Mandrou underlined the conservative nature of this discourse: "The Troyes collection cultivates social conformity."[33] Bollème did not dispute the high culture origins of these books, but that was not important for her. She considered this collection popular because it won a large following. It activated a particular economy of reading and writing that Bollème called popular. For her there was no mystification or alienation. On the contrary, the collection she presented was resolutely turned toward reality. Roger Chartier has rightly questioned the validity of their disagreement: "French historians have perhaps taken the wrong path in trying to describe the contents of the category 'popular culture,' without questioning beforehand the pertinence of such a categorization."[34] He suggested replacing this unsuccessful search for an authentically popular culture with an attempt to identify the different uses of similar material.

The cultural domain is then a source of conflict and dispute. It is for historians to decide what is at stake and to fix the sight lines. But they can only do that by keeping tabs on both the social and the cultural ends of the analysis. Culture is diffused by social groups and thus through a series of mediators and mediations that we have to know in order to characterize that culture. At this level social analysis should be particularly fine since it is most often in the cracks of social structures that the cultural intermediaries interact most effectively. There are places that are specialized in cultural diffusion, either official, like church or school, or unofficial, like the tavern, against which the church struggled because it was the site of an uncontrolled culture. We have moved from cultural to cultural. As for reality, it remains in the margins of the nonessential. Today's *Annales* has again succeeded in adapting its discourse to the dominating power.

The turn of history toward ethnography corresponded to the invading power of the media, which transmitted cultural history and imposed its own norms and laws. Subject to the media's power, disarticulated man is powerless, passive, and severed from society. This man has no potential other than passive. The *Annales* offers us a good example of adaptation to this media-dominated society. This school has become a cultural fashion, presenting the crumbs of history to a more and more fragmented society. These retreats back to the individual or back to unchanging former times are symptoms of a potential that has been abandoned to the sometimes crazy logic of increasing and uncontrolled productive forces. The public's fascination with *Annales* historians in the seventies and eighties corresponded to the extra soul needed to duplicate and perpetuate this system. The fragmentation of the social body is such that we think of ourselves only in our historical nature as individuals. This is the exaltation of everyman for himself and the marketplace for all. The most lucid moviemaker and decoder of our society, Jean-Luc Godard, ended his 1972 film *Tout va bien* with the comment that the two heroes, Jane Fonda and Yves Montand, "began to think of themselves historically." Behind this retreat lies discouragement and political disenchantment. Commitment is old hat. Caught in the contradictions between north-south and east-west, our society prefers to ebb toward the glorification of individual values, toward the exoticism offered by former generations that popular memory has brought to life, and toward an ethnographic, cultural history that, having denied its own potential, has no meaning.

■ NOTES

1. "La mère Denis" is an old woman who seems plucked out of France's past and who is paired with a brand new washing machine in television commercials and billboard advertisements—Trans.
2. Ph. Ariès, *Un Historien du dimanche* (1979), 212.
3. D. Roche, *Mélanges de l'école française de Rome* (Mouton, 1979), 19.
4. "Lundis de l'histoire," France-Culture, Jan. 1971.
5. J. Le Goff, *Le Monde de l'éducation,* May 1980. He is punning, especially in the last sentence, on the two meanings of "faire l'histoire," do or make history—Trans.
6. See H. L. Wesseling, "The *Annales* School and the Writing of Contempo-

rary History," *Review* 1 (Winter-Spring 1978). J. L. Oosterhoof collaborated on this study.

7. J. Hexter, "Braudel and the monde braudélien," *Journal of Modern History* (1972): 481.

8. Interview, *Espaces-Temps* 34-35 (Dec. 1986).

9. Ibid.

10. G. Duby, *L'Histoire et ses méthodes* (1961). R. Mandrou, "Histoire des mentalités," *Encyclopedia Universalis*.

11. K. F. Werner, *Histoire de France*, vol. 1 (Fayard). P. Brown, *Genèse de l'antiquité tardive* (1983) and *La Société et le sacré dans l'antiquité tardive* (Gallimard, 1985).

12. J. C. Schmitt, "Le Suicide au Moyen Age," *Annales* (Jan. 1976).

13. M. Sot, *Espaces-Temps* 7 (1978): 76.

14. J. Le Goff in *L'Historian entre l'ethnologue et le futurologue* (Mouton: 1972).

15. A. Burguière in *La Nouvelle Histoire* (Retz, 1978), 45.

16. J. M. Pesez in *La Nouvelle Histoire*, 130.

17. Ibid., 129.

18. J. J. Hamardinquer, *Pour une histoire de l'alimentation* (A. Colin, 1970), Cahiers des Annales, no. 28.

19. J. L. Flandrin, *L'Histoire* 85 (Jan. 1986): 12–19.

20. N. Elias, *La Civilisation des moeurs* (1939; rpt. Calmann-Lévy, 1974).

21. C. Ginzburg, *Le Débat* (Dec. 1981).

22. P. Aron, *Le Mangeur au XIXe siècle* (Denoël, 1974).

23. A. Burguière in *La Nouvelle Histoire*, 48.

24. P. Ricoeur, *Temps et récit* (Le Seuil, 1983), 156.

25. Interview with E. Le Roy Ladurie, *Maintenant* (Aug. 1979).

26. E. Le Roy Ladurie, *Les Paysans du Languedoc* (Flammarion, 1969), 367.

27. G. Duby, *Dialogues with G. Lardreau*, 79.

28. Ph. Joutard, *La Légende des Camisards, une sensibilité du passé* (Gallimard, 1977).

29. "Lundis de l'histoire," France-Culture, 25 Feb. 1980.

30. M. Soriano, *Les Contes de Perrault: Culture savante et traditions populaires* (Gallimard, 1977).

31. R. Mandrou, *De la culture populaire aux XVIIe et XVIIIe siècles: La Bibliothèque bleue de Troyes* (1964; rpt. Stock, 1975). G. Bollème, *La Bibliothèque bleue, anthologie d'une littérature populaire* (Archives-Julliard, 1975).

32. R. Mandrou, 21.

33. Ibid., 162.

34. R. Chartier, *L'Histoire* 8 (May 1981): 95.

SIX

Serial History

A short while ago history was still being written with a capital *H* and in the singular. Empowered by its seniority and its ability to synthesize and to rationalize all aspects of reality, history sought out if not *the* meaning at least one of the meanings of time. The *Annales* recently de/re-constructed history, which henceforth is written with a small *h* and in the plural. It is no longer History but histories. It is the history of this fragment or that one, and no longer the History of reality. Pierre Nora, for example, who is series editor at Gallimard for the "Bibliothèque des histoires," underlined this epistemological break with the original intention of historians in his introduction to that collection: "We are living the breakup of history." Is it an expansion of the historian's horizons? Of course, the multiplication of new subjects and the expansion of the field seem to indicate a good state of health. But historians, by attempting to absorb all the social sciences, risk losing their originality and their special talent, which is to synthesize. They seem to have given up. Behind the expansion of the historians' discourse lies, it appears, a confession of their inability to make reality fully intelligible. That was the price of moving forward. Historians are no longer defenders of a society that is progressing according to sure and accepted values. Like everyone around them, they are, on the contrary, buffeted by the relativity of the values the West has transmitted. Connecting different spaces has also made time more relative. In a world that is less and less coherent and based on singularity, there has developed an exploded history that is the result of a total change in the individual historian's perspective. He no longer tries to capture a total reality. According to Pierre Nora, "The historian attempts to find all of history through a single subject."[1] The trick of continuing to speak about total history allows the *Annales* to claim a direct filiation with the journal of yesterday, but we must understand that this "total" applies only to a single piece of the whole reality. There is no attempt to connect the multifarious parts of history into a single rational whole. This constitutes a fundamental break with the intentions of Bloch, Febvre, and Braudel: "It is this notion of total history that poses a problem today.... We are living an eclectic history, one that is in bits and pieces and extends toward curious subjects that we should not avoid."[2] Michel de Certeau admits there has been a change in perspective compared with the *Annales* of yesterday: "We should give up on the global history that was Febvre's dream."[3] The historian's field of investigation belongs in time, which has undergone a process of deconstruction. Single time has proliferated into many heterogenous times. Thanks to the computer's capacity to quantify historical material, a new approach to time in history has been proposed and called serial history by Pierre Chaunu. Serial history was made possible by aligning in series facts belonging to homogenous groups whose fluctuations can be measured according to their own time frame. At this point "time is no longer homogenous and has lost its global meaning."[4] Krystof Pomyan conceptualized this evolution toward temporal plurality and applauded the historian's rejection of any philosophy of time or of any preestablished direction: "It is the processes studied that, as they unfold, impose on time a specific topology."[5] For Jacques Revel, history should not weep over total history. He thinks that the fragmentation of historical knowledge is due to a scientific space that is different from the one in which the *Annales* worked from the thirties to the sixties: "The horizon is no longer total history, but a structure totally composed of discrete objects."[6] Total history would be valid only for a strict programmatic plan. However, even as it begins to experiment, that totality breaks up into a myriad of individualized objects that all have to be identified and constructed. For Revel, this modification in the historian's discourse is the most basic split with Bloch, Febvre, and Braudel, who never stopped proclaiming the totalizing purpose of history. Their model, Marcel Mauss, used historians as an example for anthropologists in his attempt to construct the total social fact because historians had reconciled the complete and the concrete. Today, in contrast, many historians confuse what is empirical with what is intellectualized. Their ever-increasing dispersion nullifies any attempt to achieve a vision of the whole.

In his *Archéologie du savoir* Michel Foucault praised the epistemological evolution that the *Annales* had wrought in history. He recognized there the same deconstruction whose theory he had set out in *Les Mots et les choses* and that he was applying in his concrete historical analyses of hospitals, insanity, prisons, and sexuality. We find that he too rejected unity, the center, the significant breakthrough, the rational whole: "A global description winds all phenomena around a single center: principle, meaning, spirit, world vision, shape of the whole. General history would in contrast unfold a space of dispersion."[7] Foucault did not aim at a global synthesis but preferred the fragments of knowledge, the institutions and discursive practices that he studied as isolated phenomena. His research gave the *Annales* the basic theory for their current orientation: "The introduction to the *Archéologie du savoir* is the first definition of serial history."[8] After having knocked the hero of our culture off the pedestal, i.e., humanity as subject, Foucault attacked historicism, history as a totality or a continuous referent. Historians had to avoid all "the unconscious continuities by which they organize in advance the discourse they intend to analyze."[9] History should give up elaborating vast syntheses and get interested in fragmented knowledge. History should no longer be the description of evolution, a notion that was borrowed from biology, nor the measurement of progress, an ethical and moral ideal, but rather the analysis of multiple transformations at work and the spotting of discontinuous flashes. Reversing history's continuity is the necessary corollary to decentering the subject: "Human beings no longer have a history or, rather, since they do speak, work, and live, they are in themselves covered all over with layers of histories that are neither subordinated to them or synonymous with them. . . . The man who appears at the beginning of the nineteenth century is dehistoricized."[10] Self-consciousness dissolves as the object of analysis in discourse and in the multiplicity of heterogenous histories. Foucault deconstructed history into a formless and dehumanized constellation. The Cubists' dissolution of the pictoral object approximates Foucault's concept of discontinuity. Temporal unity is nothing but an illusion. Still, he did not avoid history since he took it as his subject. Nonetheless, the discontinuities he discovered and the notions of evolution he destroyed were so many enigmatic figures. He was interested in real eruptions and explosions whose nature and place he noted without asking about their genesis. In this approach, events just happen and remain basically enigmatic. His is a work of dehistoricizing: "Such an effort implies that everything that belongs in time, that is formed by time should be questioned... so that we see the rip whence time comes without chronology and without history."[11] Discontinuity is unique and cannot be reduced to a causal system because it has been cut off from its roots, an ethereal figure that walks out of the morning mist on the day of creation.

Foucault's approach thus repudiated the search for systematic causality. He replaced it with multiple causes, a polymorphism that negated any global example of reality or any totality that might be recovered: "We are not and we should not place ourselves under the sign of a single necessity."[12] He acknowledged he was continuing the ideas expressed by Raymond Aron in his *Introduction à la philosophie de l'histoire* (1948): "There is no first mover to move total history."[13] Aron rejected any global approach to reality. He noticed in historical reality such inexhaustible and such equivocal dimensions that they could not fit into any global rationalization. History should therefore retreat to a more modest position and abandon its pretense of being a science: "History is never objective."[14] The historian's discourse could only have partial, local, and individual value. As for the meaning of history, for Aron it had none or a circular one. Foucault dissected the real into analytic slices so that each series had its own rhythm and its own meaningful breaks outside the general context: "From now on the problem is to constitute the series."[15] Each series constituted a specific entity with its own chronology. There was no more center, only layers. There was no motor in evolution, only discontinuities in revolutions. The historian's discourse should be limited to describing the object and the series and thus become an archeology of knowledge.

The return to description and the rejection of a meaningful totality borrowed a highly scientific discourse to decompose the material of history. Foucault's terms, like series, discontinuity, corpus, ensembles, field, system of relation, or transformation, all come from one particular area of scientific knowledge: mathematics and the logic of physics. Despite a lexical apparatus taken from the hard sciences, this approach affords no room for the global rationalization of what is real. Foucault has become the theoretician of what the third generation of the *Annales* took as its credo: serial history. "What is important is that history not consider an event without defining the series it belongs to."[16] Of course, Foucault's preference for discontinuities is different from Le Roy Ladurie's immobile history. Foucault worked with events whereas the principal historiographic flow tended to marginalize the weight and the role of events. But events have returned to current historical research because they belong in the series and their meaning comes from their position within those series. It is interesting to note that the document is no longer accepted passively but has become a monument to construct out of the pieces, ensembles, connections, and units that the documentary fabric has been cut up into. Nonetheless, history has lost its totalizing function: "There is only regional history."[17]

Historians of modern times are, according to Michel de Certeau, wanderers who seek the phantoms of the past and the discourse of the dead at the margins of society. Their purpose is no longer to seize the center but the circumference of reality. They are relegated to the periphery after having been the heart pumping the blood that nourished society. The starting point for this serial history is economic history, which has recently opened up to other dimensions of human history. *Mentalités,* social psychology, feelings have all fit into series without difficulty. This is what has been called the third level. The itinerary of serial studies is "from the cellar to the attic," to use Michel Vovelle's expression. Based on the most scientific techniques in counting and computers, serial history has produced descriptive and empirical studies. Since a causal system that could make the totality intelligible is not sought, any cause is arbitrarily or mechanically chosen according to the moment's inspiration. This refusal to distinguish among causes is viable because series change independently of each other. History then retreats into empiricism: "Our aim is no longer to seek truth.... We have decided to situate truth in the relationship between what produces a fact and the object thus constructed."[18] Paul Veyne practices this serial and partial history. When he studied conspicuous consumption (evergetism) in Rome, he refused any ultimate explanation.[19] He reconstituted the phenomenon in all its dimensions, but he refused to seek a primary factor or a central cause in the global Roman society. In his book on historical epistemology, *Comment on écrit l'histoire,* Veyne explained that history can only be a plot, a story. Here empiricism reached its high point by according history only a descriptive function: "History is not a science because it is on the side of praise (doxa)."[20] No effort at constructing a hierarchy or ordering convergent lines can justify a rational explanation. Each level of events requires its own chronology and cannot be situated in a defining hierarchy. The logic of reality escapes from today's historians. This same resistance to any explanatory schema can be found in Philippe Ariès: "I remained committed to an impressionistic approach.... The spectacle of the world and its diversity are more important to me than the explanations that I am forced to give for them."[21] Lacking explanations, Ariès recounted, commented, described. He also innovated since he investigated the unknown field of *mentalités* but he never integrated them into any rational overview. When a phenomenon has several causes, he explained, it really has none and therefore remains inexplicable.[22] He contrasted his history of specifics and legacies with massive and total history.[23] This break stemmed from the decentralization of humanity, which was no longer considered an active subject or basic to historical evolution or capable of mastering its own history. Alain Besançon attacked the "illusion of a historical totality" that affected his generation.[24]

Today's historians are interested in the discontinuities between the partial series of fragments of history rather than in the continuity of historical change. Against the universality of historical discourse they juxtapose the multiplication of unusual phenomena that finally escape from the limbo where they had been confined by the powers that be. The insane, the child, the body, and sexuality thus take their revenge on the world of reason that had hidden them. This overthrow of reason is lauded paradoxically at the very moment when the historian's discourse claims to be more scientific. The fetish of quantification is the fig leaf covering this retreat toward empiricism.

Everything begins with serial and quantitative history for Pierre Chaunu. There is a before and an after whose dividing line is defined by the computer that relegates older work to the domain of archeology. Le Roy Ladurie's famous phrase "Tomorrow's historian will be a computer programmer or he will no longer exist" demonstrates this absolute belief in the miraculous powers of the technical fix.[25] While Le Roy Ladurie proposed American methods to French historians, he theorized the denial of history as the master discipline devoted to synthesizing reality: "Historians are like pit miners. They seek the facts in the bowels of the earth and bring them to the surface so that other specialists, economists, climatologists, or sociologists, can exploit them."[26] We cannot better describe the (de)mission of historians, their relegation to the role of unskilled pieceworkers, or the loss of all that made them special. We are far from Febvre's *Combats pour l'histoire* or Bloch's *Apologie du métier d'historien*. But there is danger afoot, the famous "American challenge"[27] that demands changes and that can be answered only by embracing the technological revolution, the last salvation of today's historian. Count, count more, and count always: that is the historian's fate. Either the quantity of wheat produced in a region or the number of invocations to the Virgin in village wills or the number of thefts in a particular place: "In the end... the only scientific history is quantifiable history."[28] Le Roy Ladurie here repeats almost verbatim the view expressed earlier by François Furet and Adeline Daumard: "Scientifically speaking, the only social history is quantifiable history."[29] This love affair with the computer, that oracle of modern times, could only accentuate the tendency toward quantification and the breakdown of history. But everything cannot be counted, and historians select, therefore, a restricted field that they can translate into equations. The other effect is perverse: using the computer favors the repetition of similar phenomena and therefore the long duration that is permanent and immobile. Inertia, which characterizes the so-called "cold" societies, defines Western civilization.

On the other hand, some historians, like Michel de Certeau, favored the discontinuities or the "splits" in these repetitive series and, as a reaction against the discourse based on the average curves in statistical runs, discovered the irregularities, the scraps fallen by the wayside, all that was rejected as unquantifiable: the insane, witches, festivals, and local culture.

While they recognized that the computer could make substantial improvements in historical research, Jacques Le Goff and Georges Duby warned against any blind confidence in its ability to write history. In Le Goff's words, "the computer is only a tool that is more and more necessary. It will make history more scientific by making it more carefully documented, but it has not taken away its nature as art."[30] Duby alluded to "the scientific illusion" created by statistics and mathematical expressions.[31]

As reality decomposes into mere description, we watch the birth of a neo-positivism, not in the sense of Comte, who sought the law behind repetition, but more like the French historical school at the turn of the century that was fascinated by the simple facts, by the event as a starting point and as the lone mark of intelligibility. This was the positivistic school against which the *Annales* was founded in 1929. New history masks under its modern and technocratic discourse the return of historical description. Régine Robin sees in this fascination "a new resurgence of empirical criticism."[32] The serial method reveals a double failure, the historian's, who has lost his global vision, and man's, who as an actor in history is cut up into numbers he cannot control. He has lost his ability to act upon reality. Series are the expression of a new alienation that precludes any chance of acting within the existing culture.

Marginalizing the kind of individual who represents a variable that does not lend itself to statistical history is particularly evident in Le Roy Ladurie. The fourth part of his book *Le Territoire de l'historien* carries the revealing title "History without Men."[33] This book marks another critical rift with the *Annales* of 1930. Bloch conceived of history as human and anthropological. Le Roy Ladurie answered: "It is mutilating history to make it only a specialist in humanity."[34] He completed a concrete historical study on climate from the year 1000 without having man as a major or minor figure. He established a periodization of changes in climate per se without worrying about their impact on human society. The effects of the history of climate on man are insignificant: "They remain marginal."[35] Le Roy Ladurie gave this decentering its full value when he called it a true Copernican revolution in history. Notions of serial history are not common in Le Roy Ladurie's work; he prefers the geological metaphor of strata. History for him is cut into strata that are independent of each other in the cumulative reality, like series. In the course of time each stage in the history of a society accumulates on the previous one in a continuous process that avoids movement or major upheavals and allows nothing more than different degrees of erosion.

The result of making history statistical is to give each object its independence in relation to the other elements of reality. Unshackled from the contingency of what is concrete, the object can take off and exist only in itself, covering other dimensions of what is real. Freed of its chains, this object seems to be atemporal. Even if we follow its fluctuations in time, the latter never depend on the strata in which the object exists, and its connections with other levels of reality become insignificant. The historian's discourse becomes idealist. The positive aspect remains nonetheless the takeover of new fields and the discovery of new objects of research, but always without any desire to find a global rationalization unless it be at the microscopic level.

Jean Chesneaux has described the new religion of the present as modernism.[36] He has shown how the computer has effected this dislocation of time. The computer reduces the future to a simulation whose programmed givens are always the same. Only the combinations change. No split or rupture is imaginable: "Modernism dislocates completely the relationship between past, present, and future."[37] Chesneaux showed a France that, under the Fifth Republic, tipped over "into the out-of-bounds and the out-of-time of modernism."[38] The computer empties its simulations of their real content; it functions by segmenting a disjointed knowledge. Man is no longer the master of his techniques, he suffers them; he is decentered, ancillary. In these characteristics of modernism we find the essential springs of the *Annales* discourse that adapted to our modern society by giving us the crumbs of statistical history, by disarticulating the historic totality into heterogenous objects, and by presenting an immobile universe where change is only technical or cultural and never social or political. In this new history there is no rationality at work over time. This crisis in historical consciousness has roots that surely go back beyond the *Annales*. They reach deep into a modernism that has finally structured our vision of the world and of time, into an international capitalism that has forestalled any potential breakup in the name of market laws of production. But in its themes and its paradigms the *Annales* has captured the loss of history's ambition to reconstitute a collective memory.

Another factor played a significant role: continuing to defend history against the increasing success of other social sciences that were newer and more innovative. All the *Annales* historians, whatever their epistemological preferences, were called to the front under history's flag to demonstrate their unity in the face of the sociologists, the economists, the demographers, the linguists, etc. This counterattack consisted of stripping the other social sciences of their attributes, their methods, and their discourse, and in taking them all over. This policy of plunder succeeded since history is enthroned at the EHESS over the other social sciences that it has hypnotized. Clio is garbed in computers, in statistics, and thus in mathematical rigor. Clio has shed her old skin and appears as new history before a public that has gotten used to change. Clio has become a welcoming muse.

Nadine Fresco has done a statistical survey of the authors cited in the three volumes of *Faire de l'histoire*. It shows the extent to which history is open to the other social sciences. Foucault, Febvre, and Louis Althusser are cited six times each; Max Weber, Lévi-Strauss, Braudel, Le Roy Ladurie five times; Marx and Freud, four times; Raymond Aron and Paul Veyne, three times; and Michelet, twice: that is to say, five historians out of twelve authors, and not the most frequently cited, in a work by historians about history. This overture to the languages of the other social sciences and this borrowing of their methods are expensive in terms of the decomposition of the temporal unit appropriate to history and the dilution of history in these other disciplines. Even if confrontation and enrichment are necessary, can we not speak of the mindless loss of history's functions, especially its total view on reality stemming from the absence of any critique of these borrowed methodologies? Who has won this battle? History seems to be the winner in terms of its enlarged sphere of influence, but if triumph is purchased at the price of all that constitutes its disciplinary knowledge, this might truly be a Pyrrhic victory.

The deconstruction of reality that is taking place today seems to be fundamentally connected to our times, which is a period of lost illusions. When the winds of history were blowing to construct a new society, that is, in the eighteenth and the middle of the nineteenth century, thinkers sought the meaning of human progress and inscribed their present within a rational logic. From Kant to Marx passing through Hegel, they tried to understand the battles underway for liberty. In contrast, when resistance to change has the upper hand, when hope is crushed and disillusion takes root, we notice the refusal to attempt any global explanation of reality. Since reality cannot fulfill its own hopes, it cannot be rational. History then loses its meaning; it breaks up into multiple fragments. Reality is only rational when we have some control over it. It loses this rationality when it escapes from our grasp.

Nonetheless, many among the new historians have not renounced total history but rather have distanced themselves from the current centrifugal forces. Heedless of fashion, they continue their research toward a better understanding of the historical totality. If we look at the career of certain historians like Georges Duby, we notice that his evolution is symptomatic of an entire generation. It led him through three successive stages: beginning with economics, he ended up in the imaginary after passing through the social. For him, these three stages are indissociable in his approach to the feudal period: "Society makes a single whole. I do not think it possible to separate politics from economics or culture. This coalescence obliges us to deal with all information."[39] He considered the idea of "determining in last resort" to be functional.[40] It inspired him to begin his work with economic phenomena, not arbitrarily but because they are, for him, what makes access to the other levels of society possible. Nonetheless, like Maurice Godelier, Duby was wary of the simpleminded schema according to which superstructure reflects infrastructure. In contrast, he located the object of historical investigation along the interface between mental and material. Duby preferred mutual relations over single causality: "I am trying to dismantle a mechanical causality. I speak rather of correlations and not about cause and effect. This leads me to think that everything is determined by everything else and that everything determines everything. The indispensable notion of globality makes me think this."[41] Historians should measure the respective weights of mental habits and economic pressures and seize their correlations in order to understand a period. Duby showed that the locus of production is important but that ethical considerations can influence economics. In medieval society, the model of the prodigal prince was propagated throughout the nobility, which stimulated growth in luxury goods and the development of the role of traders. In this case, one model of comportment modified economic activity. Blood and family ties were also basic to medieval society. Duby pointed out the extent to which social metaphors referred to the family.[42] Historians should then reconstitute a pluridimensional reality and investigate each portion of human activity not only with what we know about that part but with what we know from the other parts of reality. Thus, Duby investigated fiscal pressures in the Middle Ages in a chapter on "mental attitudes" and placed them in the context of gift giving in a society that still did not have money. In this example, economics was not envisaged as an activity fully distinct from the other levels, because that would have been an anachronism.

Similarly, the interpretations given today by some historians about religious phenomena establish a new viewpoint that is concerned with globality. Religious history is no longer the exegesis of theological texts set between their successive variations and a first truth. On the contrary, theological declarations are connected to the society in which they constitute the basis for behavior and social hierarchy: "They have become symptoms, signs of things other than what they intend to say."[43] The interrogation is external, a dialogue between the concrete and its ideological representations. When Pierre Vilar worked on the Spanish theologians of the sixteenth century, his aim was to find the origins of a macroeconomic theory in gestation. When Alain Corbin studied prostitution in the nineteenth and twentieth centuries, he articulated his periodization around the evolution of socioeconomic structures.[44] Classical historians from Jean-Pierre Vernant to Pierre Vidal-Naquet, including Marcel Détienne, Pierre Lévêque, Moses Finley, and others, were inspired by anthropology when they renovated classical methodologies. They also recognized the need for a globalizing approach to history. Taking the case of religion in Greece, Jean-Pierre Vernant criticized the traditional conception that placed religion in a separate compartment when to understand it, historians had to "think together" politics and religion, ethics and daily life.[45] This was the only way to account for the essential articulations of a society in dialectic development. In addition, it was a means of avoiding anachronisms and not projecting our way of thinking onto a society whose motivations were quite different. Vernant showed how politics were established in Greece and included all aspects of production. If he used the analytical tools of ethnology and anthropology, it was always in the service of a dynamic historicization, for: "Would ethnology without history be anything but a kind of classy tourism?"[46]

In contrast to this globalizing approach, statistics has impoverished history instead of enriching it. Happily, not everyone uses that approach. Serial history in fact restricts the historian's approach in two ways. First, its series of events erases structures, and, second, it does not solve the problem of moving from one series to another. It is content with causes that are specific to one series or another. In contrast, the path being taken by a number of historians is to seek, beyond the multiplication of time frames and historical objects, a dialectical interaction of these factors in the articulation that best suits whatever characterizes a particular historical moment.

■ NOTES

1. "Lundis de l'histoire," France-Culture, 12 Aug. 1974.
2. Comment by P. Nora, *Le Nouvel Observateur,* 7 May 1974.
3. "Les discours de l'histoire," France-Culture, 31 July 1978.
4. F. Furet, *Le Débat* (Dec. 1981); reprinted in *L'Atelier de l'histoire* (Flammarion, 1982).
5. K. Pomyan, *L'Ordre du temps* (Gallimard, 1984), 94.
6. Interview, *Espaces-Temps* 34-35 (Dec. 1986).
7. M. Foucault, *L'Archéologie du savoir* (Gallimard, 1969), 19.
8. Comment by E. Le Roy Ladurie, France-Culture, 10 July 1969.

9. M. Foucault, *L'Archéologie du savoir*, 36.
10. M. Foucault, *Les Mots et les choses* (Gallimard, 1966), 380.
11. Ibid., 343.
12. M. Foucault, *L'Impossible Prison* (Le Seuil, 1980), 46.
13. R. Aron, *Introduction à la philosophie de l'histoire* (Gallimard, 1948), 316.
14. Ibid.
15. M. Foucault, *L'Archéologie du savoir*, 15.
16. M. Foucault, *L'Ordre du discours* (Gallimard, 1971), 57.
17. Comment by M. Foucault, "L'Histoire et les histoires," France-Culture, 17 July 1969.
18. Comment by J. Revel, "Lundis de l'histoire," France-Culture, 12 Aug. 1974.
19. P. Veyne, *Le Pain et le cirque* (Le Seuil, 1976).
20. P. Veyne, *Comment on écrit l'histoire* (Le Seuil, 1971).
21. Ph. Ariès, *Un Historien du dimanche*, 131.
22. Ph. Ariès, *Magazine littéraire* (Sept. 1980).
23. Ph. Ariès, *Le Temps de l'histoire* (1954; rpt. Le Seuil, 1986), 244.
24. A. Besançon, *Histoire et l'expérience du moi* (Flammarion, 1971), 71.
25. E. Le Roy Ladurie, *Territoire de l'historien* (Gallimard, 1973), 1:13–14.
26. Ibid.
27. Comment by E. Le Roy Ladurie, *Le Nouvel Observateur*, 8 May 1968.
28. E. Le Roy Ladurie, *Territoire de l'historien*, 1:20.
29. F. Furet and A. Daumard, "Méthodes de l'histoire sociale: les archives notariales et la mécanographie," *Annales* (1959): 676.
30. *Le Monde*, 25 Jan. 1969.
31. G. Duby, *Dialogues avec G. Lardreau*.
32. R. Robin, *Dialectiques* (1975).
33. E. Le Roy Ladurie, *Territoire de l'historien*, 1:423.
34. E. Le Roy Ladurie, *Histoire du climat depuis l'an 1000* (Flammarion, 1967).
35. E. Le Roy Ladurie, *Territoire de l'historien*, 1:513.
36. J. Chesneaux, *De la modernité* (La Découverte, 1983).
37. Ibid., 48.
38. Ibid., 71.
39. G. Duby, *Le Magazine littéraire* (Nov. 1982).
40. G. Duby, *Dialectiques*, no. 10-11, 121.
41. Interview, *Vendredi*, 4 Jan. 1980.
42. G. Duby, *Dialogues avec G. Lardreau*, 180.
43. D. Julia in *Faire de l'histoire*, 2:140.
44. A. Corbin, *Les Filles de noce: misère sexuelle et prostitution au XIX–XX siècle* (Aubier, 1978).
45. *Le Nouvel Observateur*, 5 May 1980.
46. P. Vidal-Naquet in *Faire de l'histoire*, 3:162.

SEVEN

A New Interpretive Grid

■ HISTORY BY MALTHUS

Behind the showcase of a history fragmented into histories, we can perceive a schema that explains historical evolution. New history has taken for its own the Malthusian model. Emmanuel Le Roy Ladurie and Pierre Chaunu are the two leading figures in revitalizing this philosophy which seems out of date. A "sort of general rehabilitation of Malthus" is taking place "in current historiography. This author has in effect supplied . . . the essential paradigms that have allowed us to formulate economic history, and especially rural demographic history, from 1340 to 1720."[1] Chronological divisions follow the double evolution of fluctuations in population and resources. The historical fabric is reduced to an implacable ecosystem in which only two variables affect its course and uncover its rifts. During periods of population growth, as in the thirteenth and sixteenth centuries, resources did not keep up the same pace. A process of pauperization began. Land was cut up by ever-smaller inheritances and the trilogy of famine-war-epidemic struck the population, which therefore entered a period of shrinkage. In the fourteenth and seventeenth centuries, when demand decreased, the population's standard of living increased. The balance between resources and demographics was thus reestablished in periods of crisis. The motor of history becomes this machine with its century-long changes. The decisive transformations between the different epochs are masked by the apparent similarities in the population figures. In *L'Histoire de la France rurale*, H. Neveu considered the beginning of the fourteenth century and the end of the sixteenth similar because the Malthusian distortion characterized them both. The population increased by 50 percent; prices and production also rose but not in the same proportion as the population. The fluctuations among these variables, which alternately rise and fall, are joined to a reality that is immobile or rather not taken in account. The social dimension is lost in these curves that span several centuries. From the fourteenth to the beginning of the eighteenth century the economy was "cold."[2] Michel Morineau has objected to this schema. He rejected the idea that an eighteenth-century agricultural revolution replaced the immobility of a rural world: "Often we are astonished by the eighteenth century because we treat as an abstraction everything that has gone before."[3] The ecosystem imposed its inexorable restraints on humanity. Society was caught in the trap of an agrarian cycle. Not only did this cycle impose its own rhythm on man but it also guided the economy which depended on demographic change, the main feature of the Malthusian dilemma. We have only to read history and line up population figures through the years. Noticing that, during this long period, the French population hovers at about twenty million, we draw this easy conclusion: "The more it changes, the more it remains the same: in both cases, 1320 or 1680."[4] Economic and social history are direct derivatives and reflections of demographic history.

Attempting to refute the efficiency of concepts about modes of production, new history has taken refuge with Malthus and learned a mechanical history that has impoverished the historian's viewpoint. History can be easily quantified by a simple equation that correlates stagnant production with a changing population. It is paradoxical to note that those who criticized the excessive weight given to economic explanations by Marxism have equipped themselves with a system that is equally reductionist in order to forge their own interpretations. The territory of the historian unfolds narrowly over a powerless society between scissors that open and close on the single pivot of resources-population. There are no longer any periods with their own specific rules of behavior; every epoch is cut to the measure of these two variables. In the sixteenth century, "it is the restoration of the medieval ecosystem."[5] The eighteenth century after 1720 as well as the nineteenth and twentieth century until 1973 belong in the same growth category. In contrast, the worldwide crisis we have experienced since 1973 repeats the long cycle that lasted from the fourteenth to the eighteenth century. Malthusian laws became the alpha and the omega of historical analysis. Increases in ground rent, decreases in salaries, malnourishment, all were seen through the bias of demographic growth: "Rural civilization in the seventeenth century is first of all demographics."⁶ In his thesis, *Les Paysans de Languedoc*, Le Roy Ladurie sought Marx and found Malthus. He wandered from the trail blazed by Bloch, who fixed his attention on the genesis of land-based capitalism in the countryside, the way of dividing up land, and agrarian structures. Le Roy Ladurie moved his subject toward other variables and other constants. The "central personage"⁷ of his thesis became an agrarian cycle that lasted from the fifteenth to the beginning of the eighteenth century. He did not find the accumulation of capital he originally sought because only demographic pulsations occurred with any significant regularity. Thus, the concentration of lands in the fifteenth century is not at all a beginning of capitalism or the promise of a new society, but simply "the inevitable redistribution of land that accompanied the demographic contraction from 1350 to 1450."⁸ Following the low water mark when humans were scarce came a period of growth in the sixteenth century that crested around 1600 before ebbing in the seventeenth century. And so it continued until the decisive break of the eighteenth century that consisted in implementing birth-control methods in order to reduce the needs of a society faced with limits its technology could not overcome. Historical demography proposed a long duration that was based on a diachronic vision of equilibrium and that excluded other parameters of historical evolution.

Demography also lies at the heart of Pierre Chaunu's system of historical exegesis. Western civilization's strength lies in its being a "full world." Demographic pressures pushed the West to play a ubiquitous role. Malthus's schema, which is coming back into favor, is, however, mistaken. Since the nineteenth century, European population growth has not brought misery but rather an unprecedented growth fed by the Industrial Revolution. If we cannot criticize Malthus for not being a good prophet, we can question the validity of his calculations that are not accurate even for the Middle Ages. The Black Plague that decimated a fourth of the European population from 1347 to 1350 was the historical event upon which he constructed his schema. Yet this swath that cut through the fourteenth century had the opposite effect. England knew a period of prosperity while the continent regressed to feudalism, tradition, and stagnation. Other parameters, therefore, enter into account, and without them, the Malthusian calculus is inoperative. In Malthus's schema population is an abstraction without value. It has a particular role to play according to the type of society and can be broken up into classes and different social categories. Rural overpopulation, which could cause crisis or famine, became in the capitalist system the very basis for economic growth and for the accumulation of capital that depends on what Marx called the industrial reserve army. To deal with population without reference to the conditions of production, exchange, social division of labor, prices and revenues, etc., is nothing but smoke and mirrors. Malthus simply forgot about technological innovation and the possibility that economic progress could permit the rapid growth of resources. The whole Malthusian schema collapses because it is founded on the inelasticity of production in the face of disquieting population growth. Rather than positing a mathematical ceiling that would limit population, we should seek the causes of social and technical immobility that beget misery. Meanwhile, changes in social relations can incorporate new discoveries and allow the population to grow within an expanding economy. No one can calculate economic periods without including changes in productivity and work, the various kinds of public and private deductions, etc. When Guy Bois studied the crisis in feudalism, he analyzed it not as the result of a simple confrontation between resources and population but rather as a global crisis for society.[9] He proposed a method comprising three analytic levels that would replace the Malthusian schema. The first level deals with the major economic and demographic indicators and is a purely descriptive look that takes into account results more than mechanisms. After this macro-analysis we move to the second level for micro-analysis. Here the profits from productions and social relationships are studied. Finally, the third level picks up the chronology of demographic and economic evolution and offers hypotheses about the factors in this evolution: "Only at the end of this triple analysis are conclusions presented, either about the socioeconomic system itself or about the economic and demographic movement in the period studied."[10] The task seems more complex because it cannot be reduced to any simplistic or mechanical schema. Rightly, Guy Bois condemned the surreptitious slipping from a descriptive to an analytic level and called it "methodologically unacceptable."[11]

Man-as-subject, already dispossessed by the Malthusian schema of which he is a prisoner, and caught inside an ecosystem that bypasses him, is even more dependent on biological phenomena that he cannot control. The microbial unification of the world between the fourteenth and the sixteenth centuries was the essential impetus in human evolution for Le Roy Ladurie, who followed Woodrow Borah on this point. The fourteenth-century crisis is no longer the symptom of a social crisis, but more simply the result of the plague of 1348: "Depopulation, born of plagues that gave it its first impetus, engenders the economic crises of slump and depression."[12] The disaster that wiped out the population of Central America in the sixteenth century (the population of central Mexico went from 25.2 million inhabitants in 1518 to 1.1 million in 1608) is presented as another illustration of the microbial unification: "The central factor is microbes."[13] The Spanish colonization and the destruction of the Inca and Aztec civilizations are treated as secondary, after the impact of bacteria. This vision allows societies to shed responsibility for their behavior: the holocaust is not human, it is bacteriological and thereby escapes from human responsibility. This also obviates the need to analyze a civilization's internal contradictions in order to explain its decline and fall: "The process that broke down classical society is, it appears, a biological process."[14]

This massive introduction of biology as the motor of historical change justifies numerous arbitrary and wholesale transpositions of animal behavior into the social domain. In order to illuminate Malthusian behavior, Le Roy Ladurie, for example, picked up the 1947 work of two American scientists, Strecker and Emlen, about white mice subject to starvation. The experiment showed that the mice limited their rate of reproduction when faced with nutritional crisis. Le Roy Ladurie saw there the Malthusian behavior of humans. The similarity with the animal world was for him total: "With women, as with female rats or mice, automatic, unconscious responses are ready to function at any moment."[15] Here was an attempt to break free of anthropomorphism at any price. History would tend to become at this rate a derivative of biology, after having been a derivative of demography. In the encyclopedia on new history, Krystof Pomyan praised this new alliance. Philippe Ariès situated himself at the point "of articulation between the biological and the social" in his studies on death and the family.[16] He accentuated this level, which he considered essential, in order to understand the changes in human conduct: "I have attempted to catch the attitudes at the lowest rung of the cultural ladder, that is to say at the biological level."[17] By trying to reduce human change to a biological reality, historians have favored one invariable while other modifications and transformations became insignificant. We agree with Jacques Ruffié who said that "we are living still an age-old misapprehension that confuses biology and culture and that has transposed arbitrarily to the social sphere a certain number of biological laws."[18] This mistake encloses man in the immobility of an inescapable nature. His actions become the sterile and useless agitations of a rat that, caught in a trap, thrashes about without any hope of escape.

■ IS THE MENTAL OUTSIDE THE SOCIAL?

The territory of the historian has recently moved toward the exploration of the human psyche by studying the evolution of its behaviors, sensibilities, and representations. This epistemological broadening is all to the credit of the *Annales;* the journal has played a dynamic role in this area. The evolution of *mentalités* has become the favored object of new history. If some work has attempted to distinguish between what is real and visions of the world, we have to recognize that most often *mentalités* course through history on a cushion of air as if they were free of any contingency. Too often new historians are happy to record the evolution of representations, the way people perceive their times, without worrying about connecting these representations to what inspired them in the real world. This indispensable back-and-forth movement between the mental and social spheres often gives way to a simple substitution, hiding the social universe behind the mental universe. The eye is fixed on the long duration that does not exclude discontinuities, which are only rarely integrated into a global social unit. Statistical methods are used for demographic research and studies on death, festivals, fear, the family, etc. This approach is based on the idea that human nature can be revealed in its eternal character.

The Ecole Normale Supérieure's colloquium held at Saint-Cloud outside Paris in 1965 and presided over by Ernest Labrousse marked an important moment in this critical reorientation toward *mentalités.* At the head of a large group of disciples who were writing regional monographs that would, with the help of statistical quantification, construct a more scientific social history aligned on categories, groups, and social classes, Labrousse indicated a new avenue for research, one that was already being exploited by sociologists. It was *mentalités,* the study of resistances and of what is most unaffected by change. "Do you want my confession? . . . Well, up until now we have done the history of movements and we have not done the history of resistances. . . . The resistance of *mentalités* which are in place is one of the major factors of slow history."[19] This was the heyday of structuralism, which influenced historians greatly by affecting both the pace of time and the choice of subjects. From this point on, a great number of those influenced by Labrousse reoriented their sociographic work to study *mentalités*.[20] Abandoning the program that Labrousse himself had defined in 1955,[21] and dissatisfied with social classifications and hierarchies, Labrousse's students produced not social history like Pierre Goubert's book on the Beauvaisis (1960) but mental history like Maurice Agulhon's *Pénitents et Francs-Maçons de l'ancienne Provence* (1968) or Michel Vovelle's *Piété baroque et déchristianisation en Provence au XVIIIe siècle* (1978). This itinerary from the cellar to the attic, from social and economic structures to *mentalités*, was followed by an entire generation. Long duration found an ideal home in mental structures. Most Labroussian historians, influenced by their precise knowledge of infrastructure, still tried to hold onto both ends of the chain. They concentrated their efforts on finding correlations between diverse mental and social phenomena. But that was far from the case with all the new historians.

One irregular, Philippe Ariès, was France's precursor in exploring *mentalités*. In 1948 he published his *Histoire des populations françaises et de leurs attitudes devant la vie*. Nonetheless he was ignored by the *Annales* until relatively recently. It was not until 1964 that he was cited by Jean-Louis Flandrin for his study on *L'Enfant et la vie familiale sous l'Ancien Régime*.[22] But Ariès's look at the traditional society of yesteryear and on the grand old households was nostalgic to the point of presenting a mystified image of a golden age. When he spoke of the economic power of women in the medieval family,[23] which they would exchange in the eighteenth century for educational power, we are far from the Middle Ages as painted by Georges Duby, where women were nothing but objects argued over by the dominant figures, either priests or knights. The family changed in the eighteenth century: the feeling that childhood was a specific age appeared in this period; the family circle narrowed. Ariès did not attribute this change to a global mutation in society. Rather, it "is explained by a psychological phenomenon that overturned the behavior of Western man starting in the eighteenth century."[24] Collective unconsciousness is the active agent that determines how *mentalités* vary in different epochs, according to Ariès. His study looks like variations on a single theme, the internal evolution of the idea of childhood, of family, and of the behavior that results from them. Ariès's contribution is far from negligible. He opened new avenues of historical research even if he did not advance beyond descriptions of the mental universe. Avoiding the question why, or else giving an unsatisfactory answer, he did succeed in telling us how. Jean-Louis Flandrin's work on the evolution of the family and sexuality in more modern times uses the same approach, which is interesting as description but limited to the area of *mentalités*. Like Ariès, he observed the same progression in intimacy and in the specialization and separation of different ages, functions, and places.[25] In the seventeenth century the single room with multiple functions gave way to the differentiation of functions among many rooms, as in the modern apartment. The house was no longer the prolongation of a sociability that opened onto the street; the habit of giving notice before each visit so as not to disturb the family's intimacy became the norm. Love and marriage never really made a good couple. Nonetheless, in the course of the seventeenth century, the affirmation of the couple and the nuclear family reconciled love and marriage.

Georges Duby's view of family, love, and marriage was quite different. He located the behaviors and sensibilities of the medieval period in the contradictions and struggles that they represented for the dominant social categories. In the family cell he saw the "matrix sheath" of medieval society.[26] The metaphors used at that time to represent society took most of their inspiration from the family. The monks were brothers, their leader was their father, the lords around their leader comprised a *mesnie*, or household. Faced with this expansive notion of family, Duby did not undertake a statistical analysis in which family and marriage were cut off from other features of reality. On the contrary, he seized marriage as the junction of the material and the spiritual: "It supports, therefore, the infrastructures; it cannot be disassociated from them."[27] In his book on the Mâcon society in the Middle Ages he established a connection between the rate of change in politics and the more or less loose nature of relations and constraints in the family.[28] Love and marriage were the stakes in the game. He showed how passion and love could be considered potential disorders that had to be restrained and redirected toward legitimate and accepted norms. Thus marriage acquired very quickly the function of upholding order. It was invested with two visions that were at first divergent, the priests' view and the knights' view. Medieval clerics saw in marriage the only remedy against fornication and concupiscence. The union of two beings was supposed to exclude physical pleasure. Marriage was evil on the face of it since it required carnal relations, a necessary evil for the reproduction of the race. Therefore, marriage had to be codified and surrounded with strict taboos that regulated it and that grounded the power of clerics over the laity: "Marriage is an instrument of control. The leaders of the church used it to cope with the laity and in the hope of subjugating them."[29] That was the conflict in the eleventh century and a major aspect of the feudal revolution. At this moment when central political power disappeared, the disintegration of the social body tended to favor the clerics. Rather than replacing medieval society, Duby's study of marriage made that society transparent. His plunge into the social through the mediation of *mentalités* was made possible by asking the question why about the changes observed, by bypassing the purely descriptive approach, and by putting different aspects of human activity and thought into perspective.

We find this same opposition between a statistical analysis of collective unconsciousness and a global approach in studies on death. When Ariès studied various reactions to death, he did not distinguish between Catholic and Protestant ways of dying. He did not take into account either the mechanisms for transmitting the dominant culture or the demographic and social conditions: "For me, the great drifts that determine the *mentalités* and the attitudes toward life and death originate in impulses that are more secret and deeper and exist only at the border between biology and culture, that is to say, on the edge of the collective unconscious."[30] With Ariès we follow, then, the oscillations of the collective unconscious and its tricks for adapting, turning around, and inverting meanings. The basic reference seemed to be, as for the family, "the world we have lost," that fetal time when happiness reigned. It was the time of "tamed death" in the Middle Ages; in that golden age there reigned a familiarity with death, which was not an object of fear, either for the self or for others. The cemetery was a social space where people danced and carried on their business in the midst of cadavers. The spectacle of death did not overwhelm the living. The dying organized the public ceremony of their own death and prepared for that moment among their next of kin. This was the time of death without long illness, without trauma, almost a happy death. Beyond the incontestable interest of his study, which teaches us a good deal about behaviors, we ask ourselves about the legitimacy of a diachronic vision that embraces centuries in a single grasp around a central parameter, death, without ever seeking their basic differences. Ariès never felt the need to contextualize these various sensibilities in the face of death because, for him, they were only variations of the collective unconscious that transcends its environment. If there is a real autonomy in the evolution of Western attitudes toward death, can we therefore opt for total independence from a given society either in its material or spiritual dimensions? The attitudes toward death in this idealist vision are in a state of weightlessness, animated by their own irrational dynamism.

Nonetheless we can find an internal logic to the evolution of our society, which has successively emptied death and turned it into a taboo. Michel Vovelle advanced a method that was entirely different from Ariès's and tried to make sense of the changes in attitudes toward death. His interpretation is organized vertically and analyzes in turn "death that is suffered, death that is lived, and the discourse on death."[31] He avoided any mechanical explanation by distinguishing among infrastructural factors, demographic evolution, changes in economic and social structures, and the relative weight of the individual and the family for the "death that is suffered." At the other extreme, the "discourse on death," he identified ideologies that retained their coherence in the face of death and their place in relation to the church and the civil powers. Finally, between these two poles, he located the *mentalités* of the time in the "death that is lived" with a description that acknowledged social differences. This analytic grid allowed Vovelle to catch the distortions and the convergences that appeared on these three levels. We cannot speak of a "death that is lived" in the Middle Ages without fixing it socially, which is what Colette Beaune did in describing noble funerals in the fifteenth century.[32] At that time the bodies of nobles were exposed for a long period in their chateaus, their faces painted and their bodies embalmed before being replaced by an effigy. This dramatization of death, this taste for pomp accentuated the inegalitarian nature of death. At the Colloque de Strasbourg in 1975, Maurice Berthe analyzed the *danse macabre* as the expression of an ideological manipulation that masked this inequality that was becoming more and more obvious.

Concrete studies can then take death as a topic and not necessarily treat it in idealist fashion. Michel Vovelle did such a study of twenty thousand wills in Provence in the eighteenth century. He found a change in *mentalités* during the Enlightenment: "Baroque pomp was finished."[33] Requests for masses in the wills fell by half, ceremonies disappeared, the tomb itself was no longer the center of preoccupations. Vovelle did not stop with this statement: "What does this evolution throughout the century represent, under what pressures was it produced, and what name can we finally give it?"[34] He rejected the schema by which elites opposed the lower classes, and he demonstrated the decisive role of the urban bourgeoisie in changing *mentalités*, a role that contrasted sharply with the defensive reaction of the nobility: "We do not like the word *elite*, which is a source of confusion and erroneous shortcuts."[35] For Vovelle, de-Christianization did not exhaust the reasons for this change. Still no study of "death that is lived" can ignore this analysis.

Fear is another field open to the history of *mentalités*. It was the topic chosen by that pioneer Georges Lefebvre, who wrote, in 1932, a book on the great fear of 1789. More recently, Jean Delumeau devoted a long book on fear in the West from the sixteenth to the eighteenth century.[36] But Delumeau left the path trod by Lefebvre. He did not study a moment or the emotional accretions around an event; rather, he sought the collective unconscious and the human nature that was revealed by a statistical study of the different faces of fear through time. Fear is an innate structure in humans: "Fear is natural."[37] On radio he said: "Man is naturally conservative."[38] We find the same mental man as in Ariès, structurally attached to order and to its preservation. But we can ask with Michel Vovelle: "Is fear really not chronic?"[39] That human being who hungers for security and who is hostile to change is the counterpart of immobile history. Delumeau's serial analysis led him to see fear as the origin of all the phenomena at the end of the Middle Ages and in the modern period. Seditions were only the expression of neuroses engendered by fear; similarly, persecutions by those in power had fear as their motive. It would have been better to connect this rash of fears at all levels of Western society at the end of the Middle Ages with the new marginal place of Christianity. The secular arm was being separated from the church, power was escaping from the clergy, who resisted by spreading fear among the faithful with their teaching on three burning topics, the heretic, the witch, and the Jew, and with their apocalyptic proclamation of the Last Judgment.

Mental man appears to be the indispensable counterweight to statistical history. He is its double. He allows historians to investigate the more human realities and to accept descriptive logic. The mental sphere covers the social field and incorporates it into a permanent and immutable human nature. Since long periods blur social tensions, studying the mental makes our awareness of these tensions and of the oppositions that flow from them more relative. Humans reduced to their mental aspect is the object of history rather than its subject. The object of counting and of quantifying, they become the psychological object, the object of *mentalités*. The breath of human action through the centuries is diluted in the descriptions given by historians. By drowning man in statistics and then by rehabilitating him through *mentalités*, historical discourse has crossed out social man, he who, in his individual relation to society, symbolizes the process of domination and the articulations of a mode of production.

An immense recent publication has tried to bypass the blurry concept of *mentalités* and to accent the idea of private life, which is related to what was called in the past the history of civilizations or of mores. Michel Winock is the force behind this series of books. He proposed the idea to Philippe Ariès and Georges Duby: "The trio Ariès-Duby-Winock chose the editors for each of the five volumes."[40] The new theme of private life fit into the movement that exploded the object of history and provoked a radical split with social history as it was practiced in the sixties. "Private life" hopes to be a more efficient tool than mental history and to move away from social contexts to concentrate on an intimate area definitively removed from anything political. Paul Veyne, editor of the first volume, defined the motives of the series as a loss of interest in politics and a search for a new post-Christian ethic.

Another recent tack for escaping from reality and cutting every link between infra- and superstructures is to seek refuge in the world of the imaginary. Since any reconstruction of the past is mythological, fantasies are just as significant as real institutions and social relationships. Gilbert Durand, the founder of a center of research on the imaginary at Chambéry, wants to develop a myth analysis: "Like Nietzsche, I believe that any culture is a network of myths."[41] For Durand, the imaginary is an underlying structure that is innate in humans. There would be a limited number of mythemes easily available to all. Myths would break the surface sometimes, at other times they would be pushed to the bottom of the unconscious. The figure of Prometheus returned to prominence in the West in the nineteenth century. After having become ahistorical and permanent in its structure and its function, the imaginary can cover all the other dimensions and become a key to contemporary life. Durand picked up Jung's concept of archetypes, which we thought had been definitively discredited, and used it to capture the form and frequency of the imaginary. He ended up with a fixed, nonrepetitive, and idealist approach to history: "Most frequently, we notice that ideologies . . . move the world more than positive facts."[42] In a slightly different spirit, Jacques Le Goff has also favored the imaginary. For him, its major interest lies in how it extends the historical field and multiplies its subjects. Climate and animals entered as valid historical subjects with Le Roy Ladurie and Robert Delors. Why then should the imaginary escape from historians?

The other factor contributing to the success of imaginary history and one that allows us to hope that the historians of the imaginary will respond to a social need is the coming of a visual society thanks to the media. Paul Alphandéry and Alphonse Dupront have already shown the extent to which images can mobilize energy. For them the essential motivation for the Crusades originated in the force of the celestial Jerusalem.[43] The history of the imaginary, that second wind of the history of *mentalités* on a larger scale, allows historians to annex literary and iconographic documents: "Finally, there is going to be a real and true entry of history into the world of art and literature."[44] The polymorphous and decentered nature of their methods allows historians to take advantage of the richness of neighboring disciplines. However, the negative consequence of this gain would be the loss of any reference point covered only by imaginary representations. This loss of reality has not deterred historians like Duby or Le Goff, for whom the imaginary adds an additional complexity to knowing medieval society, whose economic aspects they have already mastered. They find themselves in fact splitting off from the dominant method of their school, which sees the history of *mentalités* or of the imaginary as a replacement for social history. The concept of *mentalité* has always been vague. Consequently it opens onto a very wide perspective but by the same token it must be used with care and meticulousness. The danger for history now is the desire to describe various representations without bothering to show how they fit into a historical reality. Le Goff admitted that this approach is no longer history: "We cannot say that we are doing history when we are satisfied with representations."⁴⁵ For Le Goff, the history of *mentalités* has its place in the historical totality that includes both material civilization and culture. Both levels communicate by asking questions that break with the traditional mechanical theory in which infrastructure reflects superstructure. Of course he believes that the relations between social and mental are more complex than those that might exist between economics and society, but they remain linked in the same structure. In his definition Le Goff integrates the study of *mentalités* into the global historical movement.⁴⁶ Unlike most *Annales* historians who see in *mentalités* a way of doing anything, of pursuing an imaginary otherworld by fixing their gaze on the evidence of the irrational and toward the margins of a society perceived through its failures, for Le Goff the mental is not an escape, a long day's journey into night, but a way to bring on the light. He locates the history of *mentalités* not in excuses fleeing rationalization but rather in the center of the social body.

Georges Duby has also defined the history of *mentalités*.⁴⁷ He does not envision it as an independent entity, but rather thinks that the connection between what the Marxists call infra- and superstructures cannot be ignored. For Duby, the mental has its own time frame, which he subdivides into three parts according to the Braudelian schema. The first is rapid, the emotions of the moment, rumors in their instantaneous echoes; second, the evolution of behaviors and beliefs that a specific social group shares; third, over a longer duration, the mental underpinnings that resist change most, the cultural inheritances, the systems of belief or models of behavior that outlast simple events. To advance the history of *mentalités*, Duby moved historians from narrating past facts to seeking the truth in the traces left behind by genealogies, hagiographies, and chronicles, and had them study, in those same sources, the representations that an age forms of itself, its subjective history. The source no longer screens historians from the reality they want to recapture, it even becomes a transparent object: "I try to do the history of verbal formations."⁴⁸ Thus Duby defined the first step required for giving official status to the study of representations, which was for a long time neglected or considered simple reflection. But he immediately added, to distance himself from a nominalist conception, that "having undertaken this social semiology, the way in which it fits into economic conditions remains to be seen."⁴⁹ He does not, therefore, make the history of *mentalités* function as a substitute for social structures. He was able to give historical status to the symbolic universe pierced by the internal conflicts of the society from which it sprang. In every instance, the systems of representation are referred to and not the individual speaker. Duby is leery of long statistical frescoes that cling to the changes of a behavior, a concept, or a representation through long duration: "The diachronic method comes unglued too often from reality."[50] The work of the historian, in contrast, consists in confronting continually diverse time frames and in displaying the discordances, the misfits between social reality and ideological representation, which do not evolve in perfect synchrony. *Mentalités* are not conceived as supplements that would allow the territory of the historian to explode into tiny bits; they demand the restitution of a whole, of a coherence that is both more difficult and more exhilarating.

Michel Vovelle has placed the work of historians of *mentalités* at the point of articulation between diachrony and synchrony. In this sense, the best position is surely that of decoding the phases of crisis, the most radical social changes, and the deepest tectonic shifts. The change from one mental model to another is read most easily in the transitions. Vovelle, although a specialist in the history of *mentalités*, does not push history toward the immutable or the immobile. He carefully distinguishes between history and anthropology. He also gives a definition that integrates the history of *mentalités* into global history. The concept of *mentalité*, so in vogue today, covers a field wider than ideology. It is the shift from the study of what is conscious and clearly formulated by institutions and individuals to what is not formulated, i.e., unconscious attitudes and representations. The mental universe should take ideology into account even as it transcends the latter. Too often the mental is presented as a formless magma without any shape. The time frame for *mentalités* evolves generally more slowly than society, as Marx understood; others have called it "a prison of long duration" (Braudel) or "resistance" (Labrousse), but Vovelle highlighted the innovative aspect of these systems of representation: "Inversely, we should speak of the real creativity of the imaginary."[51] Great is the complexity of this whole that has to be reconstituted, in which a double-phase action and reaction move back and forth between the real and the imaginary. At each crucial turning point, we notice a global crisis in society. Such was the case at the end of the eighteenth century when economics tipped over into politics as well as into attitudes about family, religion, and death. Similarly, the macabre spurt of the fifteenth century expressed the crisis of feudal society and not the resurfacing of repressions nor the impact of the Black Plague. The fluctuations of a society's representations are therefore in the prolongation, sometimes distorted, sometimes harmonious, of its social evolution. This is how Michel Vovelle approaches the history of *mentalités*. It remains "the sharp point of social history"[52] while the function of historians consists in "formulating the question, which is essential for us, of the hierarchy of reciprocal actions, of causes, and of effects."[53]

Mentalités are no longer understood as discursive formations detached from reality; rather, they constitute an integral part of the study of society. It is in this sense that history has been enriched while preserving its own ambition to be global, even as it has avoided the fragmentation of its own field of analysis.

■ NOTES

1. E. Le Roy Ladurie in *Y a-t-il une nouvelle histoire?* (Institut Collégial Européen, 1980), 5.
2. E. Le Roy Ladurie, ed., *Histoire de la France rurale* (Le Seuil, 1975), vol. 2.
3. M. Morineau, *Pour une histoire économique vraie* (Presses Universitaires de Lille, 1985), 356.
4. E. Le Roy Ladurie, *Territoire de l'historien*, vol. 2.
5. Ibid., 165.
6. Ibid., 1:147.
7. E. Le Roy Ladurie, *Les Paysans de Languedoc*, 135.
8. Ibid., 24.
9. G. Bois, *Crise du féodalisme: économie rurale et démographie en Normandie du début du XIVe siècle au milieu du XVIe siècle* (FNSP, 1976).
10. Ibid., 23.
11. G. Bois in *La Nouvelle Histoire*, 387.
12. E. Le Roy Ladurie, *Territoire de l'historien*, 2:85.
13. Ibid., 90.
14. P. Chaunu, *Histoire, science sociale* (SEDES, 1974), 3 vols.
15. E. Le Roy Ladurie, *Territoire de l'historien*, 1:346.
16. "Radioscopie," France-Inter, 4 Jan. 1974.
17. Ph. Ariès, *Un historien du dimanche*, 172.
18. J. Ruffié, *De la biologie à la culture* (Flammarion, 1976), 501.
19. E. Labrousse in *L'Histoire sociale* (Presses Universitaires de France, 1967), 5.
20. See interview with M. Vovelle, *Espaces-Temps* 34-35 (Dec. 1986).
21. E. Labrousse, "Voies nouvelles vers une histoire de la bourgeoisie occidentale aux XVIIIe et XIXe siècles (1700–1850)," *Congrès International des sciences historiques de Rome* (1955).

22. J.-L. Flandrin, "Enfance et société," *Annales* (1964): 322–29.
23. "Radioscopie," France-Inter, 4 Jan. 1974.
24. Ph. Ariès, *Un Historien du dimanche*, 136.
25. J.-L. Flandrin, *Famille, parenté, maison, sexualité dans l'ancienne société* (Hachette, 1976).
26. G. Duby, *Dialogues avec G. Lardreau*, 181.
27. G. Duby, *Le Chevalier, la femme et le prêtre* (Hachette, 1981), 23.
28. G. Duby, *La Société aux XIe et XIIe siècle dans la région mâconnaise* (A. Colin, 1953).
29. G. Duby, *Le Chevalier, la femme et le prêtre*, 303.
30. Ph. Ariès, *Essai sur l'histoire de la mort en Occident* (Le Seuil, 1975), 222.
31. M. Vovelle, *Idéologie et mentalités* (Maspero, 1982), 103.
32. C. Beaune, "Mourir noblement à la fin du Moyen Age," in *La Mort au Moyen Age* (1977), 125–45.
33. M. Vovelle, *Piété baroque et déchristianisation en Provence au XVIIIe siècle* (Le Seuil, 1978), 275.
34. Ibid., 305.
35. M. Vovelle, *La Mort et l'Occident* (Gallimard, 1983), 216.
36. J. Delumeau, *La Peur en Occident* (Fayard, 1978).
37. Ibid., 9.
38. "Dialogues," France-Culture, 7 Mar. 1979.
39. M. Vovelle, *L'Histoire* 22 (Apr. 1980).
40. P. Veyne, *Magazine littéraire* (Dec. 1985): 106–9.
41. *Le Monde*, 15 June 1980.
42. G. Durand in *Histoire et imaginaire* (Poiesis, 1986), 143.
43. P. Alphandéry et A. Dupront, *La Chrétienté et l'idée de croisade* (Albin Michel, 1954–59).
44. J. Le Goff in *Histoire et imaginaire*, 13.
45. "Lundis de l'histoire," France-Culture, 19 Aug. 1978.
46. J. Le Goff in *Faire de l'histoire*, vol. 3.
47. G. Duby, "L'Histoire des mentalités," in *L'Histoire et ses méthodes* (Gallimard, 1961), La Pléiade.
48. G. Duby, *Dialogues avec G. Lardreau*, 136–37.
49. Ibid.
50. Interview, *Vendredi*, 4 Jan. 1980.
51. M. Vovelle, *Idéologies et mentalités*, 93.
52. Ibid., 101.
53. M. Vovelle, *La Mort et l'Occident*, 23.

EIGHT

A Metahistory of the Gulag

History forms the historian as much as the historian forms history.
—J. MICHELET

■ A SOCIO-LIBERAL DISCOURSE

During the 1950s many new historians identified with the French Communist party in the throes of the cold war. The world was seen in Manichean terms, the just in the lap of the Soviet god, the unjust to its right and left. We can understand the disillusionment of those who made the Soviet Union their model as the truth filtered back little by little, from the Twentieth Congress to Solzhenitsyn. One invasion after another turned the Red Army into an army of oppression and scraped away the mythological vision of the historians who belonged to the Communist party. In 1952, the group of those holding the *agrégation* in history and membership in the party was rich in future VIPs. We find in it Claude Mesliand, the future rector[1] of Amiens, Pierre Deyon, future rector of Strasbourg, Jean Dautry, Jean Nicolas, François Furet, Robert Bonnaud, Jacques Chambaz, Denis Richet, and Emmanuel Le Roy Ladurie. When the results of the *agrégation* were announced, François Furet and Jean Chesneaux counted up those who passed and announced in the courtyard of the Sorbonne: "We left a few spots for the bourgeois."[2] At the time Albert Soboul, the leading authority on the French Revolution, was having difficulty with the sectarian wing of the party, whose spokesman was the young François Furet. This was the opening round of a polemic that never ended, even if the dividing line between the two adversaries moved around quite a bit. Many of these Communist historians, to whom we can add Alain Besançon and Jacques Ozouf, found themselves at the most prestigious vantage points of the *Annales* and put their organizational skills in the service not of the party but of the journal.

François Furet, former president of the Ecole des Hautes Etudes en

Sciences Sociales (EHESS), joined the Communist party in 1947. This militant period fixed uncrossable boundaries and shaped his historical discourse through the Stalinlike practices of that time and the rancor that resulted from them. Recently he reaffirmed how much this past counted for him and for his comrades: "When twenty-five years later I try to understand what we all still have in common, excluding memories and feelings, I ask myself if our prolonged adolescence in the ranks of the Communist party does not play a larger role than our work as historians at the Ecole des Hautes Etudes."[3] That experience vaccinated him and taught him the discreet charms of liberalism to such an extent that he was named to Edgar Faure's cabinet after May 1968: "I feel I am close to the most enlightened representatives of liberal thought."[4] There is no solution other than the one currently in power, the system now in place, the acceptance of the established order: "I mean that there is no struggle in the twentieth century that is not compromised."[5] Furet recently converted wholeheartedly to Aronism and has directed since 1984 a new institute created by the Ecole des Hautes Etudes, the Raymond Aron Institute.

His fellow traveler Emmanuel Le Roy Ladurie has become the idol of the masses interested in history. Without a doubt he is the most representative of the current tendencies within the *Annales*. This globetrotter through the territory of the historian came to us from Normandy, the son of the minister of agriculture and supply in the Vichy government in 1942. His childhood was so wrapped in hymns that he dreamed of becoming a priest. Nonetheless, after his arrival in Paris to attend the Ecole Normale, he joined the French Communist party in 1949 and remained a member for eight years: "I left my little chouan [provincial] shell. But at the same time I became a Stalinlike crustacean."[6] Protected by his ideological shell, Le Roy Ladurie swallowed all the Stalinist pap without any digestive problems so as to atone for the faults of his father at Vichy. In 1956, the Twentieth Congress ended the purges. He had by then won salvation for his father, and he turned in his party card a year later. The French Communist party leads to everything, but only if you leave it. Times were hard in the fifties. A bitter campaign against "Tito the cop" had to be carried on, and Le Roy Ladurie was in the middle of it as the editor of a student Communist journal, *Clarté*. Talking about the Slansky affair, he said that he had to show that a son should denounce his father if the party interest were at stake.[7] His Stalinist madness even prompted him to ask Louis Althusser, a comrade in his cell, to break off with his wife, Hélène, who was accused of being a heretic by the party leaders. Having been Charles Tillon's friend, Le Roy Ladurie abandoned him without a murmur as a renegade of the working class. How was all that possible? He explained it quite well: "I believed in paradise."[8] This faith was his guide, but there was also his personal life, rooted in family in the widest sense of the term: "In the party, I finally met the other, the comrade, the worker. Of course it was an illusion, but not completely. Some of my best friends, François Furet, Denis Richet, Alain Besançon, and others, date from that period. I owe the party my marriage, my family...."[9] After all that, how can you proceed by half measures? The temptation was great, as they used to say in the party, to throw the baby out with the bathwater. And that is what Le Roy Ladurie did, with a vengeance. Why the split? "My father had 120 cows, I liked them. I read in a journal in the 1950s that the Russians had fewer cows than in 1913. I thought they were unfortunate with so few cows."[10] He took a firm stand against the united Left in 1976. But he did have a weakness for Giscard d'Estaing's administration: "Giscard is first of all a liberal, a Tocquevillian. He is of course aware of the isolation and the fragility of his liberal positions in this century of fanaticisms ... between the traditional Right that wants to be nationalistic and strong and the Marxists of every persuasion."[11] In 1978 he joined a new organization, the Committee of Intellectuals for the Europe of Liberties (CIEL), whose president was Eugene Ionesco. In the face of the crisis in Western values, the committee was mobilizing to oppose any possibility of global revolution in our society. Marxism was presented as the sergeant of the firing squad and public enemy number one. Le Roy Ladurie became a guaranty of order and his writing an antidote, after having been the credo of the Stalin poison. To denounce the totalitarian risk, he cited a philosopher who was then quite à la mode: "Karl Popper frames the problem quite well: revolutions cannot be controlled, because they unleash unforeseen processes that touch the entire society and thus inevitably take on a totalitarian character."[12] He ended up leaving *Le Nouvel Observateur* for *L'Express*.

The decade of the fifties was crucial in defining a generation that denies today with the same absolute vigor what it adored yesterday. Yesterday's god is today's devil. We have only to read Alain Besançon, another comrade from that same period, a Sovietologist after having been a Sovietophile, to understand the motives they shared. Besançon was eighteen in 1950: "I belong to a generation that has been strongly marked by the idea of communism."[13] Today, his rejection of the Soviet Union is more than extreme: "The Soviet system appears to me to be the antithesis of civilization. . . . To describe the USSR as barbarian is unjust, not for the USSR but for the barbarians."[14]

History is stuttering. This phenomenon of a mystical belonging, the prelude to a period of expiation, has been repeated for some in the generation of May 1968, especially those who embraced Maoism. When the Great Helmsman deceived them, out of spite they invented a new philosophy built around the mystical book *L'Ange*.[15] In its pages revolution was declared impossible or, rather, totalitarian. Guy Lardreau, Christian Jambet, Bernard-Henri Lévy were hunting in these philosophical fields the nasty ferret whose name became, in a regressive process, Marx, Hegel, Rousseau, or Plato. Scrape away as much as you want, something will always remain. The slipping of some drags down others in an unforeseen direction, which leaves the bitter taste of disenchantment hovering over the research and the intellectual activity of historians. Now is not a time for commitment. When Pierre Nora, in charge of historical publications at Gallimard, started the journal *Le Débat* in 1980, he defined the undertaking: "*Le Débat* is a counterweight to *Les Temps Modernes* and to its philosophy of political commitment."[16]

Ideology terrifies those who have seen it used to negate reality in the name of higher interests. The historian's gaze passes, therefore, through the deforming prism of the gulag. It has been marked by the consequences of Poznam, Budapest, the Twentieth Congress, Prague, and Jaruzelski's coup, even as historians pretend that they use an objective and scientific discourse, beyond any political leaning, devoted to historical science alone. Certainly, Stalin's totalitarianism demands an attempt at explanation from historians, but this necessary effort is not what we are now noticing. Rather, it is a chilly retreat into the past to avoid the future. The choices made in each period, the angles of observation, the different rhythms of each sequence are determined most often by the political position of each historian's school. Pierre Vidal-Naquet explained the reasons behind his choice of classical Greece as a specialization.[17] His democratic hopes naturally pushed him to study how the city was constituted. Claude Nicolet, ready to join the radical party, was more taken with the study of Rome where political politics were already hierarchical if not hieratic. In the nineteenth century, Guizot, Thierry, and Thiers directed their attention to the French Revolution in order to legitimize 1830 and liberalism, as well as the innovating role and the vast aspirations of the French bourgeoisie. They stopped, therefore, at 1789–90. In contrast, Michelet and Louis Blanc, as partisans of a social republic, emphasized 1792 in their histories of the French Revolution. As Georges Duby wrote, "We notice that every generation of historians makes a choice."[18] The young generation of the *Annales,* inheriting the disillusionment of its mentors, went even further in its efforts to dress Clio as the vestal of the existing order. Emmanuel Todd, a disciple of Le Roy Ladurie and a member of Communist Youth in 1968,[19] attacked every form of militancy, but only on the left. He assailed "the doctrinal flabbiness" of the Socialist party for its Marxist-Leninist language and considered its alliance with the Communists "a morbid psychological manifestation of the schizophrenic type."[20] For Laurent Theis, of the same generation, history is a safe haven in a world without faith or law. He felt he was an orphan of those fine days of the golden past when "our ancestors were happy with their candles and their wooden shoes."[21] He wished that our future could return to this past: "What interests me is the society where tradition and rules govern everything."[22] This nostalgia is one of the unifying characteristics of much current historical research. It is in the name of this conquest of the past, of rehabilitating our ancestors' times that former and reformed Communists have been able to work with conservative historians along the same historical lines, claim to belong to the same school, and use the same methods despite their different commitments.

Somewhere along their path those who escaped Stalinism met Pierre Chaunu, the most prolific historian of his generation. An apostle of Protestantism, a Cassandra for modern times, he put our Christian humanity on alert. The Western fortress was invincible, but danger lurked nearby. The crusade was inside our walls. Be careful not to turn the West into a desert that would soon be invaded by the dark hordes of the Third World. He hoped to save us from the apocalypse before the year 2000. The father of six children, he exhorted the white population to increase its birth rate and violently rejected abortion, which, for this militant pro-lifer, was tantamount to a crime. The survival of the race was at stake: "We are in the process of making a powder keg. We will provoke civil wars by producing people in the Third

World and sending them to work in Paris or the Ruhr basin. As a historian whose task is to illuminate what is happening now, I tell you: this is crazy."[23] Chaunu's ideological positions have the advantage of being perfectly clear. After having denounced abortion clinics, he declared: "We, the parents of three and four children, do not want to become shoeshine boys, slaves, street cleaners, domestics for other people."[24] He intended to demonstrate the superiority of our traditional, Christian civilization under the cover of the historian's scientific outlook.[25] White Christians deserve credit for socializing asceticism and controlling sexual impulses; they succeeded in establishing continence as a general rule through a praiseworthy effort of willpower. From this model derive two characteristic marks of our modern era: the postponement of marriage (until twenty-five to twenty-eight years of age) and the affirmation of the narrow, matrimonial family. The practice of continence allowed Western intelligence to flourish: "It resuscitates aggressivity and intellect. It provokes creative tensions. Aggressivity and creativity are indissolubly intertwined."[26] Thanks to the repression of its sexual appetites, Western Christianity has taken up the role of guide that fell to it in the name of God, the Bible, and its message, which is "the only one." A new crusader, Chaunu looks like the pope in the midst of his brothers at the *Annales*.

Another conservative Christian, this one a Catholic, was accepted late into the ranks of the *Annales*. Philippe Ariès specialized in the history of *mentalités*. Descended from a royalist family, he remained a royalist. A militant in *Action française* ever since high school, he was courageous enough not to hide this conservatism: "I am a man of the Right, a true reactionary. . . . I am in favor of continuity. That is, I believe, the essential."[27] Ariès was like a fish in water since the topics in vogue with the *Annales* school matched those of his conservative heart. Still he was ignored for a long time, despite the defense he wrote for the *Annales* discourse in 1954.[28] He has told why he had not been satisfied since 1946 by the kind of history filled with politics and legends that Jacques Bainville wrote and that he had read throughout his youth. He replaced this indefinite chronicle of edifying memoirs with a history that sought the gist of local sociabilities and basic solidarities with scientific and mystic care: "Historical creation is a phenomenon that is religious by nature."[29] He was then overjoyed to discover the *Annales* discourse that separated history from the state and that searched out daily life in its concrete manifestations and in its own particular space. From that moment on, he proposed to imitate the *Annales* way of writing history, which would allow him to "reconcile his family and political loyalties with his scientific interests."[30] His assimilation was late in coming, however.

The word *nostalgia*, which in the past eliminated whatever was too old, today has assumed a positive connotation. Rallying to a preindustrial society coincides with what Ariès has always defended as a world that had to be preserved against either liberal or Marxist progress. The current cult of the past and of the traditional community with its old solidarities corresponds accurately to the practice of history as ethnology of the past. Reading Le Roy Ladurie, Furet, and many others, we understand how historians from so many different backgrounds came together under the same heading. Dazzled by the durability of the structures in family, agriculture, and households that outlasted the ancient *ostal*, Le Roy Ladurie cited past models that we could reproduce if we could not create new foundations for a future society: "I'm tipping my hand: I love the Rouergue area. I appreciate the way this little region was able to throw off its misery and underdevelopment in a century and a half. . . . Why not reverse utopia? Without hoping too much, of course. For our planet, which is largely poor and rural, I wish a counter-utopia in the future, as green as it is undoable. On behalf of the twenty-first century, I wish for a global Aveyron as it was in 1925, enlarged for all humanity."[31] These two ideological currents, one composed of defrocked Stalinists, the other of nostalgic conservatives, met a third current flowing from left-wing Christians or intellectuals politicized by the Algerian war and the deception of Mollétism. Such was the case of Jacques Julliard, Pierre Nora, Pierre Vidal-Naquet, and Michel Winock. This current was attuned to self-management, antistate pronouncements, the defense of civil society, and social experimentation.

This catchall group of the *Annales* historians, in which varied backgrounds tended toward consensus, fostered not only the meeting but even the syncretism of different ideologies that found a common credo in the *Annales* discourse. As a result the dialectic between the past/present and the future was lost, which was the basis of the historian's discourse. Jacques Julliard championed this loss explicitly: "Since 1968 freed us from Utopia, i.e., the future, despite itself, while 1981 freed us from doctrine, i.e., the past, we can today try to live in the present."[32] This is weightlessness in the age of vacuum. Julliard started to strip yesterday's revolutionaries by attacking Jean-Jacques Rousseau, one of the leading figures of the French Revolution, as being out of date and as the cause of the Revolution's loss of direction and of the leftist themes of the nineteenth and twentieth centuries. He especially indicted the use made of Rousseau's work because there was, according to Julliard, a major confusion. Rousseau a revolutionary? You're mistaken, no one is more conservative! The builder of a new society founded on the social contract? A fairy tale for children, a philosophical parable at best! Popular sovereignty? A monster that crept out of its lair, an incongruous, unthinkable concept! "I declare Dr. Rousseau to be entirely incompetent!"[33]

Rather than constructing theoretical models that do not measure up, historians can troll in our past and enumerate the best recipes of our ancestors. History changed function. The science of changes and transformations specialized in the inertia of immobile societies. That warned us of the uselessness of change while feeding us with a vague nostalgia for what we had lost. The reactionary character of this kind of history was recognized and accepted by Furet: "I willingly accept that this history (the history of long durations and of the average man) has a conservative vocation because right from the moment when you begin to compare, not the events that mark a change but the elements that are always the same through a period, it is obvious that, in theory and by definition, you risk finding inertia. Consequently, this kind of history seems to me to be a good antidote to, let's call it, the Marxist-Manchesterish history of the nineteenth century."[34] The revolutionary horizon or the temptation to restore having been rejected, only immobile history remains. History risks losing its identity despite the plethora of current work. Immobile history tends to dilute the historical field with the other social sciences. Skepticism replaces the construction, based on the past, of human progress in the name of lost meaning. Consequently, narrative filled with events has reached its low point and has lost status because it is not inscribed in a problematics that is intelligible from before and after on the scale of time. Societies that were formed by historic consciousness are seen to be inert material, "cold" matter like those primitive societies Lévi-Strauss studied. Régis Debray analyzed this phenomenon as nature's revenge against the twentieth century for the arrogant attitude that dominated the nineteenth century. Nature was conceived as an obstacle to conquer while today it appears as an ideal standard or a paradise to be recaptured: "Crisscrossing from one century to another, from old-fashioned to new fashioned; nostalgia and expectations."[35] Human acts and deeds are lost in a universe without meaning. Everything is reduced to the same level. There is no more global discontinuity from one society to another, and that allows historians to compare the realities of different epochs in their repetitive manifestations. Le Roy Ladurie analyzed the phenomenon of crisis in Western society.[36] The period from 1720 to 1973 was globally one of growth, and today we are experiencing a penury similar to what happened from the fourteenth to the eighteenth century. Nothing has changed under heaven: it is the same crisis marked by the short supply not of grain but of petroleum. Demography is just as affected. Gross national product declined in the twentieth as in the seventeenth century. If the predictions of the Club de Rome come true, "it will be a return to the *ancien régime*." History is no longer stuttering, it is actually repeating itself. Reactions to the crisis should follow the paths of the past. Our reaction should be that of the *ancien régime*. It is best to hunker down, to suffer through the adversity and the shortages so as to preserve continuity and prepare for the future by trying to compensate for poor economic performance with cultural creations. That was how the West overcame the crises of the fifteenth and the seventeenth centuries, and we just have to repeat the recipes of yesteryear.

The complement to losing any dialectic connection between past, present, and future is the all-out attack against Marxism, which is being denounced as a theory of oppression and the source of all our troubles. More and more firmly the Marxist teleology is being denounced as colored by a Judeo-Christian vision and as the impetus for creating a false paradise on earth. The history of the gulag would be in Marx's thought if history were reduced to the production of ideas. Practice would only be a mirror, the simple excrescence of theory. At that rate, law courts would be in session nonstop. Jesus would have to answer for the Inquisition, Rousseau for the Terror, Nietzsche for Hitler's abominations, Sorel for Italian fascism, and Marx for the horrors of Stalinism. With this reduction of history to discourse, we are astonished to see a good number of new historians humming the same funereal chant as the new philosophers.

The diversity and heterogeneity of the *Annales* obviate any facile overgeneralizations. There are those who refute Marxism and those who think their work continues it. Emmanuel Todd wrote to banish

Marxism from his intellectual horizon. His book *Le Fou et le prolétaire* attempts to be a "non-Marxist reinterpretation of European history, a counterhistory." Marxism is denounced as the symptom of our society's psychotic state: it is a morbid temptation, a modern totalitarian variation belonging to the same psychic level as Platonism or Protestantism. Besides, for Todd, there are significant correlations with the morbid nature of Marxism, which permeates those societies where the rates of suicide, alcoholism, and insanity are rising and affect the bourgeoisie. For Todd, Marxism is related to psychiatry. That should not drive Billancourt[37] to despair, however, for it can be cured. According to Furet, "Marx, today, cannot escape his inheritance, and the boomerang effect is stronger for having been delayed so long."[38] Le Roy Ladurie's view of Marxism is full of sarcastic irony. He does not see why Marxist historians who claim to belong to the *Annales*, like Guy Bois or Michel Vovelle, should not have the right to their little "hit" of Marxism.[39] But we should not confuse hard and soft drugs. Only going over the wall can lead to the gulag. A joint of Marxism never did any irreparable harm. For Pierre Nora, Marxism has finished living as a revolutionary idea; it is condemned to extinction.

This ideological drifting has not dragged along all the historians of the *Annales* school. A significant number of them consider their work as a direct or indirect continuation of historical materialism. Georges Duby discovered Marxism as a senior in high school in 1937. It was for him a major revelation that has never stopped inspiring his work. Reading Louis Althusser and Etienne Balibar also influenced him. Duby's Marxism will always have a heuristic value; it will never be the basis for a political commitment. This limit allowed him to escape from under Stalin's lead cape and from today's nonsensical elucubrations: "In my evolution, the influence of Marxism has always been deep. I react violently against those who pretend today, in keeping with the Parisian fashion, that Marxism did not count for the historians of my generation. It counted a lot for me and I want that to be said."[40] Guy Bois, another medievalist, has continued the Marxist method in his globalizing approach to history. Jacques Le Goff can be called a Marxist even if, recognizing that Marx was "one of the masters of new history,"[41] he disputes the "clumsy" primacy of economics that relegates *mentalités* to superstructures fashioned by the infrastructure. When he evokes official Marxism, he refers to the use made of it by the Stalinist movement. In this regard we can only share his wariness. Until the fifties, it was through economic history that Marxism influenced history. A certain number of modernists in the *Annales* school follow in the wake of Marxism, including Michel Vovelle and Robert Mandrou, specialists in the history of *mentalités,* and Pierre Vilar, who has continued to improve the Marxist conceptual system in his studies on Catalonia.

For a large number of specialists in classical Greece, Marxism was a fundamental analytic tool. Yvon Garlan, Pierre and Monique Lévêque, Claude Mossé and Jean-Pierre Vernant: my list is far from being all-inclusive. Looking at these divergent approaches to the function of history, it seems that the *Annales* has assembled historians whose ideological positions are far from being identical. At the heart of this school a friendly confrontation is taking place among its diverse components. Most recently, we have to admit that the conservative, nostalgic discourse has won out over those who were resisting the tide of despair and holding on to the mooring of a history that was committed to collective progress.

■ NEGATING THE POLITICAL

Politics sprang up when the city was born. The feeling of belonging to a community that was larger than the unit of a family or clan first appeared on the open perspective of the *agora.* This world that defined itself by opening up, by questioning its own identity and its relationship with reality and truth produced a major rift in the history of humanity. History, or the need to bear witness and to leave some trace for future generations, was born of the political.

The advent of history was the event that begat the tale of the Persian wars by Herodotus.[42] Time became humanized and formalized by a Hellenistic awakening when faced by the "barbarians." Herodotus's tale revealed a new consciousness of man's situation in the world. He contrasted the Greek law of the fifth century B.C. to absolute monarchy, citizenship to slavery, civilization to barbarism. It was a binary world, the source both of identity and resistance. It was the apology of *dikè* (justice) against *hubris* (exaggeration), of equality, and of the people (the *demos*) at the apex of the Athenian achievement that was presented as the model for civilization in the fifth century B.C. Born of politics, history grounded politics in the solidarity of a collective destiny.

Similarly, Thucydides, that other father of history, recounted the Peloponnesian wars to give meaning to human potentiality based on an Athenian model that was the antithesis of Sparta. The explanation that Thucydides gave for this schism among the Greeks was essentially political. It was already the conflict between a democracy and a statocracy. Historical time pulsed according to political desires. As François Châtelet has shown, the crisis of the city led to the crisis of historical discourse. Facts lost their coherence, the conflict between Athens and Sparta bogged down. Politics broke down, broke into pieces, and antihistory replaced history. The Sophists abandoned the idea of evolution because political salvation seemed impossible. They invoked a return to the past, to the good old days of Hellenistic solidarity, and denied progress any meaning. The disintegration of Helos continued in the fourth century as historical discourse disappeared behind the individual preoccupations of Xenophones.[43] Time lost its political meaning; historical narrative could no longer attain the level necessary for making reality intelligible. History became contingent, an individual affair. Xenophones and Aristotle, who were both caught in the incoherence and the conflicts of their times, turned back toward systematic empiricism. Already history had decomposed into singular histories written in the plural.

This detour into classical Greece is not unmotivated. It leads us back to the connection between new history since 1929 and politics, and thus to the definition of history's function. This evolution or involution from the fifth to the fourth century, from Herodotus to Aristotle, can be perceived in the nineteenth and twentieth centuries. The current eclipse of all that is political is connected to the loss of our awareness of historicity. Progress having no meaning, our historical consciousness is now dissolving into a single empiricism: "No one has wondered about the contribution of history to a better political awareness. Is this because the *Annales* school has chosen to not intervene in this area?"[44]

Michel Foucault, one of the best historians of our time, chose power—the powers that be—as his target. But, and this change is significant, he tracked them down to their furthest reaches where they extended beyond their internal rules. He wanted to reconstitute the reality of those bodies that were peripheral, neglected, and until then considered epiphenomena. His method had the advantage of uncovering hierarchy and order behind what was disorganized and inorganic. But power in Foucault hid its own political dimension by diluting and dispersing it. Power was not shared dichotomously between those who held it and the others. It could only be confiscated by one class; it was not homogeneous. Power circulated through a network of individuals, it functioned in chains, it passed through each one before collecting in the whole. If there was no nodal locus of power, there could be no resistance to this power. Omnipresent, it could not rock back and forth, it was inside us. Everything is power. Resisting it has no purpose. It would be wrong to deny Foucault's insight, which invites us to not confuse power and the state in a single reality. However, his major shortcoming is the occultation of the state. This displacement toward the periphery was also influenced by the failure of May 1968 and its mythification. All liberation would be resubjugated by its logical link to the devices of this power. The Foucauldian trilogy, body/discourse/power, functioned at its extremities. Body and power were the equivalent of being and nonbeing, liberty confronted constraint, desire the law, revolt the state. The schizophrenic faced the paranoid, multiplicity faced unicity. The inevitable subjugation of the individual passed through a third term and not a constellation of forces. That third term was discourse, or the discursiveness that belongs to the field of power. This dilution or dissolution of the political was a trace of the repulsion felt for the modern monster of the state, that source of oppression and evil. Unable to knock it down, we walk around it. To avoid any recuperation through contamination, we deny its existence.

The rejection of whatever is political on the part of today's *Annales* is in total harmony with the journal's first generation. There is in fact an analogy between the spirit of the thirties, virulent antipolitical feeling, technocracy, planning, and the climate of the eighties, when the state is presented as something outside civil society. To yesterday's hyperliberalism we hear today the echo of Reaganism even within the "second left." There is a perception shared by the core leadership of the *Annales* and by the feeling on the "second left" that denounces "the barbarous age where everything is politics."[45] The overwhelming presence of the *Annales* school at the *Nouvel Observateur*, at least until 1981, demonstrates this ideological agreement, this wholesale acceptance of a consensus, the strike, treaty, or peace of those classes that are resigned to their fate in the existing order of things. This thought agrees nonetheless to give people their rights through their popular culture and by recognizing their values, on condition that the latter not become dominant. The people see their status recognized, but in a situation where they remain dominated. Technocrats take account of its identity to better control it without difficulty. This sociolibéral ideological discourse includes just about all those in the power structure of the *Annales*.

Rejecting political analysis caused the *Annales* to miss the major historical phenomena of its day. It is the same today. The encyclopedia on new history published in 1979 has no entry for *politics* or *political*. Add to this the present climate that encourages depoliticization and reinforces the rejection of politics. "Long duration so dear to the new history is depoliticized long duration."[46]

The *Annales* has succeeded in decentering politics. François Furet set himself outside political history, which he considered the special repertory of change.[47] Since history should deal with what lasts, it should borrow from the social sciences and abandon political illusions. When he demonstrated that literacy triumphed in France without going through the schools, Furet emphasized the reduced role of the state and of its ideological apparatus in the cultural domain.[48] Philippe Ariès, disillusioned because the ideas of Maurras that he had professed were becoming more and more marginal, retreated into a history that was radically depoliticized. This was the path that led him into the embrace of the *Annales:* "Yes, a connection does exist between my growing dislike for political action and my definitive embrace of the kind of history that reduces the importance of the state and its ideologies in favor of a more ethnographic culture."[49] When Yves-Marie Bercé studied peasant revolts up to the nineteenth century, he stuck to an ethnographic "morphology" to depict the unfolding of that collective violence. He distanced himself from their political context and presented what was permanent.

The state disappeared in the vast movement that made our knowledge planetary. Similarly, the takeover by multinationals has diminished the role of national enterprises. As for *mentalités*, as André Burguière has shown, the oldest of new ideas, happiness, has tended to become private and apolitical.[50] In the past those who worked for change counted on the state to guarantee human happiness. From Voltaire to Diderot, the Enlightenment philosophers counted on an enlightened despot. Today, pleasure and emotional independence are sought outside the framework of the state. The period lends itself to the slow ebbing of politics. Le Roy Ladurie commented: "Historical research should be separated from politics."[51]

We cannot say that Jacques Julliard has abandoned politics since he is chief editor at Seuil for the collection "Politique." He considered it normal that a serious journal like the *Annales* keep away from political history: "Political history is psychological and ignores conditioning; it is elitist, indeed biographical, and ignores comparisons; it is narrative and ignores analysis; it is idealist and ignores matter; it is ideological without knowing it; it is biased without knowing that either; it clings to the conscious and ignores the unconscious; it deals with single points in time and ignores long duration; in one word, since this word sums up everything in the jargon of historians, it deals with events."[52]

Not everyone has marginalized or displaced the political dimension. Some take it as an essential part of the reality of the society they study. Georges Duby thinks that feudal society was characterized first by the decomposition of the monarch's authority.[53] The inability of the Carolingian kings to confront external aggressions produced a dispersion of power and a breakup of political authority. Local feudal authority was based on the debasement of the central royal authority. But in general, politics remained a dead issue in the *Annales* discourse, and this was due to the loss of any dialectical play between the present and the future. The essential political basis was inscribed in the desire for revolution and change, just as it bogged down when any possibility for a rift vanished. Jacques Le Goff ratified this rejection of politics which he equated with an elitist conception of history, since for him politics belongs to the decor of an aristocratic style exercising irrelevant power. What was political was restricted to a thin superficial layer of history. But he called for a new approach to the political using a larger, anthropological perspective centered on the notion of power: "Political history conceived as the history of power recovers a verbal dignity that refers back to a change in mentality."[54] But this renovation of the political would displace the interplay of classes over the power of the state in favor of a purely cultural history that is based on immobile anthropological models.

The modern context has aggravated the split between progress and the present for the French "who don't belong," as Gérard Mendel called them. It is in this phase of individualistic retreat and of confinement to a narcissistic igloo that politics returns to the margins and that the stakes increase. The historian's discourse outside politics expands even better in a society founded on the extension of the private domain and the erosion of social identities. There are no more historical projects that rally many forces. An "era of emptiness" is beginning as Gilles Lipovetsky noticed: "Postmodern society is one where the indifference of the masses rules, where the feeling of being scrutinized and trod upon dominates."[55] While this new era may initiate a soft, relaxed period, it also signifies an atomization of the social body, a lack of political commitment, an atrophy of organized labor's strength. It leads to indifference and the inability to act. The political loses its reason to exist, except for the body of specialists that would be the political class.

■ NOTES

1. The "recteur" is the chief governmental official responsible for all levels of education, elementary through graduate study, in a particular geographical area called an academy. The academies are named after the principal city of the region in which a major university is located. Rectors are somewhat comparable to our state superintendents of education—Trans.
2. Personal interview with R. Bonnaud, 16 Jan. 1986.
3. F. Furet, *Le Débat* (Dec. 1981): 113–14.
4. *Le Nouvel Observateur,* 20 Nov. 1978.
5. Ibid.
6. E. Le Roy Ladurie, *Le Débat* (Nov. 1981).
7. Ibid.
8. Ibid.
9. Ibid.
10. "Apostrophes," 12 Mar. 1982.
11. *Le Nouvel Observateur,* 23 May 1977.
12. Interview, *Maintenant* (Aug. 1979).
13. *L'Express,* 1978.
14. *Le Quotidien de Paris,* 18 Dec. 1981.
15. G. Lardreau and Ch. Jambet, *L'Ange* (Grasset, 1976).
16. *Le Monde,* 2 May 1980.
17. *Le Nouvel Observateur,* 18 Apr. 1977.
18. G. Duby, *Dialogues avec G. Lardreau,* 40.
19. "It is an adolescent transition" he said. "Radioscopie," France-Inter, 12 Nov. 1976.
20. E. Todd, *Le Fou et le prolétaire* (Laffont, 1979).
21. "Radioscopie," France-Inter, 11 Apr. 1979.
22. Ibid.
23. P. Chaunu, reception speech for Louise-Weiss Foundation Prize, 17 Jan. 1977.
24. France-Inter, 14 Dec. 1978.
25. P. Chaunu, *Histoire, science sociale* (1974).
26. Ibid.

27. Ph. Ariès, *Un Historien du dimanche*, 202.
28. Ph. Ariès, *Le Temps de l'histoire* (1957; rpt. Le Seuil, 1986).
29. Ibid., 42.
30. R. Chartier, "Préface," in Ariès, *Le Temps de l'histoire*, 18–19.
31. E. Le Roy Ladurie, *Le Territoire de l'historien*, 2:335–36.
32. J. Julliard, *La Faute à Rousseau* (Le Seuil, 1985), 247.
33. Ibid., 242.
34. F. Furet in *L'Historien entre l'ethnologue et le futurologue* (Mouton, 1972).
35. R. Debray, *Critique de la raison politique* (Gallimard, 1981).
36. E. Le Roy Ladurie, *Le Territoire de l'historien*, vol. 2.
37. A Paris suburb where a Renault auto factory is located, and hence a working-class neighborhood. In France working class always suggests leftist and this area is associated with the other suburbs comprising the "Red belt" around Paris—Trans.
38. *Le Nouvel Observateur*, 4 July 1977.
39. *Le Monde*, 11 Mar. 1977.
40. Interview, *Vendredi* (Jan. 1980).
41. J. Le Goff in *La Nouvelle Histoire* (Retz, 1978), 236.
42. F. Châtelet, *La Naissance de l'histoire* (10/18, 1962).
43. Ibid., 2:118.
44. F. Ewald in *Y a-t-il une nouvelle histoire?* (Institut Collégial Européen, 1980).
45. E. Maire, quoted by H. Hamon and P. Rotman, *La Deuxième Gauche* (Ramsay, 1982), 399.
46. J. Chesneaux, *Du Passé, faisons table rase* (Maspero, 1976), 129.
47. F. Furet, *Le Débat* (Dec. 1981).
48. F. Furet and J. Ozouf, *Lire et écrire* (Minuet, 1977).
49. Ph. Ariès, *Un Historien du dimanche*, 98.
50. *Le Nouvel Observateur*, 10 Sept. 1973.
51. Interview, *Maintenant* (July 1979).
52. J. Julliard in *Faire de l'histoire*, 2:229–30.
53. G. Duby, *Guerriers et paysans* (Gallimard, 1973).
54. J. Le Goff, *L'Imaginaire médiéval* (Gallimard, 1985), 338.
55. G. Lipovetsky, *L'Ere du vide* (Gallimard, 1983), 11.

NINE

Immobile History

■ A STRUCTURAL APPROACH

The inaugural speech of Emmanuel Le Roy Ladurie at the Collège de France on 30 November 1973 had the revealing title "Immobile History."[1] Hidden in this provocative expression, which seems to combine fire and water, lies the desire to reconcile opposites and to unite, under the aegis of history, anthropology and ethnology, whose advances have been marked by structuralism.

We find that that new historians in their work have adapted those operations used by Lévi-Strauss for his "cold societies." Unchanging time has an advantage in seizing the unconscious structure of each institution. Series of combinative rules (exclusion, inversion of signs, and pertinence) are employed to make sense of reality and allow the system to regulate itself and reabsorb, according to internal and logical operations, what is new or contradictory. Change and rupture are no longer meaningful. Historical movement is conceived as repetitive and permanent; what is invariable takes precedence over what has changed. Differences located within the system are only local differences, and unity overwhelms their oppositions. Contradictions that might emerge from the historical process are reabsorbed by substituting one term for another and preserving the initial given. Society continues without any major rifts in a contrapuntal modulation that repeats according to the rules of a harmonic system that avoids any wrong notes. The system cannot be changed in itself. Only an external shock can rock it since it possesses no internal contradictions.

The conflict between historical and structural is not recent. Auguste Comte had distinguished static from dynamic societies and had favored the former. As Henri Lefebvre noted: "Structuralism is the ideology of equilibrium. . . . It is the ideology of the status quo."[2] How can historians use this legacy when they are confronted by movement, process, and change? They can do it only at the price of seeking a final equilibrium as the parameter of their studies, around which they arrange the oscillations that record illusions, accidents, insignificance. New history is a war machine aimed at dialectic thought. It favors becoming over being and sees the motor and impulse of history in the fission and not in the fusion of contraries. This distinction becomes dialectical through a network of correlations that unifies the historical moment in the act of fission and of resolving the contradiction. Historical thought can only be the thought of splitting, the thought of rupture working toward the future, toward transcending the past and not returning to it so that contradictions may be reabsorbed. The new cannot be absorbed in the old, but remains resolutely new in a thought that attempts to catch what is in the process of no longer being, that is to say in its transition to a new reality.

Anthropology has supported this tendency and has made contingent all the divisions established up until then by history. Century-long continuities and constant regulating comprise the basis of new history: "Behind the crowded history of governments, wars, and famines can be seen the immobile histories, slow-moving history: the history of maritime routes, of wheat or of gold mines, the history of drought and irrigation and crop rotations, the history of the equilibrium reached by the human race between hunger and proliferation."[3] Le Roy Ladurie's model is also Lévi-Strauss's, but applied to Western civilization. In his view change can only unfold from the top of society. In terms of both culture and the state, an elite overturns certain values from the top of the social hierarchy. Antagonisms and struggles for hegemony disappear in favor of this new social entity, the elite. Contradiction does not take place; it has lost all meaning. The system adapts, replacing the ruling layers by substitution or osmosis, and thus preserving stability and continuity. The time frame of structures does not have the same rhythm as the history of humanity. It belongs to the very long duration. It is important to emphasize not the break points but the repetitive nature of human activity. Our attention is directed to what is regular, the seasons, cycles, and the continuity of daily life. History has become structural: "Social science ... abandons events and even facts, unique facts that are not events, all in favor of repetitions."[4] History imposes new restrictions in which social structures can be reproduced even as it eliminates anything that upsets this process of repetition. The ideological foundation of this approach is a profound pessimism in which the real world escapes from humanity and is destined to survive without any changes, conforming to a human nature that is as immutable as the nature of animals or plants. Historians plunge into the depths of historicity, leaving behind the superficial phenomena where individuals struggle.

The status of the event has changed. After being the significant symptom, it has become the artificial and mythological crystallization of insignificance. It is pushed back into the margins. Historians may even "not be interested in it at all."[5] The American school of cliometricians has even elaborated some history-fictions using the computer. They eliminate a certain number of facts that are considered major in American history, the Revolutionary War, for example, and show at the end of a statistical study that economic growth would have been the same without them. Events dissolve in long duration. At the same moment that philosophers are discovering the death of man, historians are proclaiming the death of the event: "Contemporary historiography . . . was forced to kill in order to live: it condemned traditional narrative history and the biography of the individual to near-death several decades ago."[6] History would then be mythological, the illusion of an unchanged society: "The interaction of man to man is not reducible to its zoological status but is subject to it."[7] According to the current vogue for repetitions, any revolutionary activity is assimilated to totalitarianism, whatever its object or period. Any desire to make a break with the ongoing evolution reveals schizophrenic behavior in the sense that it attacks a timeless operation in an unchanging society. Emmanuel Todd equates France in 1793 and 1848, Russia in 1917, and Hilter's Germany in 1933. In each case, he uncovers behind the causes of these upheavals evidence of the petty bourgeoisie that was experiencing both social and sexual frustrations. The bourgeoisie was subject to morbid and hysterical impulses that underlay its totalitarian tendencies. The "dangerous classes" are not those analyzed by Louis Chevalier, but the petty bourgeoisie. It is a sick social class, marked by alcoholism and a high rate of suicide, which are the result of its morbid sadomasochism. Consequently, its ideological commitment is nothing but the product of its schizoid tendencies. The petty bourgeoisie is a real social class but one filled with crazies. For Todd, progress engenders regression and imbalances that are fatal to the social body. Progress in literacy and raising the cultural level of the European population brought intense psychic troubles: "The rates of literacy and of hysteria seem to change according to the same hidden factor."[8] Progress and history are the enemy for some of these historians! Scorn knows no limits. When reality does not correspond to the hypothesis, reality has to be eliminated to exorcise once and for all these suicidal attempts. One chapter of Todd's book is entitled "Rejecting the History of France." The loop is looped. Once it's all over, it begins again. When history moves and reveals undeniable shifts, it is better to erase those pivotal moments by imputing them to psychotic delirium. Vain human activity can do nothing, the world is immobile, nature immutable, and man insane. If we want to worry about this evolution of historians' discourse, we must paradoxically read Philippe Ariès, who, while insisting upon his own conservative point of view, declared "that this situation carries a risk: the loss of our awareness of time."[9]

■ THE FRENCH REVOLUTION IS OVER

The contemporary historian's gaze tends to erase the phases of acceleration in the historical process, the turns and the pivotal moments when one system self-destructs and gives way to another. Having become an immobile structure, history has to eliminate what heretofore was considered its essential rifts. Revolutionary phases are treated like periods of restoration closely connected to the past. They could even be reactionary in the sense that they react against new disputed factors. Far from esteeming what seems to be innovative in every attempt at change, historians fix their attention on what endures despite the will to change, on what is inert. Obviously they reduce if not eliminate the upheavals that create new systems. Discontinuities disappear. The historical horizon becomes flat and repetitive, regardless of the time or place studied. Any upheaval is thwarted by the perspective of long duration. Seen as macro-history, events are reduced to impotency, they cease being the motor and the accelerator to become simple symbol, myth, or fantasy.

And so it is with all historical phases. Here we will limit ourselves to that founding gesture and topic of historical polemic without peer that is the French Revolution in order to illustrate this new negative reading of rifts. On the eve of the bicentennial of 1789, and as a kind of exorcism, former president of the EHESS François Furet proclaimed the death of the French Revolution: "When I wrote: The Revolution is over, it was a way of expressing a desire and a fact."[10] It is no longer possible to draw a line of demarcation that puts Frenchmen on the Right or the Left. Hasn't the new historians' research led us to ask if the famous revolutionary phenomenon even existed? Or if it was only a nightmare? Opening our eyes wide would suffice to rid us of that bad dream. This was tried in two phases.

First, the Revolution was placed in brackets, reduced to an episode that was both tragic and insignificant. Once the monster was thus tied up, all that was needed was to throw it out, to put it outside consideration. This is what allowed Furet to say in 1979: "The French Revolution is over."[11] The French Revolution was cumbersome from the perspective of the long duration of peaceful history. For Furet, the Revolution was only a myth, just as the British historian Alfred Cobban had said in 1955. Furet's view pretends to be removed from political polemics and distant from the participants, in order to sound the correct scientific note. Nonetheless, we find here and there traces that safeguard a social model that functions "from the top down" and revitalizes itself through elites. The peaceful revolution of the eighteenth-century Enlightenment achieved the osmosis of enlightened nobles and cultivated bourgeois and it offered the possibility of change without upheaval. Capitalism grew strong without class struggle and without the intervention of the masses, whose intrusion upon the scene appeared incongruous and backward. Eliminating the Revolution was therefore possible for the good of a France whose people had rushed into the Empire's continental wars and who spurned economic progress.

Far from being a new discourse on the Revolution, new history picked up the long legacy of liberal thought that was hostile to the Jacobin revolution. There was a trauma, a fracture in the heart of liberal thought: the French Revolution was felt to be necessary and yet finished. Liberals claimed the first moments of the revolutionary act, but they wanted to exorcize it, to repel any risk of experiencing another phase of revolutionary excess. The political aspect had to be rethought so as to allow considering the revolutionary events foreclosed. French liberal thought is first and foremost antirevolutionary. The paths leading to it are, however, diverse. For Madame de Staël there was a hiatus in the revolutionary block 1789–94. For her as for most liberals, there were two distinct phases in the Revolution. The liberal revolution of 1789 was turned toward England and was welcomed as the harbinger of liberty and progress. The other phase belonged to the lower classes and was known as the "reign of the Jacobins." For de Staël, the people were located between noble landowners, the basis of the social order, and savages. She turned a look full of condescension toward the people on the condition that it keep its place: "The secret of the social order is in the resignation of the largest number."[12] To avoid disorder, she recommended bicameralism because it would counterbalance any possible popular pressure. Guizot picked up on this split between 1789 and the Terror and opposed the good and bad sides of the Revolution so as to better identify the July monarchy as the continuation of the ideals of 1789. His entire history of European civilization was nothing but an immense fresco depicting the different elites in power. The Revolution was presented as the result of a century-long evolution toward an egalitarian society based on law that ended in the dominance of an overly ambitious middle class. In 1875 Taine also placed the Revolution in brackets because it prevented the natural elites and the upper classes from managing the state. Popular uprisings were like mud welling up from the depths to the surface; the people looked like wild beasts. "A lewd gorilla . . . an enormous beast that takes the bit in its teeth."[13]

François Furet and Denis Richet are not the innovators they pretend to be, for they have repeated a traditional argument about the dualism of the French Revolution. Rejecting the apologists of Danton and Robespierre, Aulard and Mathiez respectively, Furet tries to appear as an outside historian, free from the direct influence of the participants in a revolution he considers a myth. This effort led him to appropriate the analysis of all those who have attempted to deny the revolutionary rift. The work of Furet and Richet is completely ideological as is clearly manifest at every moment.

In their 1965 version,[14] events were placed within the long duration that made them appear ridiculous and out of phase with the general tendencies that dominated the period 1750–1850. In the vast rise of liberalism, the Terror seemed an incongruous monstrosity that had to be put in brackets in order to discern the meaning of history. We are amazed that those who attacked a teleological vision of history denied reality any significant status in the name of a preestablished meaning. Furet and Richet divided the revolutionary play into two acts according to a schema that has since become classic: a positive time of unity, a negative time of conflict. Everything began well enough and 1790 was called the "Happy Year."[15] The will to reform was incarnated in the Assembly, which held from then on most of the power. In the eyes of our authors, this was the only valid revolution. The two other revolutions that took place at the same time, one in the cities, the other in the countryside, were only anachronistic movements. Everything was ready at the top to proceed without being hindered by the masses. Forgotten, in passing, was that at this point the Revolution was far from realizing the principles it proclaimed. Legally, equality did not yet exist since voting was still limited to those owning property and paying a certain amount in taxes. Socially, only a few rich land-owning peasants, who were able to prove that the right to collect feudal taxes had been usurped and who had bought up a lot of land, could hope to be free. But the situation deteriorated, war was not far away, and this lovely equilibrium cracked, to the regret of our authors who entitled one chapter "The Revolution on the Skids."[16] An accident caused the liberal evolution to fail and everything flipped over.

Furet and Richet attempted to pick out the people and the parties that opposed the radicalization of the Revolution. They defended the monarchists who had moderate opinions in 1789. Then they played another card: the Feuillants in 1791 did all they could to maintain peace. "The last quarter of 1791 is the twilight of a fine and grand epoch."[17] The failure of the Feuillants was attributed to the king alone. This explanation is, to say the least, surprising for historians who want to emphasize the deepest phenomena of history. The elimination of the Feuillants was the critical point of deviation when the French Revolution took the wrong road. On the threshold of failure in 1793, the Girondins suddenly become sympathetic and irresistible: "The Girondins surrounded the Revolution with a halo of charm, youth, and enthusiasm."[18] Their defeat on June 2 was not just the defeat of the Gironde, but the defeat of the Revolution. The Montagnards steered the Revolution toward more radical aims. In the beginning they took their strength from the popular movement that demanded more equality in the social body and the legal repudiation of privileges. Our authors called this chapter "The Time of Misery."[19] For them, the abomination came from the populace. The *sans-culottes* repeated the actions taken by the urban movements of the sixteenth and seventeenth centuries so they could only be archaic resurgences. Hébert became a vampire who "thirsted for blood."[20] The popular pressure in the streets and in the clubs was far from being the expression of class antagonism; rather, it derived from jealousy of those who had talent. The Revolution skidded off the tracks laid down by enlightened reformers, "outside the path traced by the intelligence and the wealth of the eighteenth century"[21] because of the interference of the motley crowd, the plebians. Denying the universal message of the French Revolution against dynastic authority, which reverberated throughout Europe in the nineteenth century, Furet and Richet saw the Revolution as historical nonsense, a military and peasant regression that championed a garden of one's own next to the factory. They used only one model, one single measure for every comparison, the British evolution, the preservation of the monarchy, the people strangled, compromise from the top down, debating rather than fighting among good fellows.

A disciple of Furet, Guy Chaussinand-Nogaret has assured us that compromise was possible in 1789 and that the Revolution was, after all, a tragic mistake among partners unsettled by popular uprising. We used to imagine that the French nobility in the eighteenth century was lazy, parasitic, and removed from a renewed social space. Chaussinand-Nogaret depicted a dynamic nobility at the heart of progress.[22] Can he be serious? He was trying to reinsert the nobility into our national patrimony and to transfer its ashes to the Pantheon. The nobility fell victim to virulent racism: "The noble, in 1789, was the Jew of the kingdom."[23] Economically, Chaussinand-Nogaret presented a nobility that, after having absorbed capitalistic notions of wealth and competence, tended to identify with innovation: "There was no need of the Revolution to free productive forces."[24] Culturally, a domain he gives even more importance to, Enlightenment was indivisible, the appanage of the elite, nobles and bourgeois mixed together. All this is forgetting the essential, that is to say the question of privilege that was at the center of the *ancien régime*'s final crisis. Attempts at compromise made at the apex of the eighteenth century between a liberal nobility and old-regime bourgeoisie were frustrated by the nobility's refusal to relinquish its caste privileges and by the constant opposition of the Parlements that blocked any possible compromise. The political and legal issue became an unavoidable stumbling block for the bourgeoisie, which had to find support in popular legitimacy in order to triumph. Unlike the British situation in the seventeenth century or even Germany and Italy in the nineteenth, the French aristocracy, as

Georges Lefebvre has demonstrated, provoked the first act of the Revolution by its conservative attitude, what is called the noble reaction, or the aristocratic revolution against royal power. The very concept of liberty hides the entrenched desire to keep feudal rights and honorific privileges intact against any egalitarian aspirations. Once we leave the antechambers of the court, we see the real nobility: a class in decline, ready to revolt even at the risk of being thrown into a revolution. Inert, resisting any change, enclosed inside its codified universe, these nobles, who were in the majority, found in Boulainvilliers the reactionary discourse of their lost legitimacy. In the name of its historical ascendancy, of its Frankish origins, and of its former liberties reduced by the monarchy, the nobility stood up to the double threat of the third estate and the king. The noble reaction slowed down the access of the bourgeoisie to the highest positions in the state, the church, and, most of all, the army. Chaussinand-Nogaret would like us to believe that France could have, like England, avoided the Revolution. Like Furet and Richet, he contrasted the dual reality of a society in revolution with the simple vision of a pyramid dominated by its elite for all eternity. Our daily life would then be anchored in a past without class struggle and could rid itself of the egalitarian fantasies that rise from the depths of society. The year 1789, already bracketed, was to become a regrettable misunderstanding between two categories of the same elite.

Furet has not stopped hoeing his row. After having seen the Revolution skid off the road, a parenthesis, he wrote in 1978 that the essence of this as of every revolution is totalitarian.[25] Between these two points, Solzhenitsyn's writings had revealed the gulag that provided Furet with his second schematic reading. In the name of what the Soviet Union had become, he attacked the very idea of revolution: "Today, the gulag leads us to rethink the Terror, given their similarities. The two revolutions remain linked."[26] This disillusionment, by a former militant of the French Communist party, derived from his rediscovery of two thinkers hostile to the Revolution, Alexis de Tocqueville and Augustin Cochin. Parenthesis turned into drift not in 1792 but in 1789. The Revolution followed an internal dynamic that had nothing to do with its social or economic bases, nor with the war that was then taking place. Revolutionary symbolism functioned by itself, cut off from society in a process from which history itself was missing. Terror at the time of the Committee of Public Safety was not presented as the response to the dilemma of being besieged by an internal aristocratic uprising and a united Europe. Contemporary events, like the two world wars, have shown that in such a situation recourse to state planning, requisitioning, and rationing are all necessary. Still, for Furet, the evil lay in the revolutionary will itself: "The truth is that terror is an integral part of the revolutionary ideology."[27] His perspective was completely different: Robespierre was no longer an actor out of place in this drama, but rather the logical incarnation of a totalitarian dynamic that reappeared in the twenties in Stalin's Russia.

Furet's approach was based on the work of Tocqueville, whom Aron had already brought to light. Tocqueville wrote in 1851 after the failure of the Second Republic, which came to grief in the coup d'état of December 2. Disenchanted by the strong state that returned to power with Louis Napoleon Bonaparte in 1851, he began thinking about the split between liberty and equality, especially since Bonaparte was voted in by almost the entire French people. His thinking about the Revolution climaxed in the publication of *L'Ancien Régime et la Révolution* in 1856. He situated the Revolution in a long duration that dated back to the *ancien régime*, continued in 1789, and accelerated in the nineteenth century. This period was marked by the centralization of power and the more efficient control of the central administration over society. In this conception of the state, the Revolution happened as a epiphenomenon. It simply terminated a process begun under the *ancien régime*, the establishment of a centralized, powerful state that regulated civil society. All the seeds were there before 1789, the Revolution only continued its legacy "in a transitory and uninteresting period."[28] Louis XIV, Robespierre, and Napoleon were connected by a continuous thread that united them in the same consolidation of a strong state. The Revolution lost its innovative look since it continued royal absolutism in its own way. Tocqueville tried just as hard to extirpate the notion of revolution in a France traumatized by 1848. Ten years later he wrote: "Moreover, there is in that sickness of the French Revolution something that I feel without being able to describe, nor to analyze its causes. It is a virus of a new and unknown kind."[29] The only vaccine for Tocqueville was to reintegrate the event into national history and avoid any new rifts. The result of the Revolution was positive, but it should have taken place without shocks or passions. We find the great liberal aspiration for reform, which protects the interests of those in power, and not for revolution: "A people so poorly prepared to act by itself could not attempt to reform everything at one stroke without deforming everything with that same stroke, without destroying everything. An absolute ruler would have been a less dangerous innovator."[30]

Tocqueville did not find the right vaccine against the virus, but Furet did, in the person of the traditional Catholic Augustin Cochin. Cochin wrote at the beginning of the twentieth century against Aulard's republican thesis. Attached to Catholic civilization as it was in the Middle Ages, he took as his hero Saint Louis. Cochin is therefore as far as one can get from the idea of revolution. He denounced its collective power, the tyranny of its clubs, and the "popular magma." Cochin waved Jacobinism like a red flag and denounced it as purveying totalitarianism disguised as the will of the people or general will. Furet saw in this concept of the people-as-king "the matrix of totalitarianism."[31] Cochin's work had already been exhumed by Pierre Gaxotte, an ultrareactionary popular historian. In 1929, Gaxotte picked up the theme of intellectual terrorism and denounced the "Communist dictatorship" of the Mountain as the logical end result of the Jacobin revolution. Furet used anything he could lay his hands on and adopted a more and more conservative line. This was a logical evolution in that he wanted to root out the very idea of revolution: "1789 opens a period of history on the skids."[32]

Even if the French Revolution was over and political history disappeared with it, the bicentennial began and Furet did not want to be left behind. He produced numerous case studies to illustrate his theory about history skidding out of control and about the organic link between revolution and despotism. To support his ideas he chose another nineteenth-century thinker, one who like Tocqueville was disillusioned by the coup d'état of December 2 and who went into exile in Belgium and later in Switzerland. Edgar Quinet, a republican deputy, analyzed the failure of the French Revolution in the light of the fall of the Second Republic. In 1865 he published his *Histoire de la Révolution* inspired by a teleology of lost battles: "Everything pushed [Quinet] exiled by December 2 toward a pessimistic meditation on the national legacy."[33] For Quinet, 1789 remained a progressive break, but the resulting balance was precarious and always threatened by a return or relapse to the tyranny of the *ancien régime*. This step backwards took place in 1792 when the Mountain revived the legacy of the royal past with the Committee on Public Safety. Like Furet, Quinet rejected the role of external circumstances like the war in this change: "No, it was not circumstance that created the system of terror. That is a wrong idea."[34] Furet drew a philosophical lesson from this and proclaimed it valid for all time, namely that there is an undissolvable connection between the phenomenon of revolution and state despotism.

These attempts to erase history, recently denounced by Max Gallo,[35] have installed a new vulgate as the dominant discourse. Among its leading practitioners we find the crusader Pierre Chaunu surrounded by young pretenders to the mantle of official discourse who have grown up on all this counterrevolutionary work. Key thinkers have been repainted to make them look modern but in fact they come directly from the traditional catechism that has been hostile to the Revolution since 1789. Edmund Burke wrote against the Revolution in 1790 and did not need the Vendée as a pretext for his horror at what was happening in France.[36] He attacked in particular French abstract thinking, which tended to neglect reality and experience in favor of metaphysics. Joseph de Maistre denounced 1789 as a diabolical manifestation: "There is in the French Revolution a satanic element."[37] He has entered the pantheon of obligatory references for those who want to vilify the essence of the Revolution. The third prominent figure for these new crusaders is the Abbé Barruel.[38] For him, it was a plot orchestrated by three leaders, Voltaire, d'Alembert, and Frederic II: "The day of the uprising was set for 14 July 1789."[39] The Revolution would then be a three-headed monster: plot, negation of reality, totalitarianism. This was a new interpretation that had to be inculcated or beaten into people, especially since it avoided everything that touched on historical circumstances. Furet, overwhelmed on the right, already considered it a "weak" argument. Barruel seems to be reincarnated in the preaching friar Chaunu, a evangelist in the style of Billy Graham: "We have never seen an order written in Hitler's hand about the Jewish genocide, but we do possess those of Barrère and Carnot about the Vendée. What's more, every time I walk by the lycée Carnot, I spit on the ground."[40] "The sadistic imagination of Tureau's army equals SS, gulag, and Khmer Rouge."[41] The Revolution is presented to us as a "minuscule segment of our history that is dangerously cancerous."[42] Like any cancer, it requires shock therapy. Chaunu gives us a feel for the tone of those works that attack the Revolution case by case and call it bloodthirsty violence and barbarous bloodbath. Frédéric Bluche tackled the September massacres, Reynald Secher the Vendée.[43] The thread connecting these works is the same surliness that was present in 1939 at the sesquicentennial. That was a more sinister time, with Pierre Gaxotte's *Je suis partout*, Léon Daudet and others madly demanding revenge for 1936, the Popular Front, paid vacations, and their own fears. As Max Gallo said, these "new Muscadins" aim at rejecting the principle of equality printed on the frontispiece of the French Republic ever since 1789.

Illusion of manipulative politics, illusion of liberation, illusion of revolutionary festivals: Mona Ozouf chose the festival, traditionally a site for transgression, for not respecting norms and taboos, and for spontaneity, to show that revolutionary festivities between 1789 and 1799 were an expression of order and not happiness, of coercion and not imagination: "The revolutionary mania for festivals is the story of an immense deception."[44] By eliminating from her concept of festival those spontaneous expressions of the people's joy that were marked by violence, Ozouf was able to use Durkheim's schema that saw in the festival the unanimous expression of a people assembled by the authorities. The festival was an integral part of establishing a system of controlling the individual who was caught in a new space occupied by an invasive political power. Power was written in transparent space, open space, outdoors, a space without boundaries, that was available for the memorial services which deserted churches and avoided mountains as a symbol of hierarchy. This transparency aided in controlling and eventually repressing any deviation. Festivals parceled out individuals just as schools lined them up in rows. Festivals became a means of subjugation. They were one of the instruments of the Leviathan state that even wanted to master time. What was at stake in this theatricalization? The message behind those massive columns erected around altars to the *patrie* was the effort to cap the revolutionary effervescence and to suspend time in the peaceful present of a mission accomplished. If all this became possible when authority broke with public pressure, then the ritual of festivals turned in fact into a lifeless allegory that disarmed revolutionary violence. It was not Louis XIV who was insulted in public squares, but the idea of royalty. Ozouf ignored the creative explosion of Year II when the people invaded the political scene with more determination and broke with official organizations. Nonetheless, the deepening of the social rifts made possible a decrease in the intensity of codes and ritual systems, including those of the new authorities. Another festival was born, the festival of dispute and imagination, the festival Ozouf refused to recognize. How can we not see a festival of the future in those revolutionary days when blue-collar workers from the suburbs walked to the convention? Spontaneous festivals multiplied. From 1780 on, peasant groups would go from village to village on Sunday, take the benches out of the churches, dismantle the weather vanes, and dance in the public squares. During the period of de-Christianization, these impulsive desires broke all interdictions. The people transformed churches into dance halls, priests threw off their holy vestments, bonfires proliferated. This grass-roots movement gathered people around pyres that were built to burn confessionals, ornaments, and pious books taken from the churches. Around these same pyres the people danced the Carmagnole. Power was nowhere and the people were everywhere. Joy twinkled in their eyes as they gazed at their resolute actions against the powers that be.

Surely the revolutionary fire still glows if it continues to provoke those whose purpose is to quench it forever from the historical horizon. As Georges Clemenceau said in 1891: "That lovely revolution, which made us what we are, is not over." Because it is a universal symbol of liberation and because of the force of what it signifies, the French Revolution continues to be a major battleground and a line of demarcation between those want to bury it to protect their own advantages and those who want to build a world with more justice. No, surely, the French Revolution is not over.

■ NOTES

1. E. Le Roy Ladurie, *Territoire de l'historien*, 2:7.
2. H. Lefebvre, *L'Idéologie structuraliste* (Le Seuil, 1975), 69.
3. M. Foucault, *L'Archéologie du savoir*, 10.
4. K. Pomian, *L'Ordre du temps*, 158.
5. K. Pomian in *La Nouvelle Histoire*, 543–44.
6. E. Le Roy Ladurie, *Territoire de l'historien*, 1:169.
7. R. Debray, *Critique de la raison politique*, 52.
8. E. Todd, *Le Fou et le prolétaire*, 61.
9. Ph. Ariès in *Y a-t-il une nouvelle histoire?* (Institut Collégial Européen, 1980), 21.
10. *Le Nouvel Observateur*, 28 Feb. 1986.
11. F. Furet, *Penser la Révolution française* (Gallimard, 1978).

12. Madame de Staël, *Considérations sur les principaux événements de la Révolution française* (1818).
13. H. Taine, *Les Origines de la France contemporaine* (1875).
14. F. Furet and D. Richet, *La Révolution française* (1965; rpt. Fayard, 1973).
15. Ibid., 99.
16. Ibid., 126.
17. Ibid., 145.
18. Ibid., 201.
19. Ibid., 203.
20. Ibid., 232.
21. Ibid., 253.
22. G. Chaussinand-Nogaret, *Le Noblesse au XVIIIième siècle* (1976).
23. Ibid., 9.
24. Ibid., 122.
25. F. Furet, *Penser la Révolution française*.
26. Ibid., 25.
27. Ibid., 90.
28. A. de Tocqueville, *L'Ancien Régime et la Révolution* (1856).
29. A. de Tocqueville, *Oeuvres complètes* (Gallimard, 1977), 16 May 1858.
30. A. de Tocqueville, *L'Ancien Régime et la Révolution* (Idées-Gallimard, 1967), 265.
31. F. Furet, *Penser la Révolution française*, 232.
32. Ibid., 69.
33. F. Furet, *La Gauche et la Révolution française au milieu du XIXième siècle* (Hachette, 1986), 30.
34. Quoted by Furet, ibid., 96.
35. M. Gallo, *Lettre ouverte à Maximilien Robespierre sur les nouveaux muscadins* (Albin Michel, 1986)
36. E. Burke, *Reflections on the Revolution in France* (1790).
37. J. de Maistre, *Considérations sur la France* (1796).
38. Abbé Barruel, *Mémoires pour servir à l'histoire du jacobinisme* (Hambourg, 1797–99).
39. Quoted by M. Gallo, *Lettre ouverte*, 48.
40. France-Culture, 24 June 1986.
41. Quoted in M. Gallo, *Lettre ouverte*, 22.
42. Ibid., 26.
43. F. Bluche, *Septembre 1792, logiques d'un massacre* (Laffont, 1986); and R. Secher, *Génocide franco-français* (PUF, 1986).
44. M. Ozouf, *La Fête Révolutionnaire: 1789–1799* (Gallimard, 1976), 19.

Conclusion

By applying its own methods to its own history, we can define the *Annales* as a school committed to long duration. It claimed a continuity and a permanency that united in a single movement Lucien Febvre's struggle for history and Pierre Nora's fragmented history. At the same time, this school wants to be untraceable, beyond any definition, a cloud without a core. This desire has several motives. Proclaiming out loud that it belongs to a group that already has a past and can take credit for various achievements allows the *Annales* to consolidate its power and to reinforce the institutional structures that constitute its strength in regard to the other social sciences, which are younger and less rooted in the university infrastructure. An overall coherence and a common identity, even if they are partially mythic, are required to manage and to preserve power. That is the strategic aim. We have, however, seen that we must disarticulate the sweep of three generations or the binary configuration of the social sciences. The continuity that the *Annales* claims hides in fact numerous changes of direction and breaks between the historical discourse of the thirties and the eighties, even if some of the original intentions remain today. The history of the *Annales* is not immobile history. On the contrary, this school has adapted successfully to the continual changes of society throughout the twentieth century and has vigorously resisted the assaults of its neighbors and rivals in the social sciences.

History has laid a heavy hand on the *Annales*. Its influence is especially evident among historians who are receptive to the outside world and its influence. Between the *Annales* of the thirties and the eighties a number of continuities and discontinuities can be found. Among the continuities: the same denial of the political, which has been an *Annales* black hole since the beginning; the same strategic policy of taking over the social sciences and their innovations; the same rallying around history-through-problems; the same alternative route between traditional anecdotal history and an atrophied Marxism. The latter led the *Annales* into unexplored fields that became both a barrier against and a replacement for Marxism, that is to say, *mentalités* but not ideology, material culture but not materialism, structure but not dialectics. Another continuity can be found in the adaptation to modern life. In the thirties the *Annales* tried to play an active, operational role (in a managerial sense) through its economic interpretations; in the eighties when the locus of power moved to the media, the *Annales* again adapted to the reigning discourse and strategically invested the positions of power and took control of the decision-making process for the diffusion and commercialization of the historical "product." One result was the transition from geographical and economic history to anthropological history or the history of *mentalités*.

Nonetheless there are real deviations. First of all, man was no longer in the forefront of history. Even if we do not go as far as Le Roy Ladurie and his "history without men," the perspective is no longer anthropologically centered on human beings. The progress of this decentering moves from Bloch and Febvre's history as a science of change through the "nearly motionless" history that Braudel defined in his inaugural lecture at the Collège de France in 1950 to the "immobile" history Le Roy Ladurie announced when he replaced Braudel there in 1973. But history cannot be motionless, for then it would no longer exist. A second important deviation was the jettisoning of any dialectic between the past-present and the future. History was no longer considered a tool for illuminating its immediate times. Le Roy Ladurie has said, "For me, history is a bit like an escape out of the twentieth century. We live in a sinister time." Finally, the most critical deviation was the deconstruction of historical knowledge, the ending of any global perspective; there are histories, but no history. Whereas the founding fathers Bloch and Febvre often repeated their commitment to a total history, today's historians are equally happy describing the plurality of their aims and methods. This fragmentation came after the Braudelian transition when time frames were pluralized within a single whole. Still, not all *Annales* historians supported this explosion of history as a discipline. Within the school itself are tendencies that run counter to fragmentation. These historians prove that history can be enriched by the social sciences without adopting their methods wholesale. History's striving for synthesis and its ambition to articulate the diverse levels of reality and to sustain a dialectic between long and short durations can be realized.

The *Annales* owed its triumph to its remarkable ability to adapt. At every turn we find the challenges that the social sciences threw at history. The *Annales* has ripened and changed to the point that for Pierre Vilar, there is no more *Annales* school: "It is dead."[1] To the Durkheimian challenge at the turn of the century, *Annales* history responded by destroying the three idols of traditional history, namely biography, politics, and events. To the challenge of Lévi-Strauss in the 1950s, the *Annales* under Braudel conceptualized long duration as a language that could unify the social sciences. In the seventies, the deconstruction of history was completed by Foucault's provisional, regional, and partial configurations of knowledge. Absorbing Vidal's geography, Durkheim's sociology, and psychohistory in the thirties adumbrated the conquest of statistics and demographics in the fifties and of ethnology and anthropology in the sixties and seventies.

This history in three time frames reveals the basic dynamism of a school that defined itself by its openness and that accepted new aims and new horizons so as to attain a particularly high level of historical production. Paradoxically, history, fertilized by the social sciences, ended by losing its identity. If it ever finds its own character, it risks getting lost again in a myriad of different purposes that lack connection. It risks disappearing like zoology or experiencing the same marginalization as geography.

While we can map this evolution in three chronological stages, we can also speak of two great movements, two specific configurations in which the history of the *Annales* is inscribed. The global, humanizing perspective belongs to the first and second generations, the period of Bloch and Febvre who founded the *Annales d'histoire économique et sociale* in 1929 as well as that of Braudel. It was Braudel's heartfelt desire to establish a common market of the social sciences confederated around history and to synthesize them in a globalizing discourse that would give birth to an interscience. The lay of the land changed in the sixties. In order to resist another attack by the social sciences, *Annales* historians renounced synthesis and began to think in terms of the disciplinary boundaries that were erected by differing historical aims and purposes. Humanity was decentered by a deconstructed history that limited fields and abandoned any globalizing purpose. Everything became a question of segmenting society and locating the stable forces that presented a systemic character. Serialization could generate enrichment only when it inquired about the articulation of distinct systems and located the active, internal forces of destruction that foretell ruptures and transitions. The deconstruction enacted by the last generation of the *Annales* has led to a discourse that is more descriptive than analytic, more positivistic and empirical than scientific. In this new configuration of the social sciences, historians lost their place as the leader of the orchestra to become, in Le Roy Ladurie's metaphor, a pit miner who drags to the surface material other social sciences study, or a vagabond like Michel de Certeau who is a specialist in deviants, undersides, and whatever is marginal. In fine, historians gave up their social legacy to better invade the field of the media.

History has always been connected to power. The strength of the *Annales* was that it stuck to the new powers in the twentieth century, which were different from those in the past. History gives us a discourse that is coextensive with society. History is the mirror of society, the transparency of power that seeks its legitimacy through history. Historians give meaning to those in power; they guarantee their legitimacy. The incessant crises in the historian's discourse are articulated according to the different phases of society's evolution; they are each and every time adaptations to the realignments in society.

Historians were political in the ancient world where the *polis* dominated Greek or Roman society. They had to find a new civic identity under the aristocratic dispensation. Clio offered coherence. In the context of the expansion, defense, and influence of the city, Clio appeared as a political discourse and the glorification of military prowess. In the Middle Ages, clerics dominated society and gave meaning to the future of Western society: "Christians, carried along by history, honor Clio by baptizing her."[2] At this point history became moral, it was incorporated into a Christian teleology that envisioned God's plan being realized. Reality was incorporated into a spiritual temporality. In the fifth century, Saint Augustine defined history as the fulfillment of the divine will. At the same time clerics imposed their vision of the world and of man's future, while simultaneously consolidating their social domination over laymen. This was the age of edifying history at the ethical level, the lives of the saints, and hagiography. History was fully religious under the influence of the regular clergy and the monks in their libraries. But in the thirteenth and fourteenth centuries, the historian's discourse followed the displacement of power from the monastery to the town, from the chateau to the emerging central state. History underwent a secularization that fit the new dominant power better. The connection with time became more human. Temporality was adapted to the rhythms of these new states. It offered a legitimacy that helped them consolidate their power. The union of the two dominant orders of society, the clerics and the nobles, preserved the social order. The kings of France immediately called upon monks to write the history of the kingdom. Royal power cannot be limited to the expression of its physical strength, it needs to speak the meaning of its power. This task fell to historians. Meanwhile, chroniclers undertook the apology of the noble class and praised its courage, virility, and abnegation, especially during the Crusades, a privileged moment when the fusion of politics, religion, and the discovery of the other took place: "Froissard is the mirror of the social class for whom he wrote."[3] Servants of the lords, the chroniclers of the Middle Ages displaced historial discourse from religion to politics. History "came of age. It earned its independence. But it only stopped serving the church to enter into the service of the state."[4] The first office of royal historian with an official title and a cash stipend dates from 1437. This position was held under Charles VII by a monk from Saint-Denis named Jean Chartier and it disappeared only during the French Revolution. Royal power nudged historians toward a discourse that reflected its positive image and justified its royal ambitions.

The aristocratic class, like the king, anchored its power on belonging to a noble bloodline. History gave the nobility the basic grounding for its roots. History was therefore an indispensable auxiliary in justifying its position. Holders of power in the corridors of power, historians wove together the continuities of the political space that organized the new society. Historians functioned as the twin of power, adapted to diverse political reigns, and grew stronger until the beginning of the twentieth century. We have already seen that the school of Lavisse and Seignobos was an effective instrument in the hands of a radical republic preparing its revenge against Germany. History was essentially political so as to homogenize the nation's diversity around a single, central objective, patriotic defense. History helped to make war.

Nonetheless, French society had changed by the end of World War I, and the economy became the essential focus of power. Always a determining force, economics became the decisive factor in the nineteenth and twentieth centuries. Covering all aspects of social life, it structured society as a whole. Historical discourse evolved to adapt to this new change. This was the *Annales* revolution of the thirties, a true epistemological rift, moving the historian's focus from politics to economics. This was the first phase in adapting to the modern world. Economic history reached its zenith with Braudel after World War II.

The *Annales* echoed changes in society. Is that still true today? A superficial view might lead us to believe that, on the contrary, there are no connections with the dominant powers, technocracy and technology, and that today's historians are huddled over an immobile and far-removed history. Wrong. The historian's new discourse, like the preceding ones, has adapted to the current ideology. In our modern world, the desire for change has been relegated to the margins and to the status of fantasy or delirium, while change itself is considered a qualifier and no longer a simple quantitative transformation or reproduction of the present. Today's *Annales* represents the phenomena of transition or rupture as failed maneuvers within continuities that follow a linear evolution. Revolution has become mythology in this discourse. Whoever wants to think about change will find nothing of value in the extensive work of the *Annales*, as Jacques Revel himself admits.[5] *Annales* discourse reflects the predominance of the media: it has adopted their norms and it offers essentially cultural and ethnographic history. It is a spectacular description of material culture along neo-romantic lines where fools meet witches and where the margins and the periphery replace the center, where a new esthetic offers an underside that is sorely needed in the surrounding technocracy with its brutal concrete. This history includes our fantasies and our repressed unconscious in its effort to achieve a consensus around the realization of our modernity. Historians are asked to search through all these deviants so as to include them in a composite world where everyone has a place in a single social whole without any contradictions.

The *Annales* has adapted to the system and acquired a hegemonic place. The *Annales* triumph cannot be contested and the extent of its domination is such that there is no place left for alternatives: "There is, therefore, scarcely any conflict inside the family of historians."[6] The time is over when history in Lavisse's style was the designated enemy and could mobilize everyone's energies. That traditional history no longer exists. The *Annales* is fixed in the seat of power, singing its own praises, and inventing its own legend. But a single school happily managing its own inheritance risks crisis because it includes no internal consensus other than the rejection of traditional history. Already voices have started criticizing, which is the first step toward eventual splits. The current vogue for historiography recognizes the need to take stock, even at the risk of encouraging a diversity that has been suppressed under the single banner of the *Annales*. Although it has been victorious in all its combats, the school is now prey to internal, centrifugal dissensions. One symptom of the crisis that the *Annales* discourse is undergoing can be seen in the acidic and critical comments made by one of the school's most eminent members. Alain Besançon has written: "Unfortunately there is one very inferior way of writing history, which unfortunately has prospered in our country since the war: systematic history, or rather history by system. This time, events are not appreciated in themselves and do not provoke surprise, astonishment, horror. They are taken, wrapped up, frozen in a schema that is always the same or in a global interpretation they serve to justify. What system? Less often Marxism than a sociology that derives unconsciously from Marxism, and that floats about in the air, in the milieu where historians are found, or in the intellectual laziness it condones. Economics, society, civilization."[7] Nothing could be clearer than this criticism aimed squarely at the core leaders of the *Annales* who are accused of diluting history in the name of an analytic rigidity that should be banned. A whiff of gunpowder is emanating from a school in which everyone is supposed to do one's own thing to such an extent that we ask, what does historical anthropology have in common with quantitative, demographic-economic history or conceptual history?

The major internal division that cuts across the *Annales* discourse confronts those who propose a fragmented history, a history that would follow the procedures of the social sciences, with those who propose a total history, enriched by the social sciences but preserving history's global aim. The first camp is that of the dominant core that holds a central position and thus the essential machinery of the school's power. Jacques Le Goff foresees that history will be diluted in the social sciences, becoming a panhistory that will absorb all the other social sciences. In this conflict that has, since the beginning of the century, opposed history, the oldest and most traditional discipline, to the new social sciences, history is foreseen as dominating and unifying the whole confederation thanks to the *Annales*. But at the price of diluting itself and losing its specific identity.

There is another possibility that a second *Annales* camp proposes, which is close to Marxism but which still accepts the original purposes of the school as valuable stimulation. This group of historians warns against the dangers of fragmented history and insists on synthesis, especially at a time when specialization is increasing. Numerous members of the *Annales* remain faithful to the first generation's total history. They see in the totalizing process the very foundation of history's uniqueness. Far from conducting a rear-guard operation, these historians refuse to change their minds even though everyone around them is encouraging them to do so. While most Annalists have given up on total history because of its totalitarian implications, those who maintain history's global dimension are the best guarantee against that danger. Humanity reclaims its stature through time, which locates it, whereas breaking up time into multiple temporalities without connection deprives humanity of its central position. Rather than fragmenting history into economic, political, ideological temporalities, each of which is studied in its own autonomous evolution, historians should prefer a globalizing approach and a conceptual frame that permits the study of causal systems and the marshaling of correlations between different kinds of phenomena. Then history would be a dialectic between a logical, abstract structure and reality; the movement would go from the structure to the instance, and vice versa, in order to reconstruct a plausible web.

The atomization of reality is sometimes accompanied by a pretense at globality among those historians who divide their analysis into two parts. Their first part is a breaking up; the second a collecting of fragments into a fictional whole that simply juxtaposes the pieces. This neo-positivistic illusion of a globalizing approach eliminates one essential component, the structural analysis, the causal hypothesis without which there can be no total history. The presupposition underlying this totalizing approach is the idea that there is rationality at work within history. The historian's task is to discover the outlines of this rationality behind the tangle of apparently confused and meaningless facts. This demands a step back. Moving from the abstract to the concrete is the arrival and not the departure point for constructing a hierarchy of determining factors at different levels of reality. "Any new history lacking a totalizing purpose is a history that is already old."[8] The causal hierarchy that has to be constructed must avoid two pitfalls, both the abstract theoretical generalization that is removed from reality and the description of exceptional cases. Historians must sustain a constant back-and-forth movement from the event to the conceptual frame and from the conceptual frame to the event. Their synthesis is not a simple collage of different parts presented like a chest of drawers but the search for causal systems.

Historians in favor of global history are today the authentic agents for change and for a truly new history. Any reclassification should follow new criteria. Will we see an explosion not of history but of the *Annales*? The answer to such a question depends less on historians than on social change. For history to become a science of change (Bloch's term), it has to break with the dominant *Annales* discourse of immobile time and with the old-fashioned notion of historians who insulate themselves against any impulse to transform the world and who depict society with its natural, regular, and unchangeable rhythms. By becoming ethnology, history denies itself, it attacks its own basis, which is duration with its slow and rapid rhythms and its upheavals. Any renascence of the historian's discourse demands the resurrection of what has been rejected ever since the beginning of the *Annales* school, i.e., events. The rejection of events led history down the path where it lost its specificity and its function. History alone can capture the dialectic between system and individual event, of long and short duration, of structure and instance. Of course even to suggest a return to the events of Lavisse's history is out of the question. Such history has been relegated to the status of diversion or evasion without any chance of redemption, even if some do hope for its revival, with its good old stories about our national heroes, our exceptional men, and our amorous intrigues. Some do want to revive the finery of aristocratic drawing rooms and the elegance of the social elites from times past with their candelabra and four-poster beds, in contrast to the cultural history of the uncultured masses. We reject this false choice between stories based on insignificant events and the negation of events. The issue is rather to recover the significant event, which is the source of innovation and which is linked to the infrastructure that made it possible: "True modern science will only be able to begin with the recognition of events."[9] Rehabilitating events is therefore an indispensable part of constructing new history. The historian's work will also have to transcend the break between past and present with an organic link between the two, so that knowledge of the past helps to better understand our society. Let us not forget, with Moses Finley, that "it is the world we have to change, not the past."[10]

NOTES

1. P. Vilar, private interview with author, 24 Jan. 1986.
2. Charles Carbonnel, *L'Historiographie* (Presses Universitaires de France, 1981), 26.
3. R. Fossier, "Le Discours de l'histoire," France-Culture, 2 Aug. 1978.
4. B. Guénée, *Histoire et culture historique dans l'Occident médiéval* (Aubier, 1980), 366.
5. J. Revel, *Annales* (Nov.-Dec. 1979): 1371.
6. J. Glénisson, "L'Historiographie française contemporaine" in *La Recherche historique en France de 1940 à 1965* (SEDES, 1965).
7. A. Besançon, "Préface," in M. Malia, *Comprendre la révolution russe* (Le Seuil, 1980).
8. P. Vilar, *Annales* (Jan. 1973); reprinted in *Une Histoire en construction* (Gallimard-Le Seuil, 1982).
9. E. Morin, *Communications* 18 (1972): 14.
10. *Le Monde*, 14 Mar. 1982.

Index

Académie Française, 10, 19, 109, 127
Aftalion, Albert, 51
Aglietta, Michel, 116
Agrégation: subject matter, 13; in geography, 17; exam questions, 53–54; Braudel attempts reform, 101–2; Braudel in middle of jury, 133; and Communist party, 182
Agulhon, Maurice, 171
Alba, Duke of, 132
Alembert, Jean Le Rond d', 210
Alphandéry, Paul, 177
Althusser, Hélène, 184
Althusser, Louis, 160, 184, 191
Amoureux, Henri, 1
Andreu, Pierre, 9
Annales: its dominant position, 2, 218, 220; rejections, 9–10, 36, 42; the spirit of the thirties, 9–10, 44; politics, 10, 33, 44–46, 148, 194, 220; attitude toward the other social sciences, 15, 33, 98, 143, 146, 152, 194–95; adumbrated by Henri Berr, 25–26; its founding myth, 27, 54; taking over other disciplines, 27, 35, 57, 100, 140, 143–44, 160, 188–89; editorial staff, 31, 98, 140–41; types of articles published, 32, 48, 103–4; polemical tone, 32–33, 130; attitude toward facts, 34, 131, 223; kinds of history, 42, 50, 115, 144–45, 155, 170, 218; disillusionment, 45, 186; and the present, 47–49, 160, 215; American model, 49; capitalistic management, 49–50; *agrégation,* 53–54; changes in title, 98; fiftieth birthday, 107; attitude toward time, 141, 147, 215; the media, 142, 150, 216, 220; special issue on South America, 142–43; interest in Elias, 145; diversity, 190–92; continuities and discontinuities, 215–17, 220; its evolution, 217–18; internal dissention, 221–22; mentioned, 7, 8, 9, 46–47, 55, 72, 99
Area studies: along American model, 102
Ariès, Philippe: nostalgic look at past, 147–48; precursor in *mentalités,* 171; on death, 172, 173; conservative Catholic, 187; mentioned, 81, 157, 169, 175, 176, 188, 195, 202
Aristotle, 87, 193
Armengaud, André, 82
Aron, Jean-Paul, 146
Aron, Raymond, 155, 160, 208
Aron, Robert, 9, 10
Attali, Jacques, 116
Augé, Marc (president of EHESS), 143
Auger, Pierre, 99
Augustine, Saint, 218
Aulard, Alphonse, 51, 204, 209

Baby, Jean, 45
Bachelard, Gaston, 34
Backman, Gaston, 49
Bacon, Francis, 13
Baehrel, René, 117
Bainville, Jacques, 187
Bakhtin, Mikhail, 64
Balazs, Etienne, 102
Balibar, Etienne, 191
Barrère, Bertrand, 210
Barruel, abbé, 210
Baulig, Henri, 28
Beaucourt, Marquis de, 20
Beauharnais, Joséphine de, 1
Beaune, Colette, 174

Bercé, Yves-Marie, 195
Berger, Gaston, 103
Bernard, Claude, 18
Berr, Henri: compared with Febvre and Bloch, 26; his principles of synthesis, 58; mentioned, 3, 13, 21, 27, 28, 64, 66, 107
Berthe, Maurice, 174
Besançon, Alain, 157, 182, 184, 185, 221
Bettelheim, Charles, 98, 100–101
Bibliothèque bleue, 148–49
Biology: its concepts in history, 169–70
Blanc, Louis, 186
Blanchard, Raoul, 12
Bloch, Gustave (Marc's father), 29
Bloch, Jules, 29
Bloch, Marc: compared with Henri Berr, 26; early career, 42–43; political commitment, 43–44; backwards reading, 47–48; comparative history, 60–61; *mentalités*, 62–63, 65–69; historical time as plasma, 71; intellectual influences on, 107–9; mentioned, 7–10, 12–18, 27–29, 31–36, 44–46, 50–58, 82, 87, 90, 95, 100, 101, 112, 128, 131, 153, 157, 159, 167, 216, 217, 223
Bloch, Raymond, 49
Blondel, Charles, 28, 29, 61
Bluche, Frédéric, 210
Blum, Léon, 43
Bois, Guy, 168, 191
Bois, Paul, 81
Bollème, Geneviève, 148–49
Bonnaud, Robert, 182
Borah, Woodrow, 168
Borkenau, Frantz, 43
Bouglé, Célestin, 8, 12, 98
Boulainvilliers, Henri, comte de, 207
Boulanger, Georges, 22–23
Bourdieu, Pierre: rival of Braudel, 89; on legitimate and popular culture, 148
Bourgin, Georges, 43
Boutruche, Robert, 81
Bouvier, Jean, 3
Boyer, Robert, 116
Braudel, Fernand: EPHE, 17, 102; influenced by Marcel Mauss, 87–88; at Collège de France, 88; struggles with Lévi-Strauss, 90–98; economists read him, 116; on capitalism, 116–22; his triumph, 126–27, 128; his ambition, 127; faithful to Bloch and Febvre, 128; his pessimism, 129; a solitary figure, 129–30; Marxist history, 133; mentioned, 13, 33, 73, 85, 89, 100–103, 107–33, 140–41, 153, 160, 179, 216, 217, 220
Bruhat, Jean, 46
Burguière, André, 70, 139, 140, 195
Burke, Edmund, 210

Caillé, Alain, 124
Camisard legends, 148
Capitalism: its genesis, 116–22
Capitalists: various kinds of, 123–24
Carbonell, Charles-Olivier, 17
Carnot, Hippolyte Lazare, 210
Castiglione, la, 1
Centre National de Recherche Scientifique (CNRS), 82–83
Certeau, Michel de, 3, 153, 156, 158, 218
Chalonge, Daniel, 45
Chambaz, Jacques, 182
Change: appearances without real change, 141–42
Chappey, Jean, 49
Charencey, Hyacinthe de, 20
Charles V, 2, 55–56
Charles VII, 219
Charles X, 22
Chartier, Jean, 219
Chartier, Roger, 87, 149
Chateaubriand, François René de, 70, 140
Châtelet, François, 193
Chaunu, Pierre, 8, 82, 98, 115–16, 126, 128, 142, 153, 157, 165, 167, 186–87, 210
Chaussinand-Nogaret, Guy, 206–7
Chesneaux, Jean, 101, 102, 159–60, 182
Chevalier, Louis, 201
Cholley, André, 54
Christianity: and new history, 186–88
City: and politics, 192
Clemenceau, Georges, 212
Cleopatre, 2
Climate: geographical determinism, 114–15
Club de Rome: predictions, 190
Cobban, Alfred, 203

Index **227**

Cochin, Augustin, 207, 209
Collège de France: Bloch and Febvre candidates, 17–18, 29; Berr as candidate for, 26; and Febvre, 43, 55; Braudel's inaugural, 88; Braudel replaces Febvre, 107; mentioned, 12, 53, 98, 130, 199, 216
Colin, Armand, 31
Committee of Intellectuals for the Europe of Liberties (CIEL), 184
Communism: and new historians, 182–86; nostalgia, 186
Computer: number crunching, 82; Le Roy Ladurie's programmer, 157; Le Goff and Duby, 158; Chesneaux, 159–60; history-fictions, 201
Comte, Auguste, 12, 199
Copernican revolution in history, 91
Corbin, Alain, 21, 48, 162
Crémieux, Albert, 60
Croce, Benedetto, 7
Crouzet, Maurice, 22, 98
Culture, material: brings people to life, 145

Dandieu, Arnaud, 9
Daniel-Rops, Henri, 10
Danse macabre, 174
Danton, Georges, 204
Dastre, A., 34
Daudet, Léon, 211
Daumard, Adeline, 158
Dautry, Jean, 182
Davy, Georges, 12
Death: Ariès on, 172–73; Vovelle on attitudes toward, 174
Debray, Régis, 189
Decaux, Alain, 1
Decentering humanity: Braudel and Febvre, 130
Decolonization, 79; and structuralism, 139
Delors, Robert, 177
Delumeau, Jean, 175
Demangeon, Albert: influence on Braudel, 87; mentioned, 12, 31, 54, 58, 59
Deng Xiao Ping, 123
Denis, Mme: and her washing machine, 139
Descartes, René, 26
Détienne, Marcel, 66, 163

Deyon, Pierre, 182
Dictatorship: during French Revolution, 209
Diderot, Denis, 195
Dion, Roger, 98
Demography: and statistics, 81–82; and resources, 165–66; "full world," 167–68
Determinism, spatial, 113–15
Discontinuity: series of fragments, 157
Doumergue, Gaston, 8
Dreyfus affair, 23, 43
Duby, Georges: computer, 158; his career and evolution, 161–62; on marriage and family, 171–73; Marxism, 191; politics, 196; mentioned, 1, 81, 128, 144, 148, 176–79, 186
Dumoulin, Olivier, 48
Dupront, Alphonse, 177
Durand, Gilbert, 176–77
Duration, long: in history, 33, 60, 92–96, 167, 171, 189, 201; in the other social sciences, 58, 60, 110, 141, 144, 217; trump card, 90–91; helpless man, 129; computer, 158; French Revolution, 203–4, 208; mentioned, 114, 125, 195, 200
Durkheim, Emile: beginning of sociology, 11–13; mentioned, 3, 27, 144, 211, 217
Duruy, Victor, 23

Ecole des Hautes Etudes en Sciences Sociales (EHESS): the *Annales* laboratory, 143; mentioned, 89, 160, 182–83, 202
Ecole Normale Supérieure, 12, 23; Febvre at, 26, 29; mentioned, 49, 58, 170, 183
Ecole Pratique des Hautes Etudes (EPHE): sociologists retreat to, 11–12; Braudel, 17; Labrousse, 51; area studies, 102; Braudel president of section six, 107; mentioned, 99, 130
Economists: read Braudel, 116
Economy, world, 124–25
Einsteinian mechanics, 18
Eisenmann, Louis, 34
Elias, Norbert, 145–46
Emmanuel, Arghiri, 119
Engels, Friedrich, 46

Epinois, Count H. de l', 20
Erasmus, 64
Espinas, Georges, 31
Eugénie, Empress, 23
Event: changed status, 201
Exchanges: importance for capitalism, 119–21

Fabrègues, Jean de, 9
Fairy tales, 148
Fauconnet, Paul, 12
Faure, Edgar, 183
Fear: a field in *mentalités*, 175
Febvre, Lucien: compared with Berr, 26; early career, 42–43; objections to Marxism, 46; political and social tensions, 55–56; geography, 57–59; *mentalités*, 62–64; literary history, 64–65; contradicts self, 71; mentioned, 3, 7–10, 12, 14, 16, 18, 27–29, 31–36, 46–47, 49–59, 80, 82, 83, 87, 93, 94, 95, 98–101, 103, 107–9, 112, 114, 115, 118, 123, 128, 130, 131, 153, 157, 160, 215, 216, 217
Fernando, Don: evangelizing the crowds, 129
Ferro, Marc, 3, 98, 128, 140
Ferry, Jules, 20
Festivals, 211–12
Feudalism: crisis in, 168
Finley, Moses, 163, 223
Flandrin, Jean-Louis, 145, 171–72
Flouquet demonstration, 42
Folhen, Claude, 98
Fonda, Jane, 150
Ford Foundation, 104
Foucault, Michel, 64, 153–55, 160, 193–94, 217
Fougères, Marc: wartime pseudonym of Bloch, 43
Fourastié, Jean, 98
Franck, Gunther, 119
Frazer, James, 68
Frederic II, 210
Free School of Higher Studies, 98
Fresco, Nadine, 160
Freud, Sigmund, 84, 87, 160; Freudian unconscious, 121
Friedmann, Georges, 43–45, 50, 98
Frioux, Claude, 101
Froissart, Jean, 219

Fuggers, the, 120, 122
Funerals: of nobles, 174
Furet, François: young communist, 182–83; political history, 195; on the French Revolution, 202–10; mentioned, 143, 158, 184, 188–91
Fustel de Coulanges, Numa Denis, 23, 24, 34

Galileo, 64
Gallo, Max, 210–11
Gallop Institute, 84
Gance, Abel: his film *J'Accuse*, 8
Garlan, Yvon, 192
Gaxotte, Pierre, 209, 211
Geography: school of Vidal at turn of century, 15–16; annexed by history, 57–58; geohistory, 109–11
Geremek, Borislov, 43
Gernet, Louis, 66, 99
Ginzburg, Carlo: microhistory, 146
Giscard d'Estaing, Valéry, 141, 184
Godard, Jean-Luc, 150
Godelier, Maurice, 162
Gold and silver: their duel and circulation, 120–21
Goubert, Pierre, 81, 98, 117, 126, 171
Gourou, Pierre, 98, 109
Graham, Billy, 210
Granet, Marcel, 66
Gravier, Jean-François, 57
Guérin, Daniel, 46
Guises, the, 20
Guizot, François: on revolution, 19–20; mentioned, 70, 185, 204
Gurvitch, Georges, 82, 88, 90, 98–100

Halbwachs, Maurice, 12, 28, 30, 43, 53, 98
Halphen, Louis, 20, 34; history textbook, 125
Hamilton, Earl, 53
Hartog, François, 66
Haupt, Georges, 101
Hauser, Henri, 8, 25, 29, 50, 53
Hébert, Jacques René, 205
Hegel, Georg Wilhelm Friedrich, 161, 185
Heller, Clemens: area studies, 102
Hemardinquer, Jean-Jacques, 145
Henry II, 22

Henry, Louis, 81
Herodotus, 192–93
Herr, Lucien, 143
Hexter, Jack, 93, 143
Hiroshima and Nagasaki, 79
Historians: as wanderers, 156; and royal power, 219
History: and the other social sciences, 14, 15, 100, 128, 199, 216; and scientific thought, 18; traditional, 18–24, 131, 166; and patriotism, 22–24; and economics, 51, 53–54, 81; through problems in *Annales*, 55; as questioning not narrative, 55–56; in Bloch, 56–57; and politics, 193, 219; immobile, 199–200; mentioned, 17, 25, 60–61, 89, 159, 185, 190, 192, 200, 210, 222
Hitler, Adolph, 190, 201, 210
Hugo, Victor, 107
Humanity: decentered, 94–95

Imaginary, world of the, 176–77
Institut Français d'Opinion Publique (IFOP), 84
Institut National de la Statistique et des Etudes Economiques (INSEE), 82
Institut National des Etudes Démographiques, 82
Ionesco, Eugène, 184
Izard, Georges, 10

Jalée, Pierre, 119
Jambet, Christian, 185
Jaruzelski, 43, 185
Jaurès, Jean, 24
Jesus, 190
Journals: of the thirties, 9
Joutard, Philippe, 148
Juan, Don, 132
Juillard, Etienne, 112
Julien, Charles-André, 22
Julliard, Jacques, 188–89, 195
Jung's archetypes, 177

Kaiser Wilhelms Universität, 28
Kant, Immanuel, 87, 161
Karady, Victor, 11
Kölhm, Serge Christophe, 118–19
Kondratieff cycle, 129
Kriegel, Annie, 101

Labrousse, Ernest: career, 51–52; mentioned, 8, 81, 93, 110, 133, 170–71, 179
Lacombre, Pierre, 14
Lamour, Philippe, 9
Lane, Frédéric, 119
Langlois, Charles, 10, 22, 24, 31, 34, 55, 64, 70
Lanson, Gustave, 64–65
Lardreau, Guy, 185
Laval, Pierre, 8
Lavisse, Ernest: his "Bible" and career, 23; mentioned, 10, 20, 24, 34, 70, 219, 220, 223
Le Bras, Gabriel, 28, 99
Leenhardt, Maurice, 99
Lefebvre, Georges, 17, 28, 54, 175, 207
Lefebvre, Henri, 199
Lefranc, Abel, 63
Le Goff, Jacques: computer, 158; global history, 177–78; Marxist, 191; politics, 196; mentioned, 7, 55, 70, 140, 141, 221
Lenin, Vladimir Ilyich, 8, 46
Le Play, Frédéric, 11
Le Roy Ladurie, Emmanuel: historian as computer programmer, 157; marginalizing the individual, 159; communist background, 183–84; at Collège de France, 199–200; mentioned, 72, 81, 116, 126, 140–41, 145, 147, 155, 158, 160, 165, 167–69, 177, 182, 186, 188, 190, 191, 195, 216, 218
Leulliot, Paul, 43, 98
Lévêque, Monique, 192
Lévêque, Pierre, 163, 192
Lévi-Strauss, Claude: in Brazil with Braudel, 85–86; criticizes history, 86–87; his struggle with Braudel and history, 90–98; mentioned, 68, 84, 141, 144, 160, 189, 199, 200, 217
Lévy, Bernard-Henri, 184
Lévy-Bruhl, Lucien, 61, 68, 99, 144
Liberman, Simon Isaevich, 123
Life, private: alternative to *mentalités*, 176
Linnaeus, 90
Lipietz, Alain, 116, 123
Lipovetsky, Gilles, 197
Lombart, Maurice, 98
Longchambon plan, 103
Loraux, Nicole, 66

Louis, Saint, 209
Louis XI, 2
Louis XIV, 69, 103, 114, 208, 211
Louis-Philippe, 19, 20, 22
Luther, Martin, 29, 62, 63, 65

Machiavelli, Nicolo, 97
Magma, history as, 90; and the mental, 179; denounced by Cochin, 209
Maistre, Joseph de, 210
Malthus, Thomas, 165–68
Mandrou, Robert, 144, 148–49, 192
Mantoux, Paul, 14, 25, 120
Marguerite de Navarre, 62
Marketplace, transparent, 122–23
Marshall, George, 100
Marshall Plan, 79, 84, 103
Martonne, Emmanuel de, 16, 87
Marx, Karl, 11, 46, 71, 86, 117, 118, 123, 125, 160, 161, 167, 168, 179, 185, 190, 191
Marxism: rival and precursor of *Annales*, 45–46; hotbed of, at *Annales*, 49; attack on, 190; as psychotic symptom, 191; and classical Greece, 192; mentioned, 216, 221, 222
Mathiez, Albert, 204
Matrix: history-through-problems, 56
Maugüe, Jean, 85, 108
Maulnier, Thierry, 10
Maurras, Charles, 195
Mauss, Marcel, influence on Braudel, 87–88; mentioned, 12, 66, 98–99, 144, 153
Maxence, Jean-Pierre, 9
Mazarin, Cardinal, 1
Meillet, Antoine, 29, 35, 65
Mendel, Gérard, 196
Menier, Charles, 98
Mentalités: origins of, 61–62; critical reorientation, 170–71; and statistics, 175–76; its second wind, 177; Duby's definition of, 178–79; diachrony and synchrony, 179–80; and happiness, 195; mentioned, 115
Méquet, Gérard, 50
Mérimée, Prosper, 140
Mesliand, Claude, 182
Meuvret, Jean, 81
Michelet, Jules, 46, 70, 160, 182, 186
Microbes, 168–69

Mignet, François, 19–20
Milioukov, Paul, 34
Minc, Alain, 116
Miquel, Pierre, 1
Molière, Jean-Baptiste Poquelin, 146
Molotov, V., 44
Momigliano, Arnaldo, 80
Monod, Gabriel: methodic or positivistic school, 20–21; mentioned, 14, 26, 55
Montand, Yves, 150
Montgoméry, Gabriel, Count de, 22
Monzie, Anatole de, 26, 29
Morazé, Charles, 98–100, 140
Morineau, Michel, 125, 166
Mossé, Claude, 192
Mounier, Emmanuel, 9
Myth of *Annales*, 130

Napoléon I, 2, 208
Napoléon III, 23, 208
Narbonne: Bloch's name in the resistance, 44
Neo-Poujadism, 123
Neveu, Henri, 165
New Deal, 8
New School: invites Bloch to New York, 44
Nicolas, Jean, 182
Nicolet, Claude, 185
Nietzsche, Friedrich, 176, 190
Nora, Pierre, 152, 185, 188, 191, 215
Nostalgia: and history, 188; and change, 189

Oosterhoof, Jean-Louis, 32, 36, 50, 143
Organic: images in geography, 15–16; images in Braudel, 111–12; inspiration for Braudel's world economy, 125–26
Orwell, George, 1
Ozouf, Jacques, 182
Ozouf, Mona, 211–12

Parisot, Jean de la Valette, 132
Parrain, Charles, 45
Perrault, Charles, 148
Perrin, Charles-Edmond, 28, 54, 67
Pesez, Jean-Michel, 145
Pessimism: the world escapes from humanity, 201
Pfister, Christian, 22, 28

Philip II, 29, 33, 55, 56, 108, 132
Piaget, Jean, 35, 144
Piganiol, André, 28, 31
Pirenne, Henri: godfather of *Annales*, 31–32; mentioned, 120
Pius V, 132
Pivot, Bernard, 55
Plato, 185
Plozévet: survey of, 139
Poincaré, Raymond, 8
Polanyi, Karl, 118
Political: abandoned by Bloch and Febvre, 10; intertwined with social, 56; avoided by Braudel, 115
Pompidou, Georges, 141
Pomyon, Krystof, 153, 169
Popper, Karl, 184
Popular Front, 8, 43
Pose, Alfred, 49
Potsdam, 79
Poussou, Pierre, 82
Power: and geography, 17; and history, 20; and politics, 193–95; and revolutionary festivals, 211
Prices: and market economy, 124
Progress: crisis in the idea of, 140
Prometheus, 176–77
Prudhon, Pierre-Joseph, 43, 123

Quinet, Edgar, 209–10

Rabelais, 62–65
Rambaut, A., 20
Ranke, Leopold von, 24, 35, 131
Ratzel, Friedrich, 36, 59
Raymond Aron Institut, 183
Recuperation: of the new by the old, 97
Rémond, René, 1
Renaudet, Augustin, 29
Renouart, Yves, 98
Renouvin, Pierre, 103, 133
Revel, Jacques, 141, 153, 220
Revolts: peasant, 195
Revolution, social: as delinquency, 96; and state despotism, 210
Revolution, French: liberal thought, 203; dualism, 204; a play in two acts, 204–6; totalitarianism, 207–8; vilified, 210; principle of equality, 211; and festivals, 211–12
Ricardo, David, 124

Richet, Denis, 182, 184, 204–7
Ricoeur, Paul, 87
Rist, Charles, 31, 101
Robespierre, Maximilien de, 204, 208
Robin, Régine, 158
Roche, David, 140
Rockefeller Foundation, 99, 101, 102
Roosevelt, Franklin Delano, 8
Roubaud, A., 34
Rousseau, Jean-Jacques, 185, 189–90
Ruffié, Jacques, 169
Ruggieri, Eve, 1

Sagnac, Philippe, 20, 125
Saint-Denis, church of, 219
Sartre, Jean-Paul, 127
Saussure, Ferdinand de, 84
Sauvy, Alfred, 82
Schmitt, Jean-Claude, 144
Schumpeter, Joseph, 118
Sciences, social: expansion of, 83; American model, 84; in conflict with history, 88
Secher, Reynald, 211
Sée, Henri, 54
Seignobos, Charles: attacked by Simiand, 13–14; his way of writing history, 22; mentioned, 10, 13, 14, 24, 31, 33–35, 55, 64, 70, 219
Selim II, 132
Series: as new alienation, 159
Siegfried, André, 31
Simiand, François: his inflammatory article, 13; precursor in statistics, 50–51; mentioned, 7, 8, 12, 14, 22, 53, 58, 66, 85, 91, 93, 103
Sion, Jules, 12, 29, 57
Slansky affair, 183
Soboul, Albert, 182
Sociology: attack on history, 13
Solzhenitsyn, Alexander, 182, 207
Sombart, Werner, 117, 118
Sorel, Georges, 190
Soriano, Marc, 148
Sorre, Maximilien, 16
Sot, Michel, 144
Smith, Adam, 123
Staël, Mme de, 203–4
Stakhanovism, 44, 50
Stalin, Joseph, 44, 184, 185, 191, 208
Stoetzel, Jean, 84

Stoïanowich, Traian, 45
Strasbourg, dissidents of, 10; breeding grounds for *Annales*, 27–28; Bloch and Febvre there, 28–29; mentioned, 103
Strecker and Emlen, 169
Structures: Braudel's historical, 91–92; diminishes humanity, 94–95
Stuarts, the, 69
Suliman the Magnificent, 132

Taine, Hippolyte, 204
Teheran, 79
Theis, Laurent, 186
Thierry, Augustin, 70, 140, 186
Thiers, Adolphe, 19, 186
Thomas, Albert, 49
Thucydides, 18, 193
Tillon, Charles, 183
Time: decomposing chronological, 95; fleeting, 92–93
Tito, 183
Tocqueville, Alexis de, 207–9
Todd, Emmanuel, 190–91, 201–2
Touchard, Jean, 9
Trotsky, Leon, 44
Tureau, General, 210

UNESCO, 83

Vacher, Antoine, 12
Vallaux, Camille, 59
Vercingetorix, 23

Vernant, Jean-Pierre, 66, 163, 192
Veyne, Paul, 156, 160, 176
Vidal de la Blache, Paul: geographical model for *Annales*, 15–16; Vidalism, 57; Vidalian potentiality, 111; mentioned, 3, 12, 15, 21, 29, 36, 59, 109, 112, 114–15, 217
Vidal-Naquet, Pierre, 66, 163, 185, 188
Vilar, Pierre: his career, 16–17; mentioned, 46, 81, 142, 162, 192, 217
Visual society: and media, 177–78
Voltaire, François-Marie Arouet de, 69, 70, 132, 195, 240
Vovelle, Michel, 101, 156, 171, 174–75, 179–80, 191, 192

Wachtel, Nathan, 142
Walesa, Lech, 43
Wallerstein, Immanuel, 119, 123–25
Wallon, Henri, 29, 35
Walras, Léon, 123
Weber, Max, 71, 89, 118, 160
Welsers, the, 122
Willit, J. H., 99
Wills: in Provence, 174–75
Winock, Michel, 176, 188

Xenophones, 193

Yalta, 61, 79

Zeldin, Theodore, 129